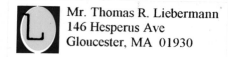
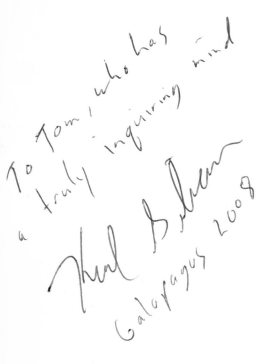

To Tom! who has
a truly inquiring mind

Galapagos 2008

Oracles of Science

*Celebrity Scientists versus
God and Religion*

KARL GIBERSON *and*
MARIANO ARTIGAS

UNIVERSITY PRESS

2007

OXFORD
UNIVERSITY PRESS

Oxford University Press, Inc., publishes works that further
Oxford University's objective of excellence
in research, scholarship, and education.

Oxford   New York
Auckland   Cape Town   Dar es Salaam   Hong Kong   Karachi
Kuala Lumpur   Madrid   Melbourne   Mexico City   Nairobi
New Delhi   Shanghai   Taipei   Toronto

With offices in
Argentina   Austria   Brazil   Chile   Czech Republic   France   Greece
Guatemala   Hungary   Italy   Japan   Poland   Portugal   Singapore
South Korea   Switzerland   Thailand   Turkey   Ukraine   Vietnam

Published by Oxford University Press, Inc.
198 Madison Avenue, New York, New York 10016

www.oup.com

Oxford is a registered trademark of Oxford University Press

Library of Congress Cataloging-in-Publication Data
Giberson, Karl.
Oracles of science : celebrity scientists versus God and religion /
Karl Giberson and Mariano Artigas.
      p. cm.
Includes bibliographical references and index.
ISBN-13 978-0-19-531072-6
ISBN 0-19-531072-1
1. Religion and science.   I. Artigas, Mariano.   II. Title.
BL240.3.G52 2006
215—dc22   2006012191

9 8 7 6 5 4 3 2 1

Printed in the United States of America
on acid-free paper

We dedicate Oracles of Science: Celebrity Scientists versus God and Religion *to William Shea, who holds the Galileo Chair at the University of Padua. Bill has been a good friend and an inspiration to both of us. We dedicate our book also to Carlos Pérez, who is no doubt looking down with delight and approval from heaven.*

Acknowledgments

The writing of this book was an exercise in collaboration: two authors, on two continents, with two first languages, with different backgrounds in both religion and science. But thanks to e-mail, the universality of Microsoft Word, and the value Europeans place on multilingualism, we could have been next door to each other.

All such writing projects owe their genesis, development, and completion to a host of contributors. We would like to thank Cynthia Read, executive editor at Oxford University Press, for encouraging us to write the book and working enthusiastically to streamline its publication by Oxford. We are both delighted that such a fine press is bringing our book to market. The title for the book was an idea of David Gallagher, a good friend and philosopher, who also helped us conceptualize this project.

We also thank our research assistant, Kelsey Towle, who cheerfully performed countless invisible tasks that helped the project move quite rapidly to completion: ordering books, tracking down details, getting footnotes in order, and carefully reading—and correcting—everything we wrote. Christi Stanforth, our copyeditor, improved our prose in hundreds of places with her careful attention to our text.

We especially thank The John Templeton Foundation for providing financial support for this project. The University of Navarra in Pamplona, Spain, and Eastern Nazarene College in Quincy, Massachusetts, have encouraged us in our careers. And thanks to our many colleagues at those two institutions for stimulating us to think hard about the issues tackled in this book.

The Canadian coauthor of this work would also like to thank his wife, Myrna, for her loving support and encouragement throughout.

We make special mention of the outstanding scholar Carlos Pérez, professor of physics at the University of Navarra and founder and president of the nonlinear physics group at the Royal Spanish Society of Physics. Pérez played an important role in the genesis of the book and started this project as our coauthor; he died tragically at the young age of fifty-two in a mountain-climbing accident.

Finally, as the familiar refrain goes, any remaining errors of fact, confused interpretations, violations of the English language, or other problems are ours and ours alone.

Contents

Oracles of Science

Introduction

Oracles of Science

Somewhere billions of miles from earth a spacecraft, ancient by all relevant standards, hurtles through space, an insignificant speck in a vast, empty, and some would say hostile cosmos. Although there is little chance that it will be noticed by alien life-forms, it nevertheless contains a message from the human race to whatever aliens find it, just in case. The message—both its content and the proposal to send it—was largely the work of Carl Sagan, a physicist who served briefly in the role of humanity's ambassador to the rest of the universe. Sagan was a dedicated, articulate, and tireless enthusiast for science; he spent his life looking through its lenses at all of human experience and subjecting whatever did not measure up, like religion, to withering criticism. His enthusiastic promotion of science turned him into a standard-bearer for the secular humanists as they pressed their case for science against religion.[1]

Back on earth, in England, one of our species' most remarkable and productive minds resides in the tragically withered body of Stephen Hawking, the best-known physicist on the planet and one of the scientific community's rare celebrities. Hawking is a cosmologist who, in a runaway best-seller, sent a message to the world—in forty languages—that, at least at face value, implied that their universe had no beginning and there was, thus, nothing for God to do.

Hawking's fellow Brit, zoologist Richard Dawkins, celebrates that Darwinian evolution provides the freedom to disbelieve, to reject God, to be an "intellectually fulfilled atheist."[2] Dawkins, whose outstanding popular science books and prestigious Oxford chair have given him a bully pulpit from which to preach, makes full use of the spotlight upon him, aggressively assaulting pseudoscience and superstition and promoting science as the ultimate arbiter of all truth. Dawkins, one of the leading public intellectuals of our time, is especially hostile to religion, regarding it as the most dangerous of the many delusions to which humans are susceptible.[3]

Across the ocean, in the New World, a trio of American scientists champion similar causes. Nobel laureate Steven Weinberg, one of the greatest particle physicists of the twentieth century, assured his readers that the universe was "pointless" in his classic *The First Three Minutes*, still selling briskly a quarter century after its initial publication. We look in vain, says Weinberg, for a purpose for human existence or anything else and must console ourselves with the knowledge that science can lift the human experience above its natural level of "farce" and give it the "grace of tragedy."[4]

At Harvard University, the prolific Stephen Jay Gould seconded Weinberg's pessimistic view of human origins. Gould wrote a series of outstanding books on evolution, several of which argued eloquently that human evolution must be understood as a random and purposeless process and it is simply our hubris that leads us to impute some kind of meaning to natural history. Play the tape of life again, he says at the end of *Wonderful Life*, and history will be different. Humans will not be here. We are the product of a random, purposeless process that would never return to the same present if restarted at the beginning. Let us not think, for one minute, that we are special.[5]

Also at Harvard University, Edward O. Wilson has won two Pulitzer Prizes for his eloquent and compelling books about the ants and about the genetic basis for behaviors of everything from ants to human beings.[6] Genes, he tells us, define human nature and profoundly shape all aspects of behavior, including our all-too-natural tendency to be religious. He looks ahead to a day when this new science of evolutionary psychology will successfully explain away religion. In fact, he speculates with gusto about a day when all of human experience will be explicable in terms of the laws of physics.[7]

Carl Sagan, Richard Dawkins, Stephen Hawking, Stephen Jay Gould, Steven Weinberg, and Edward O. Wilson are all larger-than-life scientific figures. They have impeccable scientific pedigrees, but it is their unusual gift for communication that has given them a platform for speaking to millions outside the scientific community, rather than the tiny audiences of specialists to whom their colleagues speak. Their popular science books become best-sellers and, in the case of Sagan and Gould, continue to sell briskly years after they have passed away. Television shows bring their ideas to even broader audiences. Six hundred million viewers worldwide watched Sagan bring his view of science to life in the thirteen-part series *Cosmos*, produced in 1980 but still available and recently enhanced with new footage and updates from Sagan's widow, Ann Druyan.

These are the Oracles of Science. Like the traditional oracles of classical Greece, Shakespeare, and even the hit movies about the Matrix, they tell us what we need to know. Are we alone in the universe? Where did we come from? Did the universe have a beginning? Is there a point to our existence? Are we the products of random chance? Where do we find answers to deep and important questions? We are a culture that looks to science because that is where we expect to find our answers. We cannot, however, find these answers ourselves, for only a specialist can navigate the complex terrain that is modern science. We need guides—Oracles—to show us the way.

Shapers of Public Views of Science

These scientific luminaries—the Oracles of Science—are ambassadors from the scientific community to the culture at large. The challenge of bringing science to large audiences, however, is considerable. In his celebrated essay *Two Cultures and the Scientific Revolution*, C. P. Snow lamented the great divide that had arisen between two different types of intellectual—the scientist and the literary scholar, or humanist.[8] The former, suggested Snow, knows calculus, thermodynamics, and genetics but little about literature; the latter knows Latin, Shakespeare, and literary criticism, but nothing of science. Neither can talk to the other. Viewed across Snow's divide, the caricatured scientist is parochial, narrow, overly pragmatic, and virtually illiterate. The caricatured humanist is obscure, pompous, and irrelevant and wears his ignorance of thermodynamics with pride. Snow lamented this divide, recognizing that such widespread ignorance of science was potentially disastrous for a culture increasingly looking to science for leadership and solutions to important problems.

Snow knew what he was talking about, having experienced the Two Cultures firsthand. A physicist by training and vocation, Snow, who lived from 1905 to 1980, became famous for a series of eleven vaguely autobiographical novels known collectively as *Strangers and Brothers*. This success as a novelist brought Snow into contact with Britain's literary culture, and he was shocked and appalled to discover how fully disconnected it was from his other, scientific culture.

In the second edition of *The Two Cultures*,[9] Snow expressed a bit of optimism that a few brave literary souls might emerge who would work to bridge this divide. After all, this particular intellectual community was filled with people trained in communication, and surely there would be some who might rise to the challenge of delivering science to broad audiences. Of course, there have always been those with a passion to write about science for popular audiences, starting with Galileo, who produced some of his seminal works in Italian, rather than Latin, so more people could read them. And Darwin's classic work was literary and broadly accessible. Snow's generation in England had grown up reading Sir Arthur Eddington's classic popularizations of science. But these are just notable exceptions, as Snow came to realize as he moved back and forth between his scientific and literary careers. There was indeed a great chasm between the Two Cultures—a divide that Snow hoped would be bridged by a few brave souls on the literary side. Snow called these anticipated bridge-builders the Third Culture.

Snow's Third Culture never appeared. Other than the occasional anomaly, like Dava Sobel, author of the surprise best-sellers *Longitude* and *Galileo's Daughter*, or Timothy Ferris, author of the acclaimed and enduring *Coming of Age in the Milky Way*, there are surprisingly few *writers* successfully bringing science to broad audiences. But an argument has been advanced by literary agent John Brockman that a different sort of Third Culture intellectual has appeared—the literate scientist.[10]

Brockman's point is worth noting. Leading scientists are now writing extensively for the general public, and a few of them are producing surprisingly popular works of substantial quality. The half dozen names that opened this introduction are certainly well known—Sagan, Hawking, Weinberg, Gould, Wilson, Dawkins. They are the "public intellectuals" of this generation, perennially present in media outlets from public television to science magazines to popular books and on the pages of the *New York Review of Books* and other leading opinion journals. Their books are often on the best-seller lists. Wander into any bookstore in America and you can find them in the science section. Hawking's *A Brief History of Time* sold one copy for every 750 people on earth, in forty languages, and turned him into a major public figure, capable of filling large lecture halls; Wilson won Pulitzer Prizes and was ranked the seventeenth most influential person of the twentieth century by *Time* magazine; Gould's column in the popular *Natural History* magazine ran nonstop for twenty-seven years and spun off seven book-length collections of essays; Sagan won the Pulitzer Prize and was for years one of the most widely recognizable public figures on the planet; Weinberg sports both a Nobel Prize in physics and the American Institute of Physics–U.S. Steel Foundation Science Writing Award; Dawkins had a chair endowed especially for him at Oxford to free him from normal university tasks and provide more time to write and lecture in public, which he does prolifically. Called the "Charles Simonyi Chair for the Public Understanding of Science," the chair is named for the Microsoft millionaire who endowed it. Hawking and Gould have even appeared as animated guest characters on the popular TV series *The Simpsons*—further testimony to their substantial cultural presence.

These are the leaders of the Third Culture, doing exactly what C. P. Snow lamented was not getting done, and doing it well. They are bringing science to the reading public in a way that engages them. Public perceptions of both science and scientists are shaped by their writings, and aspects of science and scientists missing from their presentation are also missing from the general understanding of what science is and what scientists do.

And herein lies the problem. The scientific community is a gigantic worldwide network of scholars trained in a broad cross section of disciplines, supported by a variety of funding entities, and assisted by a vast technical and publishing infrastructure. When a small handful of leaders step forward to speak for the whole, there arises the possibility that their portrayals of science may be skewed or even distorted and science might be misunderstood.

Origins and Religion

The popular writings of Sagan, Hawking, Gould, Weinberg, Wilson, and Dawkins, if taken in their totality as a representative portrayal of science and the scientific community, suggest the following:

1. *Science is mainly about origins, and most scientists are working on some aspect of either cosmic or biological evolution.* Weinberg won his Nobel Prize for his work on an esoteric event in the very early universe that determined the strength of two of the four forces in nature. His most popular book is *The First Three Minutes*. Hawking's best-known work and the topic of his *A Brief History of Time* concern the question of whether the universe had to have a beginning. Wilson won a Pulitzer Prize for *On Human Nature*, an analysis of the genetic, evolutionary origins of our psychological predispositions, such as our aversion to marrying our siblings. Gould's many essays were about "natural history"— a euphemism for evolution. His 1,464-page opus was titled *The Structure of Evolutionary Theory*. Sagan's prodigious output ranged broadly but was infused with considerations of origins. His most famous book and series, *Cosmos*, began with his most famous sentence: "The cosmos is all that is, ever was, or ever will be."[11] And every one of Dawkins's many books was about evolution. Like Gould, he has published an opus on evolution, the 688-page *The Ancestor's Tale*.

2. *Scientists are either agnostic or atheistic.* We have selected the six scientists profiled in this book solely on the basis of their stature as the leading English-language spokespersons for science. Their philosophical and theological perspectives did not come into play. Nevertheless, we note that none of them believe in God in any conventional sense. Dawkins has claimed that Darwin made it possible to be an "intellectually fulfilled atheist." Weinberg's *Dreams of a Final Theory* contains an entire chapter about God, where he states, "It is hardly possible not to wonder whether we will find any answer to our deepest questions, any sign of the working of an interested God, in a final theory. I think that we will not."[12] Sagan was the 1981 Humanist of the Year,[13] an award presented by the American Humanist Association, whose definition of humanism reads: "Humanism is a progressive philosophy of life that, without supernaturalism, affirms our ability and responsibility to lead ethical lives of personal fulfillment that aspire to the greater good of humanity."[14] Hawking, whose physical limitations have resulted in a relatively smaller volume of material, nevertheless noted that his "no boundary" version of the big bang did away with both the beginning of the universe and any interesting role for God. Wilson's work on the genetic basis for human behavior has led him to infer that belief in God is simply something that evolution programmed into us. And Gould, who actually wrote an entire book trying to make peace between science and religion, nevertheless insisted that theology must restrict itself to statements about values and must make no factual claims about the world. Only E. O. Wilson, who concedes that the deep rationality and rich complexity of the universe might not be self-explanatory, admits any possibility of there being a God, and then only an impersonal deistic God.

3. *Science is incompatible with and even hostile to religion.* It is not surprising, of course, that people who don't believe in God are not interested in religion, although there certainly are atheists who study religion and various aspects of belief in God. What is surprising, however, is the remarkable hostility toward religion that characterizes so much of the writing we will be examining in this book. The most generous attitude toward religion is that of Gould, who made a valiant but broadly rejected attempt to eliminate the conflict between religion and science. Gould assigned science the responsibility for dealing with the "factual character of the natural world," restricting religion to the "realm of human purposes, meanings, and values."[15] Few scientists shared this view of religion, however. Sagan, for example, treated religion as a set of explanations for the empirical realities of the world that should be accepted or rejected on the same grounds as their scientific counterparts. Against those who would "explain" the origin of the universe as an

act of God, Sagan asks "where God comes from," suggesting that "if we say that God has always existed, why not save a step and conclude that the universe has always existed?"[16] Like Sagan, Hawking insists that God can be invoked only within the context of a scientific explanation. In a 1992 interview he suggested that God could be the answer to the question: "Why does the universe bother to exist?"[17] Hawking has outlined cosmological models that he says make God optional—with "nothing to do." Bringing the same agenda to his sociological extension of evolutionary biology, Wilson, who abandoned a rather substantial childhood faith when he encountered science, looks for science to not only explain God away, but also explain our inclinations in that direction: "The final decisive edge enjoyed by scientific naturalism will come from its capacity to explain traditional religion, its chief competitor, as a wholly material phenomenon."[18] In stark contrast to Gould, who saw in religion something valuable, Weinberg sees religion as not merely false, but evil: "With or without religion," he writes, "you would have good people doing good things and evil people doing evil things. But for good people to do evil things, that takes religion."[19] Similar sentiments have been expressed repeatedly by Dawkins; shortly after September 11, he wrote, "Only the willfully blind would fail to implicate the divisive force of religion in most, if not all, of the violent enmities in the world today."[20] Dawkins has assaulted religious belief with such an aggressive tone that Alister McGrath, one of the world's leading theologians and a professor at Oxford University, has written a book-length response.[21]

The scientific community, through the lenses of its six leading spokespersons, is hostile to religion, atheistic, and primarily engaged in the investigation of origins.

None of these characterizations are true. Science is not hostile to religion, scientists are not consistently atheistic, and origins are not the primary focus of scientific investigation.

Pick up any general scientific journal—*Science, Proceedings of the National Academy of Science, Nature*—or any of the discipline-specific journals—*Physical Review, Cell, Chemistry and Biodiversity*—and peruse its contents. Virtually none of the articles will be about origins. There is a good reason for this—scientific research is expensive and someone has to pay for it, usually taxpayers, or the research departments at large corporations, like Merck, Hewlett-Packard, and IBM, who pass the costs on to consumers. Very few of the funding sources for scientific research are interested in origins. Research funds for, say, biochemistry are much better spent trying to understand how the human body responds to certain drugs, rather than how life may have originated in some sort of primordial soup, or near an ocean vent, or on a meteorite, or on Mars.

The superconducting supercollider that was started in Texas got axed because Congress developed reservations about spending so many billions of dollars on a machine to help us understand the very early universe, a project that had no foreseeable benefits to the taxpayers footing the bill.

Scientists are also not, as a group, substantially more atheistic than the general population. A survey of religious beliefs among scientists revealed that 39.6 percent of scientists believed in a God "to whom one may pray in expectation of receiving an answer."[22] These results echoed a much earlier study showing similar results, suggesting that the scientific community is not "secularizing."[23] A recent survey reports that "more than half of scientists in all disciplines identified themselves as spiritual to some degree."[24]

And as for the scientific community being hostile to religion, other than a tiny minority of scientists, there is simply no widespread opposition. No scientific body, for example, has ever endorsed a "position" critical of religion. It simply does not come up, and it is hard to imagine how it might do so. Furthermore, there are important leaders in the scientific community, such as Francis Collins, the leader of the human genome project, who are deeply religious and yet encounter no difficulties coordinating substantial scientific projects. The same could be said for Allan Sandage, one the greatest astronomers of the twentieth century; Charles Townes, who won the Nobel Prize for inventing the laser; and, more recently, physics Nobel laureate William Phillips. What is most likely is the experience that Sandage reported, in an interview with philosopher Philip Clayton,[25] of discovering to his great surprise that many of his colleagues were deeply religious. The scientific community, like the crowd at a baseball game, at the symphony, or in the shopping mall, simply has no reason to be talking to each other about religion, and no reason to wonder collectively about it.

Oracular Utterances

The Oracles of Science speak to big questions of life, God, creation, purpose. They place our universe, our planet, our species, and even our human natures in context. Who are we? Where do we come from? Why are we here?

The problem is that these are not scientific questions. They may be informed by science, but they are most certainly not purely scientific questions. When Sagan assures us that "the cosmos is all that is, ever was, or ever will be," he is not reporting on the latest scientific discovery, or even the latest theory. How could science possibly determine that this present cosmos is all that will ever be? When Weinberg laments that "the more the universe seems comprehensible, the more it seems pointless,"[26] he is going beyond what he—or anyone else, for that matter—ever wrote in any scientific journal article. Such profoundly oracular—and controversial—utterances are what give popular science writing much of its excitement, but such statements are not scientific statements at all. They are philosophical and theological claims cloaked in scientific rhetoric, presented on the concluding pages of highly literate books that masterfully open science to broad audiences. But these grand now-here-is-the-point conclusions articulate the personal worldviews of the scientists making the claims, not the implications of the discussion that has preceded them, and certainly not the consensus of the scientific community.

There is nothing wrong with making philosophical and theological statements, of course, and there are entire disciplines—philosophy and theology, for example—devoted to training specialists how to do this. But these are not disciplines typically engaged by scientists. Virtually no scientists take any more than an undergraduate survey course in philosophy, and even fewer take courses in theology. So when scientists wander onto philosophical turf and begin to pronounce about ultimate realities, they sometimes do so without the requisite tools, and often without any awareness that the requisite tools exist.

Curiously, many scientists are fully aware of this but do not consider it a limitation. Dawkins, for example, when challenged about his ignorance of theology, responded that this "presupposes . . . that there is something in Christian theology to be ignorant *about*. The entire thrust of my position is that Christian theology is a non-subject. It is empty. Vacuous. Devoid of coherence or content."[27] Weinberg devotes an entire chapter in *Dreams of a Final Theory* to an assault on philosophy—titled, appropriately, "Against Philosophy."[28] Hawking speaks confidently of God and Creation in *A Brief History of Time*, apparently oblivious to the fact that he is using these terms in ways that bear little resemblance to how they are used by theologians, or even by ordinary religious people.

When the Oracles of Science write about the big questions, they occasionally alert the reader that they are moving beyond science and into realms where they have little expertise. But more often they do not, presenting personal opinions and reflections in the same vein as the science they popularize so well. Widespread popular misunderstandings about science would be reduced if the Oracles would be careful to maintain the distinctions between science and philosophical speculation that are maintained so scrupulously in the scientific literature. If Weinberg, for example, were to conclude one of his papers on theoretical physics with the claim "Now we know the universe is pointless," the referees would assume he was making a joke and simply cross it off. No such statement has ever appeared in a scientific journal. Of course, when Weinberg writes a popular book explaining the exotic early history of the universe to nonphysicists, he is not doing peer-reviewed research and is free to say whatever he wants. He could even, were he so inclined, misrepresent the science under discussion. Fortunately, he does not do that; he actually takes great pains to craft ingenious analogies and compelling metaphors to help the reader understand some rather deep ideas that normally require advanced mathematics. But after 154 pages of almost mesmerizing prose about truly amazing natural phenomena, he shifts subtly and imperceptibly into a more reflective mode as he summarizes, contextualizes, and concludes the grand story he has just told.

"It is almost irresistible," writes Weinberg, "for humans to believe we have some special relation to the universe, that human life is not just a more-or-less farcical outcome of chain of accidents."[29] But we are deceived by our self-promoting hubris; science has discovered otherwise. Gould does the same thing in _Wonderful Life_, which has to be the most captivating book on paleontology ever written. After 322 pages of discussion of fossils, replete with photos, drawings, and winsome anecdotes about scientists, he moves into a reflective phase, drawing his grand story to a close. "And so," says Gould, "if you wish to ask the question of the ages—why do humans exist?—a major part of the answer, touching those aspects of the issue science can treat at all, must be: because Pikaia survived the Burgess decimation." (Pikaia is the world's first chordate and may have been the ancestor of all the vertebrates, including, of course, us.) Pikaia's survival, Gould reflects, was just a "contingency," one of countless accidents which populate natural history and to which we owe our existence. "We are," he says, "the offspring of history, and must establish our own paths in this most diverse and interesting of conceivable universes—one indifferent to our suffering, and therefore offering us maximal freedom to thrive, or to fail, in our own chosen way."[30]

Dawkins's opus, _The Ancestor's Tale_, moves sure-footedly through 614 pages, unfolding the natural history of life on this planet; then, almost suddenly, it abandons its subject matter for a grand finale bashing religion. Dawkins objects, on the very last page of _The Ancestor's Tale_, to supernatural creation stories of the sort that undergird religious views of the world because "they miserably fail to do justice to the sublime grandeur of the real world. They represent a narrowing down from reality, an impoverishment of what the real world has to offer."[31]

These deeply philosophical conclusions—part science, part poetry, part personal religion—flow so naturally from the eloquent exposition that led up to them that it is easy to think they are also a part of the science under discussion. And therein lies their strength.

After centuries of rapid scientific advance, our culture has great faith in science. From miracle cures to cool technologies and exotic theories, we have learned to trust science and to look to it for solutions to our problems. Our cultural symbol for both genius and wisdom is Albert Einstein, a scientist, but larger than life. Our gurus—the Oracles who tell us what we need know—increasingly come from science. So when an eloquent scientific exposition, written by a respected scientist, concludes with an assurance that the universe has no point, or that human evolution is a series of accidents, or that God did not create the universe, it is hard not to see these extraordinary, if disconcerting, claims as anything other than deep truths resting on the firmest of foundations.

Intelligent Design and Scientific Naturalism

The present work appears at a time when science, especially in the United States, is increasingly under assault by conservative religious forces fearful that the *naturalism* of "natural science" (which they call *materialism*) is eroding traditional religious beliefs. Conservative religious opposition to science, particularly evolution but also cosmology and even psychology, has been a persistent feature of American culture almost from the moment Darwinism first arrived from England.

The twentieth century in America witnessed a number of celebrated legal confrontations as conservative forces tried to weaken the teaching of science in public schools. The Scopes Monkey Trial was fought in 1925 in Dayton, Tennessee, after that state passed a law making it illegal to teach evolution in the public schools. In 1982 in Little Rock, Arkansas, another legal challenge was launched, attempting to mandate "equal time" within high school pedagogy, requiring that creationism be taught alongside evolution. One of our Oracles, Stephen Jay Gould, was an important witness at that trial, which concluded that there was no basis for teaching creationism alongside evolution in Arkansas's public schools.

Persistent legal challenges to the teaching of evolution worked their way to America's Supreme Court, where, presumably once and for all, creationism was declared to be unscientific, religious, and not appropriate for America's high school biology classes.

Throughout these challenges a rhetorically charged literature emerged from both sides. Cartoons appeared that heaped ridicule on those who oppose evolution, portraying them as "missing links"; spokespersons for science decried the illiteracy and backwardness of the creationists; Isaac Asimov, who wrote over four hundred books and was an important science popularizer in his own right, wrote that "creationists are stupid, lying people,"[32] and insulted them as "cavemen" on the back cover of one of Dawkins's books.[33] Elsewhere, Dawkins charged that people who did not believe in evolution were "stupid, wicked, or insane."[34] Creationists countered that science was trying to destroy belief in God; their leader, Henry Morris, wrote a full-length book arguing that evolution was a part of Satan's strategy to destroy faith in God.[35] And while science won all the court battles, it gradually lost the hearts and minds of millions of Americans whose interest in science did not extend much beyond making sure that it did not undermine their faith in God as the creator of the universe.

Out of this grassroots antiscience populism rose the Intelligent Design (ID) movement, a well-funded and politically savvy assortment of lawyers, scientists, polemicists, philosophers, and bandwagon jumpers. With considerable financial support from the Seattle-based Discovery Institute, this movement has posed a major challenge to high school science teaching, working through local school boards instead of the courts. Led by a lawyer named Phillip Johnson, the ID movement has, in its public pronouncements, avoided overtly religious claims, asking only that high school students be alerted to the "problems" with evolutionary theory and that "alternative explanations" be provided. The alternative explanations are, of course, that evolution cannot explain much of the natural world, and there are countless things in nature that are so well designed that an "intelligence" must be invoked to explain them. While claiming agnosticism on the particulars of this intelligence, virtually all ID proponents are conservative Christians, and when they speak to religious audiences, they make the identity of this intelligence crystal clear, as ID is fashioned into an apologetics argument buttressing the Christian faith.[36]

ID proponents claim that this conflict is between rival scientific theories and that, in the name of fair play and open-mindedness, both explanations should be taught. This approach sounds generous and appeals to America's sense of fair play. But it is a false claim. There is no scientific theory of Intelligent Design. William Dembski, a major architect of ID, begins one of his books with the claim: "Intelligent design is three things: a scientific research program that investigates the effects of intelligent causes; an intellectual movement that challenges Darwinism and its naturalistic legacy; and a way of understanding divine action."[37] The problem is that you cannot have the three things at the same time. A way of understanding divine action cannot be a scientific research program, unless modern empirical science is changed into something very different. The study of divine action is theology, not science. Dembski also notes, "Intelligent design therefore intersects science and theology."[38] But then it is not science. The modern empirical sciences—physics, chemistry, astronomy, biology—do not "intersect" theology. There is no point in claiming that ID should be introduced in the teaching of the sciences. How, for example, is chemistry to be taught from the perspective of Intelligent Design? What new ideas are to be introduced to students? The teaching of ID is not about fair play or open-mindedness. It is about common sense.

ID, at its philosophical best, engages the concern that *scientific naturalism* is, and has been, often pitted against religion. If we define and measure science by the standards provided by the Oracles, for example, it can certainly appear that scientific progress validates a naturalism that leaves no room for the spiritual dimensions of life. If you are convinced that science and religion are opposed and incompatible, and your primary loyalty is to your religion, then you have no choice but to suppose that something must be faulty in science. ID can look attractive in this case.

That ID has effectively captured the attention—and the allegiance—of so many Americans can be understood in part by looking at the prominent role played in the ID controversy by the writings of our Oracles, which are quoted heavily in the literature of the ID movement. The index to Phillip Johnson's *Reason in the Balance*, for example, has thirteen entries for Gould, ten for Dawkins, nine for Hawking, seven for Weinberg, and six for Sagan.[39] The context is always the same: Here are the leading thinkers from the scientific community. They are hostile to religion and believe that science has rendered belief in God irrelevant. Their central theory is evolution, which they fanatically support, despite its many flaws, because without it they would have to acknowledge the reality that God created the world. Evolution is thus an atheistic, materialistic ideology, not a scientific theory. Johnson writes, "Darwinism is not really based on empirical evidence. Its true basis is in philosophy, and specifically in the metaphysics of naturalism. . . . Naturalism does not have an answer for the ultimate question of why there is something instead of nothing."[40]

As we will see in the chapters that follow, the Oracles do indeed make a great many negative comments about religion and belief in God. ID polemicists gather these comments and fashion them into a compelling argument that science is hostile to religion. Since most Americans are more loyal to their faith than to science, this argument works effectively to turn them away from science and make them open to ID. Lost in this culture war over origins is the fact that the majority of scientists are not hostile to religion and many are, in fact, quite religious.

Both the Oracles of Science and the proponents of ID start with a false dichotomy: An adequate explanation of the natural world must be based on either God or the natural causes of science, but the two are mutually exclusive.

ID chooses God, concluding that there is something faulty in science that must be changed. The Oracles choose natural causes, concluding that there is no room for God.

Structure of the Present Work

Oracles of Science intends to be a serious and wide-ranging introduction to the six thinkers who have done the most to shape our culture's present views of science. The chapters that follow tell six two-part stories: a biographical narrative of each scientist's ascendancy to oracular status, and the message that each scientist is delivering to the broader culture about humankind's place in the grand scheme of things.

The key ideas of each Oracle are presented in their own words, through extensive quotation of their own writings, complemented by things they have said in interviews and public presentations. Analysis and commentary is provided primarily by examining what the Oracles' more thoughtful peers have said about their work. Where appropriate we offer our own analyses.

We have tried our best to be fair and avoid unnecessary polemics in our discussion, even to the point of providing enough background that readers may draw an opinion different than our own as they read each chapter. While it is true that the Oracles of Science figure prominently in current controversies that pit science against religion, it is not our intent to participate only in that conversation. The cultural relevance of the Oracles goes well beyond their role in these disputes.

Although our analysis of the Oracles is primarily critical, as opposed to defensive, or celebratory, we share with them an abiding respect for and confidence in science. We are both scientists by training and are fully convinced that modern science is one of the greatest developments in human history and that it has done immeasurable good for the human race. We also note, in concert with the Oracles, that science has helped to spread in our societies an appreciation for the values implicit in the scientific enterprise: the value of searching for truth in humility; the importance of objectivity and intersubjective testing; and the value of independent validation. We note that for many decades science has been a major (if not *the* major) vehicle for international cooperation; science has demanded, and in the main achieved, an enviable transparency and freedom from prejudice. And given the incredible resources devoted to science, we are impressed that the incidence of fraud in the scientific community is so small. When, for example, was the last time a major public scandal erupted out of the scientific community? Such events are so rare that most people cannot recall even one, whereas leaders in the political, business, and even religious communities are routinely implicated in scandal. Furthermore, science has done much to mitigate some of the greatest problems faced by humanity: racism, sexism, hunger, pain, sickness, depression, and so on.

As scientists who are also religious believers, we agree with many of our fellow scientists and intellectuals—not all of them believers—who find no fundamental incompatibility between science and religion. Nevertheless, we are quick to note that within the overall framework of peaceful coexistence of science and religion there are examples of conflict. One of us has written extensively on the Galileo affair,[41] the most infamous historical example, and the other has written extensively on the creation-evolution controversy,[42] the enduring modern example.

We believe it is important and intellectually healthy to spotlight overly polemical and unwarranted assaults of religion on science and vice versa. Everyone is better off when both sides exercise appropriate restraint and mischief-makers are called out.

Although this book is loosely within the broad field of "science-and-religion," we do not construe it narrowly as such and thus do not articulate any particular norms for how this dialogue is supposed to work, other than to note that science and religion are two very different human enterprises and, although there certainly are points of contact, each has considerable autonomy that should be respected by the other. Our primary goal in this book is simply to introduce six important scientific voices to our readers.

Because this is not explicitly a work of "science-and-religion," we are not engaging with the leading voices in that community, who, while important in their own right, have nowhere near the cultural influence of the Oracles. This book is mainly about Dawkins, Weinberg, Gould, Wilson, Sagan, and Hawking and not what various critics think about them. By avoiding excessive analysis and critique of the Oracles, we hope to provide a more useful treatment, one that will certainly make a contribution to the burgeoning field of science-and-religion but will go beyond the boundaries of that conversation into larger questions of science and culture.

Each chapter in the present work has been written to be read independently of the rest and, thus, in any order. Readers interested in the physical sciences can, for example, read the chapters on Weinberg, Sagan, and Hawking without having to also read the chapters on the biologists—Gould, Dawkins, and Wilson. Global comments about the Oracles as a group appear primarily in the introduction and the conclusion.

In our selection of these Oracles we used four criteria: (1) They must be professional scientists and must have made substantial contributions to science (and not just its popularization). (2) They must be best-selling authors and have written books that have shaped the opinions of a large reading public. (3) They must have written on the larger cultural, philosophical, and humanistic implications of science. (4) They must be contemporary and shaping the opinions of this generation. This is why we do not consider important authors who died a long time ago. Two of our Oracles have died recently, at a relatively early age, but many of their books are still in print, some selling briskly, and their influence continues unabated.

There are, of course, other thinkers who could have been included in the present work. But books must be of a finite length, and we have limited the present work to these six. We believe that any informed process is likely to arrive at a list essentially the same as ours. Perhaps the ideas of the authors not included in the present work will be engaged in a subsequent volume.

We note that all six of the Oracles are white males, an unfortunately narrow demographic but unavoidable and easily understood as the legacy of a scientific culture still without any semblance of gender and racial balance. That no junior scientists appear on the list derives from the simple fact that most junior scientists are diligently doing science and have no time for oracular pronouncements about science as a whole. Writing books for popular audiences often interferes with getting tenure in the sciences, rather than advancing it.

Three of our Oracles—Dawkins, Gould, Wilson—are from the life sciences; the other three—Hawking, Sagan, Weinberg—are from the physical sciences. This fortuitous division, which nicely broadens the scope of the present work, is purely coincidental. Hawking and Dawkins are British, and the rest are American.

I

A Good Devil's Chaplain

Richard Dawkins

Richard Dawkins is one of the most effective science popularizers of all time, awarded recognition by both scientific and literary societies. His best-selling popular science books, like *The Selfish Gene* (1976) and *The Blind Watchmaker* (1986), have created vocabulary, examples, and arguments widely used in discourse about evolution. Passionately convinced that science rules out the supernatural, Dawkins has become an increasingly aggressive and outspoken foe of religion, using science to discredit religious beliefs. In this latter capacity he has become a strange bedfellow of those, like Phillip Johnson,[1] who would convince religious people they must not accept evolution. In fact, there are probably more people who know about Dawkins from his critics than from his own work.

Clinton Richard Dawkins was born in Nairobi (Kenya) on March 26, 1941. Educated at Oxford University, he remained there for his doctorate, working with the Nobel Prize–winning ethologist Niko Tinbergen. From 1967 to 1969 he was assistant professor of zoology at the University of California at Berkeley. In 1970 Dawkins became a lecturer and reader in zoology at Oxford University; he has been a Fellow of New College ever since. In 1995 he became the first Charles Simonyi Professor of the Public Understanding of Science at Oxford University, an endowed chair created especially for him. He was elected a Fellow of the Royal Society in 2001. Readers polls place Dawkins among the top public British intellectuals.

The Selfish Gene

In 1976 Richard Dawkins exploded into view with the publication of his first and most famous book, *The Selfish Gene*, which became an international bestseller. Three decades later, his name and ideas remain closely associated with this book, partly due to its catchy title. How can a gene, a piece of DNA, be selfish? Provocative metaphors like this contribute to Dawkins's success, and in fact, no one has done more to shape the vocabulary of their own field than Dawkins.

The Selfish Gene introduces a simple idea: Living organisms behave as if they have aims and goals. In the end, however, the apparent purposefulness derives from the genes of the organisms and their efforts to survive through replication. Living organisms are vehicles that secure the continuity of the genes that give them structure, pattern, and instinct. Individuals are short-term homes for long-lived genes; individuals are born, live, and die, but their genes are copied and passed through other individuals from generation to generation. They survive for thousands, even millions, of years. Genes are the enduring heart of a vanishing reality that passes away while they live on. We all have genes from someone who died centuries ago, and we will pass these genes into the future.

Natural selection, as Darwin argued, is the driving force of evolution, and genes are the basic *unit* of selection. Though the visible competitors in the struggle for existence are individual organisms, they are just temporary. The real protagonists are the genes. Successful genes are those that have built up successful organisms to house them. Viewed by these lights, genes are indeed selfish, ruthless parasites manipulating their host organisms for their own survival. This is Dawkins's compelling view.

Like all grand ideas in science, the concept of *The Selfish Gene* did not come out of the blue. It was advanced to solve the problem of exactly how we should understand evolution. From a Darwinian perspective, evolution results from two synergistic factors: changes in the hereditary material of an organism, and natural selection of the organisms better adapted to their environment. Viewing the individual organisms in this struggle as the competitors is a natural, almost default, way to think about evolution. But it does not take much imagination to realize that there are other perspectives on the basic competitive unit being selected by nature. Groups of individuals that share common characteristics, for example, are also good candidates. Some biologists, in fact, insist that evolution works at the level of individuals, while others point to groups of individuals, or even species, as the unit of natural selection. Dawkins makes the extraordinary claim that evolution works on genes—not individuals, not groups, not species, but genes. After all, he argues with great eloquence, evolution is all about surviving, reproducing, and leaving descendants, and this depends mainly on genes.

Evolution, as Darwin understood it, differs from this interpretation by Dawkins, but then Darwin didn't know anything about genes. Dawkins, however, claims that his view is really profoundly Darwinian, a natural reframing of a classic argument in the light of new data. In fact, Dawkins is often seen as a fully orthodox Darwinian, vigorously defending an entrenched position that his critics sometimes describe as fundamentalist.

Darwin's genius, of course, was not the idea of evolution per se, which had been floating about in a variety of forms from the beginning of the nineteenth century. For example, Darwin's grandfather, the eccentric Erasmus Darwin, had proposed an evolution of sorts decades earlier. The novelty of Darwin's *On the Origin of Species by Means of Natural Selection* derived from its articulation of the *mechanism* of evolution: natural selection. Nature *selects* organisms better adapted in the struggle to survive just as farmers select breeding animals with certain characteristics to improve their offspring. The choice of the farmer, of course, is conscious and deliberate and has a goal in mind, while the "choice" of nature is blind and unconscious, but the results are similar: Organisms better adapted to their environment are produced, and eventually the historical trajectory of accumulating change can lead to the appearance of new species.

Evolutionary theory in its modern form retains the overall conceptual structure outlined by Darwin, with the addition of insights from genetics. That Darwin could propose his theory in total ignorance of genetics was remarkable, an achievement made even more remarkable when the science of genetics confirmed his basic intuitions. The development of genetics in the twentieth century, jointly with work on populations and statistics, led to the so-called modern synthesis, or neo-Darwinism.[2]

A Gene's-Eye View of Nature

Dawkins's ideas are rooted in the work of leading twentieth-century geneticists, like William Donald Hamilton (1936–2000) and George C. Williams. Hamilton published *The Genetical Evolution of Social Behavior* in 1964. His groundbreaking work on the genetic basis of evolution is now standard, and in 1980 he was elected to the Royal Society. Williams, emeritus professor of biology at the State University of New York at Stony Brook, wrote *Adaptation and Natural Selection* (1966), another gene-centered view of biology. Dawkins explains that taking the genes as the subject of natural selection was not a novelty: "I must argue for my belief that the best way to look at evolution is in terms of selection occurring at the lowest level of all. In this belief I am heavily influenced by G. C. Williams's great book *Adaptation and Natural Selection*."[3] He also recognizes the influence of Hamilton on his work, saying, "His two papers of 1964 are among the most important contributions to social ethology ever written."[4]

A fascinating corollary to the selfish gene perspective emerges in the study of *altruism*—apparently selfless behaviors that offer no advantage and even compromise the organisms that engage in them. Biologist H. Allen Orr explains the problem this way:

> When a small bird spots a hawk overhead it will often issue an alarm
> call, warning its flock-mates of the predator's presence. The odd thing
> is that this behavior—which we'll assume is instinctive, that is, ge-
> netically based—is "altruistic." By sounding the alarm, a bird may
> well save its flock-mates but it simultaneously calls attention to itself,
> increasing the odds of an attack by the hawk. How could such a
> behavior evolve? If you think of Darwinism in traditional terms—
> competition among organisms—the answer isn't obvious. A bird
> sounding a call putting itself at risk of getting eaten is unlikely to
> have more offspring than a bird who keeps quiet. And having more
> offspring is what Darwinism was supposed to be all about.

Orr goes on, explaining how the problem is solved from the gene's-eye perspective:

> But if you think of Darwinism in selfish gene terms—as competition
> among different *genes*—the answer is clearer. A gene that makes a
> bird emit an alarm may decrease the odds that the calling bird survives
> but it can increase the odds that the gene for alarm-calling survives.
> The reason is that the flock-mates who are saved by the alarm are, like
> all flock-mates, likely to be related to the caller; and relatives, by defi-
> nition, tend to carry the same genes, *including* the gene for sounding
> the alarm. In effect, then, the alarm-call gene is warning—and sav-
> ing—copies of itself. Those copies just happen to reside in other or-
> ganisms. The counterintuitive conclusion is that a gene that
> sometimes causes an organism to sacrifice itself can increase its fre-
> quency by natural selection. The alternative kind of gene—one for not
> emitting an alarm call—can decrease in frequency, since such genes
> are on average less likely to be passed on to the next generation. To

Dawkins and other advocates of the selfish gene view, such examples reveal something deep about Darwinism: natural selection acts at the level of competing genes, not competing organisms.[5]

In *The Selfish Gene* Dawkins popularizes a specific perspective in biology. He provides the biological ideas with compelling, memorable metaphors and illustrates them with effective examples. He warns the reader that he is not proposing a new biological theory. In the preface to the 1989 second edition he writes: "The selfish gene theory is Darwin's theory, expressed in a way that Darwin did not choose but whose aptness, I should like to think, he would instantly have recognized and delighted in. It is in fact a logical outgrowth of orthodox neo-Darwinism, but expressed as a novel image. Rather than focus on individual organisms, it takes a gene's-eye view of nature. It is a different way of seeing, not a different theory."[6]

Is all this selfish gene business *genuine* science—advancing our knowledge of the natural world—or just *popular* science—advancing the public's understanding of science? Dawkins describes what he is doing like this:

> Rather than propose a new theory or unearth a new fact, often the most important contribution a scientist can make is to discover a new way of seeing old theories or facts. . . . A change of vision can, at its best, achieve something loftier than a theory. It can usher in a whole climate of thinking, in which many exciting and testable theories are born, and unimagined facts laid bare. . . . I hasten to disclaim any such status for my own modest contributions. Nevertheless, it is for this kind of reason that I prefer not to make a clear separation between science and its "popularization."[7]

Dawkins thus considers his work to be both popular science and original contribution to science.

Dawkins identifies three very different readers for whom he was writing: laymen, for whom he avoided technical jargon; experts, who he hoped would find something new—a new way of looking at familiar ideas, or even stimulation of new ideas; and students, whom he hoped to encourage by showing that there is a very good reason to study zoology, namely "that we animals are the most complicated and perfectly-designed pieces of machinery in the known universe. Put it like that, and it is hard to see why anybody studies anything else!"[8]

Dawkins obviously delights in defending radical ideas, like the gene's-eye view of evolution. Against some experts, he rejects "group selection," arguing that natural selection operates on genes. His ideas received their most severe criticism from Harvard paleontologist Stephen Jay Gould (1942–2002), also a brilliant popular writer on evolution. Shortly after *The Selfish Gene* appeared, Gould launched what would become a long-running and acrimonious war: "The identification of individuals as the unit of selection is a central theme in Darwin's thought.... English biologist Richard Dawkins has recently raised my hackles with his claim that genes themselves are units of selection, and individuals merely their temporary receptacles."[9] Gould identifies a fatal flaw in the selfish gene view: "No matter how much power Dawkins wishes to assign to genes, there is one thing that he cannot give them—direct visibility to natural selection. Selection simply cannot see genes and pick among them directly. It must use bodies as an intermediary."[10]

Gould's main target is genetic atomism and determinism. On the one hand, Gould notes, "Bodies cannot be atomized into parts, each constructed by an individual gene. Hundreds of genes contribute to the building of most body parts and their action is channeled through a kaleidoscopic series of environmental influences."[11] On the other hand, he adds, "I think, in short, that the fascination generated by Dawkins' theory arises from some bad habits of Western scientific thought—from attitudes (pardon the jargon) that we call atomism, reductionism, and determinism. The idea that wholes should be understood by decomposition into 'basic' units; that properties of microscopic units can generate and explain the behavior of macroscopic results; that all events and objects have definite, predictable, determined causes."[12]

This was only the beginning of a long quarrel between Gould and Dawkins. However, it was *not* a dispute about the fact of evolution, although one of America's leading journalists did accuse Gould of aiding and abetting the creationists.[13] The debate was about the complex *mechanisms* of evolution. Some interpreted the dispute as a clash between two opposed views of evolution.[14] In his 2004 review of Dawkins, cited earlier, Orr writes, "Selfish gene thinking is now orthodox in evolutionary biology and, among many evolutionists, represents a near reflex. It is certainly true that Dawkins' early rhetoric was sometimes extreme. But it is more true that selfish gene thinking has delivered a number of important insights. The same cannot be said for hierarchical selection, as Gould himself lamented in his final major publication, *The Structure of Evolutionary Theory*. Indeed while many of us suspect that higher-level selection occurs, the evidence for it is, so far, frustratingly weak."[15]

Gould was probably right to emphasize the complexity of evolution, and the corresponding complexity of the relevant factors and their scientific explanations. We still don't know all the mechanisms central to explaining evolution, and new insights are regularly overturning old ideas. In a recent article discussing genetics, at the heart of evolutionary thinking for decades, we are told that we may be witnessing a turning point in our understanding of genetic information. What used to be considered "junk DNA," a useless remnant of evolution,[16] now is considered a potential explanation for how genetic information is regulated and for when, during development, certain genes are "turned on,"[17] therefore playing a pivotal role in evolution.

In *The Selfish Gene*, Dawkins has little to say about humans, other than to lament their irrational tendency to believe in God and hold bogus beliefs based on blind faith. But he is explicit about one thing: "Darwin provides a solution, the only feasible one so far suggested, to the deep problem of our existence."[18] Of course, this is to be expected if the gene's-eye view of nature is enlarged into an all-encompassing explanation for the entire human experience. But it is unclear why Dawkins's particular version of Darwinism, or even evolution itself, should be expected to provide a comprehensive overall explanation for all aspects of our existence.

The Long Reach of the Gene

An ambitious and extraordinary extrapolation of the ideas in *The Selfish Gene* appeared in 1982 with the less-than-memorable title *The Extended Phenotype*. Dawkins's advice to the reader, right on the cover of the 1989 paperback edition, suggests that he viewed this idea as the highlight of his career: "It doesn't matter if you never read anything else of mine, please at least read *this*."[19] (Apparently readers did not heed the advice and continued reading *The Selfish Gene*, so to the 1989 edition of that work Dawkins added a chapter that was essentially an abstract of *The Extended Phenotype*.)

In the preface to *The Extended Phenotype* Dawkins writes, "Although this book is in some ways the sequel to my previous book, *The Selfish Gene*, it assumes that the reader has professional knowledge of evolutionary biology and its technical terms. . . . I have also tried to make the book as near as possible to being enjoyable to read. The resulting tone may possibly irritate some serious professionals."[20] *The Extended Phenotype* tried to balance a specialized presentation for Dawkins's colleagues with an accessible work for Dawkins now-substantial popular audience.

Dawkins's extension of the biological concept of the phenotype is intriguing: "The technical word *phenotype* is used for the bodily manifestation of a gene. . . . The phenotypic effect of some particular gene might be, say, green eye color. In practice most genes have more than one phenotypic effect, say green eye color and curly hair. Natural selection favors some genes rather than others not because of the nature of the genes themselves, but because of their consequences—their phenotypic effects."[21] Dawkins coined the phrase *extended phenotype* to convey the idea that the effects of the genes go beyond the individual where they reside. In his own words, the gene "should be thought of as having *extended* phenotypic effects, consisting of all its effects on the world at large, not just its effects on the individual body in which it happens to be sitting."[22]

Dawkins is probably correct to note that this idea is his most extraordinary. What he is suggesting is the following: Genes—selfish genes—are the "puppet masters" that not only direct the *development* of the bodies in which they reside, but also influence the *behaviors* of those bodies. Genes that motivate birds to sound alarms are an example of this. But birds also have genes that direct them to build nests. Why not, says Dawkins, view nests as extensions of the phenotypes of the birds? Viewed by these lights, the phenotype is just the *preliminary* physical manifestation of the "will" of the genes. Over the course of the lifetime of an organism, this full, extended manifestation will be considerably larger. The genes of beavers, for example, have them building huge dams that alter acres of wilderness; prairie dogs and chipmunks build networks of tunnels; and humans build great cities and ways to travel between them.

Again we face a highly original and suggestive idea that is not strictly scientific, but could inspire new scientific theories and facts by looking at the world differently. Dawkins is careful to acknowledge this:

> What I am advocating is not a new theory, not a hypothesis which can be verified or falsified, not a model which can be judged by its predictions. . . . What I am advocating is a point of view, a way of looking at familiar facts and ideas, and a way of asking new questions about them. . . . I am not trying to convince anyone of the truth of any factual proposition. . . . The vision of life that I advocate, and label with the name of the extended phenotype, is not probably more correct than the orthodox view. It is a different view and I suspect that, at least in some respects, it provides a deeper understanding. But I doubt that there is any experiment that could be done to prove my claim.[23]

Memes and Viruses

Dawkins's work on selfish genes provides a way of looking at survival through reproduction. Genes create congenial hosts that in turn create congenial environments that ensure the survival and spread of those genes. If they are good at this, genes flourish; if they are not, they disappear. This very general concept, curiously, is not limited to genes. Take books, for example. Books, like those by Dawkins, compete to survive in a competitive marketplace with other books. A book that sells many copies will flourish. It will remain in print for many years, there will be new editions, and it may even get translated into other languages. The ideas and even the phrases in the book will take up residence in the culture at large and outlive the book itself. The analogy with genes is obvious.

This analogy, and its extension beyond genes and books, highlights the value of a general category that includes anything that flourishes by spreading around copies of itself. Such entities can be called *replicators.*

Genes are *active* replicators because they contain instructions for being copied and are directly involved in their own copying, via protein synthesis and the creation of the associated phenotypes. On the other hand, *passive* replicators exert no influence on their own spread. Dawkins says that some might dispute whether a photocopied sheet of paper is really passive: Some sheets are more likely to be copied by humans than others. A really passive replicator might be a section of DNA that is never transcribed. When speaking of biology, evolution and natural selection, we are obviously interested in *active germ-line* replicators, specifically genes in gametes, which are potentially the ancestors of an indefinitely long line of descendant replicators.[24] Any particular gene in existence right now has the potential to exist almost indefinitely if it is successful at replicating itself.

Dawkins is particularly interested in a nonbiological replicator for which he coined the term *meme.* The term, a fusion of "gene" and "memory," refers to a *cultural* replicator. The last chapter of the first edition of *The Selfish Gene,* "Memes: The New Replicators," is devoted to introducing and explaining memes.

Dawkins notes that the analogy between cultural and genetic evolution has been made before—there are selection effects at work on culture just as there are on genes/organisms. Ideas, products, entertainment vehicles, and so on all compete in an environment with limited money, attention, and time. Some survive and some do not. But Dawkins is not satisfied with the various attempts to exploit this analogy. He says that even though some of them are plausible, "they do not begin to square up to the formidable challenge of explaining culture, cultural evolution, and the immense differences between human cultures around the world." He says, "We have got to start again and go right back to first principles. The argument I shall advance . . . is that, for an understanding of the evolution of modern man, we must begin by throwing out the gene as the sole basis of our ideas on evolution. I am an enthusiastic Darwinian, but I think Darwinism is too big a theory to be confined to the narrow context of the gene. The gene will enter my thesis as an analogy, nothing more."[25]

Dawkins's ready abandonment of the "all-is-genes" perspective may be surprising, especially as it occurs at the end of the very book that earned him this label. But Dawkins rejects both this label and the claim that he is a genetic determinist. He does indeed see the world as a pitiless battlefield where organisms struggle to survive. But he hastens to add that we should—and can—partially escape our biology and build a world guided by our ethics, not just our genes. Understanding and appreciating the challenges posed by our selfish genes can help us overcome those very challenges and rise above the mere battle to spread our genes about.

Memes were introduced by Dawkins to illuminate human culture. They are replicators, doing for culture what genes did for biology. A meme is

> a unit of cultural transmission, or a unit of *imitation*.... Examples of memes are tunes, ideas, catch-phrases, clothes fashions, ways of making pots or of building arches. Just as genes propagate themselves in the gene pool by leaping from body to body via sperms or eggs, so memes propagate themselves in the meme pool by leaping from brain to brain via a process which, in the broad sense, can be called imitation. If a scientist hears, or reads about, a good idea, he passes it on to his colleagues and students. He mentions it in his articles and his lectures. If the idea catches on, it can be said to propagate itself, spreading from brain to brain.[26]

For a meme to be successful, it simply needs to be memorable, in the most general sense of that word. It can be memorable in a good way, like Martin Luther King's powerful "I Have a Dream" speech, or Paul McCartney's winsome song "Yesterday." Or it can be memorable in a bad way, like an irritating advertising jingle that you can't get out of your head, or a powerful prejudice inherited from your family. Dawkins identifies religions as bad memes, calling them "viruses of the mind."

Oddly enough, in the endnotes to the 1989 edition of *The Selfish Gene*, Dawkins is ambivalent about the memes he created. On the one hand, he is pleased that in 1988 the word joined the official list of words being considered for future editions of the *Oxford English Dictionary* (*OED*). Very few people have their own entry in that august compilation of the world's leading language. But on the other hand, he notes that he had a much larger vision for memes than simply explaining human culture:

> I want to claim almost limitless power for slightly inaccurate self-replicating entities, once they arise anywhere in the universe. This is because they tend to become the basis for Darwinian selection which,

given enough generations, cumulatively builds systems of great complexity.... The first ten chapters of *The Selfish Gene* had concentrated exclusively on one kind of replicator, the gene. In discussing memes in the final chapter I was trying to make the case for replicators in general, and to show that genes were not the only members of that important class.... Chapter 11 will have succeeded if the reader closes the book with the feeling that DNA molecules are not the only entities that might form the basis for Darwinian evolution. My purpose was to cut the gene down to size, rather than to sculpt a grand theory of human culture.[27]

Dawkins did not formulate a grand theory of human culture and how it came to be. But, as is always the case with thinkers who create new ways of understanding the world, Dawkins's enthusiastic followers have enlarged his idea. Thus we have a new science, a "memology" purporting to explain human culture in general and human consciousness in particular. For example, Tufts University philosopher Daniel Dennett, author of *Darwin's Dangerous Idea*,[28] has used memes in the context of a universal Darwinism applauded by Dawkins. And Dawkins wrote the foreword to a book that articulates "the meme's eye view"[29] of the world. Dawkins's real aim is an ambitious universal Darwinism where genes and memes play important roles as manifestations of a more general central figure, the replicator.

Although Dawkins is clearly pleased with the success of his meme idea, he is cautious to the point of ambivalence about some of the ways it is being used. "It is a matter of dispute," he says, "whether the resemblance between gene and meme is good scientific poetry or bad. On balance, I still think it is good, although if you look the word up on the worldwide web you'll find plenty of examples of enthusiasts getting carried away and going too far. There even seems to be some kind of religion of the meme starting up—I find it hard to decide whether it is a joke or not."[30]

The meme *idea*, ironically, has clearly proven itself to be a good meme.

The Blind Watchmaker

In *The Selfish Gene* and the conversations that flowed from it, Dawkins adopted a negative view of religion, although the topic was not emphasized. In contrast, a disproportionate response from readers, reviewers, and the public focused on these portions of his writings. Particularly in the United States, Dawkins became a symbol of the perennial tension between science and religion and the latest in a long line of evolutionists attacking belief in God as the Creator.

Dawkins's negative view of religion moved front and center in 1986 when he published his third book, *The Blind Watchmaker*. With a jacket blurb from *The Good Book Guide* praising it as possibly the "most important book on evolution since Darwin," this best-seller was simultaneously a defense of Darwinism and an aggressive attack on the argument from design. The title refers to William Paley's famous version of the argument from design in his *Natural Theology*, published in 1802. Facing Paley's argument head-on, Dawkins affirms that the complex design of a watch does indeed require an intelligent watchmaker. And living organisms, with their enormous complexity, also require a "designer." However, there is no need for an *intelligent* designer, traditionally God, to explain the complexity of living organisms. Blind natural selection is enough. The watchmaker crafting living organisms can be a blind watchmaker. The subtitle of the American version of the book makes this crystal clear: "Why the Evidence of Evolution Reveals a Universe without Design."

The Blind Watchmaker had predecessors, most notably a famous and influential 1970 book by the French biochemist Jacques Monod, who won the Nobel Prize for his work in molecular biology. Titled *Chance and Necessity*, Monod's best-seller shaped discourse on this topic for a generation that included Dawkins, then a lecturer at Oxford. (Dawkins refers to Monod in the preface to *The Blind Watchmaker*.)

Monod argues that there is no place for goals or purpose in the natural world. Science is based on the "postulate of objectivity," which requires that we accept only theories that can be tested against experiments, independently of subjective ideas. Therefore, the old alliance between man and nature, the "covenant" which inspired us to see the world as the creation of God and to find meaning for our lives within that ordered creation, has been broken. Monod's whole approach was quite demoralizing, in consonance with the existentialist philosophy prevailing in France at the time. At the end of his eloquent, if sobering, manifesto he writes: "Man knows at last that that he is alone in the universe's unfeeling immensity, out of which he emerged only by chance."[31]

Dawkins picks up the torch from Monod, arguing that natural selection solves the problem of design and order in the world, so that there is no need for further explanations. *The Blind Watchmaker* begins with a statement of its purpose: "This book is written in the conviction that our own existence once presented the greatest of all mysteries, but that it is a mystery no longer because it is solved. Darwin and Wallace solved it. . . . The problem is that of complex design."[32]

Lest the reader suspect that he fails to fully appreciate the problem of design, or that his analysis is aimed at a straw man, Dawkins devotes the whole of chapter 2, titled "Good Design," to explaining the "radar" system in bats, an example sure to impress Paley and anybody else, even today.[33] He addresses the typical objections: that such sophisticated design cannot be the result of blind natural forces, or that evolution cannot gradually generate such perfect multi-component organs when each component would be useless until all of them were present.

The Blind Watchmaker emphasizes that natural selection is *cumulative*. Evolutionary theory holds that genetic changes are random in that they are not programmed to reach any particular end. Many people, however, have trouble understanding how evolution produces very sophisticated results if the process is truly random. How can such an unguided, random process produce results requiring a long, carefully sequenced chain of events? No problem, says Dawkins. We need only note that each new step in natural selection begins where the previous one ended.

Dawkins illustrates this with a now-famous computer simulation based on the traditional claim from probability that "given enough time, a monkey bashing away at random on a typewriter could produce all the works of Shakespeare." Dawkins goes easy on the monkey, however, and assigns him a simpler task: "Suppose that he has to produce, not the complete works of Shakespeare but just the short sentence 'Methinks it is like a weasel,' and we shall make it relatively easy by giving him a typewriter with a restricted keyboard, one with just the 26 (capital) letters, and a space bar. How long will he take to write this one little sentence?"[34]

With the monkey now assigned to a more manageable task that can be simulated on a computer, Dawkins specifies that the monkey gets a series of discrete trials, each consisting of twenty-eight bashes at the keyboard. The probability of producing the desired phrase by a series of independent tries would be almost completely negligible, however, even with this more modest goal. To get around this, Dawkins introduces an apparently small change in the program. The first random-produced phrase is duplicated repeatedly but with a certain random change in the copying, and then, "The computer examines the mutant nonsense phrases, the 'progeny' of the original phrase, and chooses the one which, *however slightly*, most resembles the target phrase, METHINKS IT IS LIKE A WEASEL."[35] The procedure is repeated time and again. In this case, the target was reached in forty-three tries the first time, forty-one the second time. Dawkins concludes that natural selection, understood not as a collection of independent mutations but as a process of "cumulative" selection that takes as the point of departure outcomes already reached, can account for the adaptations and apparent design of our world, thus eliminating the need for an intelligent "watchmaker."

Dawkins's argument is subtle. He introduces a direction in his monkey computer game when he instructs the program to examine the randomly generated phrases and "choose the one which most resembles the target phrase." Dawkins warns the reader that his monkey-writing-Shakespeare-with-a-target-phrase illustration is misleading because evolution has no long-term goal. There are no "targets" in nature toward which random variations are moving.

Even if we grant, however, that living beings have developed through evolution by natural selection, this does not imply that there is no design in the universe. Design arguments have a long and varied history that predates evolution by centuries, and some of those arguments are quite subtle. But evolution, as was pointed out over a century ago, actually facilitates some of those arguments. Near the close of the nineteenth century, John Zahm, an American priest and professor of natural science at the University of Notre Dame, published *Evolution and Dogma*, arguing for the compatibility between evolution and Christianity.[36] Zahm juxtaposes evolution and the traditional argument from design and concludes that evolution suggests a purpose much richer and more interesting than the old one. It is not difficult to see why. The unfolding of evolution over billions of years supposes potentials that are realized step by step, in such a way that the process as a whole would be unintelligible without a grand plan. Zahm cites authors who saw in evolution a new way to prove, in a more profound way than before, the existence in nature of purpose and a higher plan.

Contemporary cell biologist and Nobel laureate Christian de Duve accepts the neo-Darwinian account of evolution but notes: "Chance did not operate in a vacuum. It operated in a universe governed by orderly laws and made of matter endowed with specific properties. These laws and properties are the constraints that shape the evolutionary roulette and restrict the numbers that it can turn up."[37] De Duve concludes, from the point of view of a scientist who also thinks as a philosopher, that evolution is compatible with the existence of a divine plan, and he offers pointers that lead us to admit the existence of such a plan. Dawkins's wholesale dismissal of design—not just in evolution but in the universe as a whole, if his subtitle is to be believed—is remarkable for its failure to even acknowledge the apparently intricate design of the physical laws that make life possible.

From Zahm to de Duve, many thinkers prepared to place evolution in a larger philosophical framework have supported this line of thought. Cosmic and biological evolution consist of a succession of many steps, each of which implies the previous existence of potentialities. The concept of "potency" was proposed by Aristotle in the fourth century B.C. to explain the possibility of natural processes. A natural process can be seen as the passage from potency to act. Apples are obtained from apple trees, and human beings are formed through the progressive development of the potencies contained in the zygote. For something to be produced, a previous state is needed containing the possibility of the new result. Evolution from primeval life to human beings implies a quantity of steps, each of them based on the previous one, plus the circumstances necessary to enable the transition. Reflection on this point easily produces a kind of awe that results in the posing of ultimate questions. The better we know the natural processes, the more we can experience the marvel of a self-organizing universe that leads to teleological questions. Nothing is gained by highlighting that many results are eliminated, as it remains true that many successive potentialities, plus the corresponding circumstances for their actualization, must exist to reach the results we observe.

Like any Darwinist, Dawkins must face the uneasy question of progress. "There is nothing inherently progressive about evolution,"[38] he reminds us. This is pure Darwinism. Should not we admit, however, that some kind of progress has been produced in evolution? Pure Darwinism would deny this, saying it is nonsensical to apply the concepts of "higher" and "lower" to living beings. Bacteria are sometimes considered more successful than other living creatures in the way they dominate the earth and have survived for billions of years. Nevertheless, Darwinists usually feel compelled to provide some explanation of the existence of some form of progress. Dawkins devotes chapter 7 of *The Blind Watchmaker* to the subject. "Coadapted genotypes," or teams of genes that cooperate, are a good candidate. There is no scientific difficulty in this. From a philosophical point of view, this again suggests the existence of potencies that cooperate in fascinating ways. The best candidate for Dawkins is, however, "arms races" between enemies that, under the pressure of competition for survival, develop new equipment: "It is largely arms races that have injected such 'progressiveness' as there is in evolution."[39] At the end of the chapter, Dawkins recognizes, "This has been a difficult chapter, but it had to go into the book. Without it, we would have been left with the feeling that natural selection is only a destructive process, or at best a process of weeding-out. We have seen two ways in which natural selection can be a *constructive* force. One way concerns cooperative relationships between genes within species. . . . And arms races constitute the other great force propelling evolution in directions that we recognize as 'progressive,' complex 'design.'"[40]

As is typical, Dawkins does not address these problems all at once. Little by little he unfolds bits and pieces of his argument, carrying the reader where he wants, disclosing his arguments here and there, laying a foundation in this chapter and then building on it sometime later. This is a powerful rhetorical strategy, and Dawkins is an expert in the fine art of argument and persuasion. The reader will quickly forget the warning made by Dawkins in the preface: "This book is not a dispassionate scientific treatise.... Far from being dispassionate, it has to be confessed that in parts this book is written with a passion which, in a professional scientific journal, might excite comment. Certainly it seeks to inform, but it also seeks to persuade."[41]

Dawkins assures the reader that his passion is truth, adding that he never says anything he does not believe to be right. There is no reason to doubt Dawkins's sincerity, for he does indeed believe what he is writing. The difficulty is that his science and his personal opinions become so entwined that they merge, making it difficult for a casual reader to distinguish one from the other. This mixture would not merely "excite comment" if written in a scientific journal; rather, it would not be published in any scientific journal. *The Blind Watchmaker* is not really a science book, despite its appearance. The argument Dawkins makes goes hand in hand with science, but it is also profoundly philosophical and theological. Monod acknowledged this sort of "mixture" by adding to his book *Chance and Necessity* the subtitle *On the Natural Philosophy of Modern Biology*. There is no sign, however, that Dawkins can see this problem with his work. He may be sincere in his arguments, he is sincerely mistaken in construing them as purely scientific.

The Meaning of Life

The biggest question posed by evolution relates to the meaning of human life, examined by Dawkins in his 1995 book *River Out of Eden*. This title is yet another memey metaphor used to signify the flow of DNA: "Another of my purposes is to convince my readers that 'ways of making a living' is synonymous with 'ways of passing DNA-coded texts on to the future.' My 'river' is a river of DNA, flowing and branching through geological time, and the metaphor of steep banks confining each species' genetic games turns out to be a surprisingly powerful and helpful explanatory device."[42] Immediately Dawkins adds that this book continues the same line of his other books, exploring the "almost limitless power of the Darwinian principle."[43]

Leaving aside bona fide scientific concerns about Darwinism's "limitless power," we cannot dispute that, for Dawkins, it excludes the existence of God. However, readers of *River Out of Eden* will be understandably—although temporarily—surprised when they discover that chapter 4 is titled "God's Utility Function."

Dawkins explains that "utility function" is a technical term of economists, meaning "that which is maximized." He speaks of "reverse engineering," where you watch the behavior of something in order to identify its utility functions (there can be more than one utility function). Dawkins argues that we should expect of God a certain maximizing of good and happiness (this would be God's utility function). Instead we observe, using reverse engineering, that "the total amount of suffering per year in the natural world is beyond all decent contemplation."[44] We are thus forced to conclude that there is no God: "The universe we observe has precisely the properties we should expect if there is, at bottom, no design, no purpose, no evil and no good, nothing but blind, pitiless indifference. As that unhappy poet A. E. Housman put it: 'For Nature, heartless, witless Nature, Will neither care nor know.' DNA neither cares nor knows. DNA just is. And we dance to its music."[45]

This is an unoriginal version of the classical argument against the existence of an all-powerful, all-knowing God based on the presence of evil in the world. Dawkins offers it up with the sort of enthusiasm that makes one wonder if he somehow thinks it is original with him. There can be no doubt that the existence of evil is indeed a powerful argument against the existence of God. However, this argument has been around for a long time, and various thoughtful responses have been advanced. In the thirteenth century, for example, Thomas Aquinas addresses the problem of the existence of God at the beginning of his classic *Summa Theologica*.[46] He lists two objections to the existence of God: (1) If we can explain the world by natural causes, then there is no need for God; (2) The existence of God is incompatible with the existence of evil. These are exactly the same objections posed by Dawkins, but clothed in his personal interpretation of biology. Natural selection, he argues, explains the apparent design we observe in nature; therefore there is no need for divine action. Second, nature seems indifferent to suffering, and there is so much suffering in the world that there is no place for a benevolent, all-powerful God.

Fortunately, God has had many talented defenders over the centuries, and objections such as those advanced in *The Blind Watchmaker* have been addressed, albeit in subtle ways, and not, of course, with knock-down arguments.

Consider the first objection above. Does natural selection necessarily exclude God from the process of evolution? Does its (possible) adequacy, in fact, argue against the very existence of God? The evolution of life on this planet has required the never-ending presence of possibilities. Every DNA replication contains the possibility of something novel; every DNA strand formed by sexual combination has potential variety; every cosmic ray that hits an organism has a chance to induce some mutation; every organism struggles in nature against a complex array of challenges, the outcomes of which are not known in advance. The trajectory of evolution is the exploration of the variations made possible by this extraordinary roster of contingencies, and each step in the process is the selection of one possibility among many. Bacteria require a great many of these steps to evolve a chimpanzee, and each step on this unimaginably long journey is the starting point for the next. This could, of course, happen entirely by natural selection, and perhaps it did; nevertheless, so little is known about the details of the process that the assertion is surely a gigantic extrapolation, like claiming that because the New York Yankees have won their division three times in a row, they will always win it. We must keep in mind that most species have appeared and gone extinct without leaving even a trace in the fossil record. To reconstruct the details of natural history requires knowledge of exactly what occurred in a great many settings about which we know virtually nothing. This is speculation—informed, perhaps, but not by much. Furthermore, it is not difficult to see that natural selection is actually compatible with the existence of a divine plan. Evolution has produced some remarkably complex and sophisticated organisms, and the process, at least on a very large scale, coheres with the oft-repeated claim that "evolution can be viewed as a mechanism for creation." This argument in no way establishes or even supports the idea of the existence of God. What it does do, however, is open *space* for God and thus for theological reflection on how belief in God might be squared with the reality of evolution. Using evolution to argue against the existence of God is simply invalid, and Dawkins should know better.

The argument against the existence of God based on the presence of evil is more difficult and very old. Likewise, the responses also date from antiquity. One response, from both St. Augustine in the fourth century and Aquinas after him, argues that God permits evil because He is able to produce greater goods out of it. Dawkins's version of this argument is actually blander than its predecessors, being based on generalizations about evolution and not human experience as a whole. For Dawkins's argument to work, he has to, in a manner of speaking, show God how to produce a world with at least some of the wonders of this one without allowing for pain. This is not simple. Could interesting living creatures exist, for example, without eating other organisms? Could natural processes somehow be prevented from introducing disorder? Could natural laws work without ever producing any damage? Would there be no goods for one species that were harmful to another?

The argument from the presence of evil in the world supposes, of course, that there is evil in the world. Identifying evil, however, requires some sort of standard against which things are measured to establish that they are, indeed, evil. Such a standard will most likely also highlight things that are "good" in the world, things that may not be self-explanatory. Furthermore, the very existence of criteria that can be used to identify evil in the world is itself in need of explanation. So the argument from evil itself is predicated on the existence of other things that also call for explanation.

Without getting overly mired in theological nuance, we should also point out that the entire paradigm under which this argument is constructed changes dramatically if God is taken into account. The existence of an all-encompassing God of the traditional sort implies the existence of spiritual goods that provide the material world with its *meaning*. The real meaning of material goods becomes a function of spiritual goods that provide a meaning in this life. And if one accepts the idea of the eternity of God, certain goods and certain sources of meaning may last forever. As before, we do not suggest that we have solved the perennial problem of evil in a few lines. But we have highlighted the fact that theology does have resources that can be brought to bear on the problem. Problems like these are big issues, with roots that run deep into philosophy and theology. They simply cannot be tackled using only the methods of science. Polemicists like Dawkins need to be reminded of the Faustian bargain that accompanied the birth of science: Scientific investigation would dramatically limit its explanatory purview to the natural world, ignoring questions of purpose and meaning, in exchange for great success at explaining natural phenomena. We can only express disappointment and frustration to see these deep philosophical issues treated as if they are purely scientific.

Curiously, and unfortunately, chapter 4 in *River Out of Eden* was published virtually unchanged in *Scientific American*, one of the most respected periodicals in the world. In the subtitle of the article we read: "Humans have always wondered about the meaning of life. According to the author, life has no higher purpose than to perpetuate the survival of DNA."[47] Like everyone else, scientists are free to express their opinions. But Dawkins presents his opinion about the meaning of human life in a scientific context, thus endowing it with undeserved credibility. This is further exacerbated when a prestigious scientific periodical adds its approval. Many people rightly consider this an inappropriate marshalling of the authority of science against theology—a Galileo affair turned on its head. A marginal introduction to the article, and the phrase "according to the author" in the subtitle, indicate that the editors probably wanted some degree of detachment. But this, of course, was a sham.

Science versus Religion

Dawkins's assaults on theology, while always present, have grown steadily more aggressive, perhaps because his readers enjoy them so much. These various polemics appeared in diverse publications over the years but were finally collected for a 2003 book, appropriately titled *A Devil's Chaplain*.

This memorable title comes from a letter written by Charles Darwin to his friend Joseph Hooker in 1856. Dawkins reproduces the letter in the first essay of the book: "What a book a Devil's Chaplain might write on the clumsy, wasteful, blundering low and horridly cruel works of nature."[48] Apparently Dawkins thinks that Darwin was looking ahead a century to him; if so, he has eagerly embraced the odd chaplainship and done very well with the appointment.

A Devil's Chaplain contains thirty-two essays and articles, distributed in seven sections. The central idea of the third section is that religion is a harmful *virus of the mind*, which causes in the religious person an *infected mind*. Dawkins insists that this virus is usually transmitted from parents to children, so that one acquires the infection when one is a child: Children need to believe and trust and are very ready to do it. The concluding essay is also strongly antireligious, blaming religion for the attack on the World Trade Center on September 11, 2001. "It has a more savage tone than I customarily adopt," Dawkins rationalizes, because it was written in the immediate aftermath of the events.[49]

In the introduction to this section, Dawkins makes no effort to temper his negative view of religion: "From 1976 onwards, I always thought religions provided the prime examples of memes and meme complexes. . . . In 'Viruses of the Mind' I developed this theme of religions as mind parasites, and also the analogy with computer viruses. . . . To describe religions as mind viruses is sometimes interpreted as contemptuous or even hostile. It is both."[50]

Dawkins uses the definition of *meme* as it appears in the *Oxford Dictionary*: "a self-replicating element of culture, passed on by imitation." He applies the concept to the transmission of religion to children, analyzing why their minds are so ready to receive "viruses of the mind" like religion. There are seven symptoms of the religious "illness." The first three are related: Faith is a compelling conviction completely alien to evidence or reason; lack of evidence is a virtue; mystery is a good thing.

Dawkins has assumed a priori that a reasonable religious commitment cannot exist, and he offers up a caricature to make his point. His other symptoms, however, are even less edifying. The religious person, labeled the "sufferer," may behave intolerantly, for example, toward "vectors" of rival faiths, sometimes killing them.

As usual, Dawkins has grossly oversimplified the religious problem. Today, in the West at least, religious authorities are often very tolerant and enthusiastic defenders of the weak. He notes this but counters that this is a manifestation of a "symptom" diagnosed earlier, namely the delusion that faith has to be respected simply because it is faith. The philosopher of science Karl Popper called these sorts of arguments *pseudoscience*: A doctrine presents itself as reasonable and supported by arguments but, in the face of contradictory information, it freely (mis)interprets the information in an arbitrary way. Dawkins's argument goes something like this: "If you are religious, you are intolerant, and if you are tolerant, this is due to some mistaken and dangerous reason." There is no arguing in the face of such dogmatism.

Dawkins insists that the religion one holds is probably an "accident of birth." When this is not the case, he has a ready explanation: It is statistically probable that one has been exposed to "a particularly potent infective agent" such as a strong personality. Religion is thus easily explained away. One may suspect, however, that similar reasons could be used against many cultural ideas. In the same way that they acquire their religion, children develop ideas about all kinds of things, from personal hygiene to common politeness. Are these also mental pathologies, because we acquired them at a time when we were gullible? This argument is very well known, is far from original, and belongs in first-year philosophy, not in Dawkins's books.

What about science, however? Science is an enduring set of beliefs about the world, and we do teach it to our children who tend to believe it. Is it also a "virus of the mind"? "Scientific ideas," says Dawkins,

> like all memes, are subject to a kind of natural selection, and this might look superficially virus-like. But the selective forces that scru-tinize scientific ideas are not arbitrary or capricious. They are exact-ing, well-honed rules, and they do not favour pointless self-serving behaviour. They favour all the virtues laid out in textbooks of standard methodology: testability, evidential support, precision, quantifiability, consistency, intersubjectivity, repeatability, universality, progressive-ness, independence of cultural milieu, and so on. Faith spreads de-spite a total lack of every single one of these virtues.... For scientific belief, epidemiology merely comes along afterwards and describes the history of its acceptance. For religious belief, epidemology is the root cause.[51]

Most people accept Dawkins's assertion that science at its best is testable, quantifiable, and generally in possession of the virtues above; but most do not think that it contradicts religion, or that religion is completely without any of these virtues. Dawkins argues that outside science we cannot find respectable truth; this, of course, is scientism, not science.

Using Dawkins's own meme paradigm, we would argue that scientism is itself a meme. Books have been written to describe it; movements have embraced it; charismatic gurus have arisen as its champions. Scientism is a belief that serves its adherents very well, assuring them that only science provides a valid paradigm for assessing knowledge claims. Scientism is, however, an obviously self-defeating ideology. Its claims about its own epistemology are not the consequence of any scientific investigation but rather reach outside itself into the very realm that it claims does not exist. The claim that there is no valuable knowledge *outside* science certainly cannot be supported from *within* science. This is an extremely simple philosophical error, akin to a child claiming that because all the people he knows are in his house, that there cannot be any people outside his house.

When we reflect on science—its aims, its values, its limits—we are doing philosophy, not science. This may be bad news for the high priests of scientism, who reject philosophy, but there is no escaping it. Dawkins is a good scientist and a brilliant communicator and certainly would have been an effective lawyer or politician, but he seems strangely unaware that he is an abysmal philosopher and an even worse theologian.

How a scientist becomes a disciple of scientism is mysterious, because science and scientism are incompatible. Science owes its success to its restricted focus—its acknowledged inability to even *address* questions like those raised by scientism, much less answer them. Scientists concentrate on very particular subjects, generally astonishingly narrow, and use rigorous methods to study them, submitting their hypotheses to careful scrutiny and avoiding extrapolations or unwarranted generalizations. In contrast, scientism is an unsupported generalization, bad philosophy masquerading as science or one of its consequences. This qualifies as a *virus of the mind*, to use Dawkins's own terminology. Most of scientism's disciples are casual and probably not even aware that they hold this philosophy, but when scientism is seriously adopted, it becomes a sort of pseudoreligion, providing a meaning to life, and an ideal for which one will fight. Conversion to this strong form of pseudoreligious scientism often derives from two related factors: a disillusionment with some form of traditional religion, and the discovery that science is wonderful and seems to provide meaning and values, in addition to knowledge.

There are indeed important values associated with scientific work, and the progress of science contributes to their spread.[52] Progress in crucial aspects of contemporary culture reflects the spread of scientific values. But as most practicing scientists have discovered, one can work in science, easily mixing its values with unrelated extra-scientific interests.

Dawkins points, repeatedly and with enthusiasm, to the diversity of religions and concludes that their very diversity proves that no one of them is reliable. Of course, Dawkins's ideas are themselves much debated among scientists, and serious disputes do indeed exist regarding the very aspects of evolutionary theory that he champions. This, however, hardly constitutes an argument that all these various points of view are equally vacuous and that there can be no serious discussion about them. Dawkins seems strangely unmoved by the large number of thoughtful scholars—including his colleagues at Oxford University, like Keith Ward, Alister McGrath, and Richard Swinburne—whose religious beliefs are accompanied by serious reflection and considerations of evidence.

There is, to be sure, a great difference between the general unanimity of science and the diversity of religions. But there is a considered response to this. We reach the peculiar agreement and intersubjectivity of natural science only when we deal with repeatable patterns in the natural world. Scientists have the luxury of gathering together in laboratories to share common, repeatable, and predictable experiences. It is no surprise that when we pose problems related to meaning and spiritual realities, it is more difficult to reach agreement. When we insist on testability, empirical control, quantification, repeatability, and so on, we should be aware that we are confining our study to those realities that meet these criteria. This study is both wonderful and exciting, but it has absolutely nothing to do with the scientism that would impose its straitjacket on the human mind, denying the value or validity of other explorations.

Dawkins, of course, sees religion and science as opposed and incompatible enterprises. He acknowledges that "science has no way to disprove the existence of a supreme being," but (following Bertrand Russell) he compares this with the equally agnostic position "about the theory that there is a china teapot in elliptical orbit around the Sun." He goes on to suggest that, if there actually are reasons for finding a supreme being more plausible than a celestial teapot, "if legitimate, they are proper scientific arguments which should be evaluated on their merits."[53] We wonder, however, why only *scientific* arguments would be valid in favor of the existence of God—a subject that, Dawkins insists, remains outside the scope of science.

This line of argument is vacuous, its content and logical structure at the level of a schoolyard argument about whose father is the strongest. Dawkins sinks even further into his quicksand of illogic when he adds, "We are all atheists about most of the gods that humanity has ever believed in. Some of us just go one god further."[54] Shall we offer the pointed—and pointless—rejoinder: "We are also all atheists about most of the scientific theories that people once believed"?

The late famous Harvard evolutionist and science writer Stephen Jay Gould quarreled consistently with Dawkins in print. Gould attempted unsuccessfully to broker a peace between science and religion by assigning them to separate realms, a scheme he called "non-overlapping magisteria." Dawkins was not alone in rejecting this initiative: "In any case, the belief that religion and science occupy separate magisteria is dishonest," he wrote. While we would agree that there are some overlappings, we reject the odd application that Dawkins makes when the magisteria are allowed to overlap. "Miracle stories," he argues, "are blatant intrusions into scientific territory." He mentions Christian miracles such as the Virgin Birth, the Resurrection, and the Raising of Lazarus and comments, "Every one of these miracles amounts to a scientific claim, a violation of the normal running of the natural world. Theologians, if they want to remain honest, should make a choice."[55] This is a strange demand, as not one of these miracles involves any sort of scientific claim. They presuppose the "normal running of the natural world" studied by science, and in the "normal" world's absence they would not be miracles at all.

Once again, we note that the arguments above do nothing to establish the credibility of miracle stories in Christianity or any other religion. We have simply protected these religious stories from unwarranted attacks by Dawkins on his crusade for scientism.

Religion and Violence

Dawkins is irritated by the expectation that religious ideas deserve a special kind of respect: Views on politics, science, or art, of course, deserve respect as far as we can argue in favor of them, but religious views have to be respected independently of their reasons. "Why," he asks, "are religious opinions off limits this way? Why do we have to respect them, simply because they are religious?" He goes further, questioning the right of parents to decide for their children in religious matters. "Society, for no reason that I can discern," says Dawkins, "accepts that parents have an automatic right to bring their children up with particular religious opinions and can withdraw them from, say, biology classes that teach evolution."[56]

Leaving aside the complex relationship of religious upbringing and science classes, we must surely note that Dawkins has traveled very far on this particular tirade. How is it that children should not be raised in the religion of their parents? For most parents, this is a matter of personal conscience. Possibly the most important acquisition of humankind's long journey on this planet is the sense of conscience—that there are things that are right and wrong, and that we should do the former whenever possible. Denying respect to religious convictions, and denying the right of the parents to raise their children in the family religion—something they believe is the "right" thing to do—undermines the very conscience that our history has bequeathed to us.

Dawkins's assault on religion reaches its peak (and he even warns the reader about this) in the essay "Time to Stand Up," written as an immediate reaction to the events of September 11, 2001. The article opens with a brief autobiographical note: "Those of us who have renounced one or another of the three 'great' monotheistic religions have, until now, moderated our language for reasons of politeness."[57] This passage suggests that Dawkins has had some personal experiences that may explain his acrimony toward religion. Brian Goodwin suggests that Dawkins was a religious man who converted to a kind of Darwinist religion: "I suspect that Richard was at one stage fairly religious, and that he then underwent a kind of conversion to Darwinism, and he feels fervently that people ought to embrace this as a way of life."[58] Indeed, Darwinism is, for Dawkins, much more than a scientific theory. It is a worldview embracing all the aspects of human life; it is a kind of scientific religion; it is a message that must be told.

At the end of the essay, Dawkins explains what he means by of "standing up":

> The human psyche has two great sicknesses: the urge to carry vendetta across generations, and the tendency to fasten group labels on people rather than see them as individuals. Abrahamic religion mixes explosively with (and gives strong sanction to) both. Only the willfully blind could fail to implicate the divisive force of religion in most, if not all, of the violent enmities in the world today. Those of us who have for years politely concealed our contempt for the dangerous collective delusion of religion need to stand up and speak out. Things are different after September 11th. All is changed, changed utterly.[59]

He says: "My point is not that religion itself is the motivation for wars, murders and terrorist attacks, but that religion is the principal *label*, and the most dangerous one, by which a 'they' as opposed to a 'we' can be identified at all. I am not even claiming that religion is the *only* label by which we identify the victims of our prejudice.... Even when it is not alone, religion is nearly always an incendiary ingredient in the mix as well."[60]

In her book *The Meme Machine*, which includes a foreword by Dawkins, Susan Blackmore devotes a whole chapter to "religions as memeplexes." We are told, "Religions teach that God wants you to spread his *True* understanding to all the world and it is therefore *good* to maim, rape, pillage, steal, and murder."[61] Blackmore regales the reader with historical episodes of violence in the name of religion. Most people, however, and historians in particular, agree that things were rather more complex than simply "Religion A went to war with Religion B and they did terrible things to each other."

There is little basis for supposing that violence in the democratic societies of the West should be laid at the feet of religion. The most terrible episodes of the twentieth century, in particular, were caused by ideologies that opposed religion, like Nazism and Communism. Anticipating this argument, Dawkins reproduces a paragraph of a speech by Adolf Hitler on April 12, 1922, where Hitler proclaims himself a Christian fighting against the Jewish people. We wonder if Dawkins really believes that "Hitler as violent Christian" is symbolic of how religions are bad. Does he really think that a secular Hitler would have left Europe and the Jews alone, content to eat sauerkraut and paint bad pictures for all of his life?

The history of religion and its abuse in the West has been thoroughly studied. Violent episodes have usually been associated with the union of religion and secular power, making it difficult to separate religious ideals from secular interests. In the first decade of this millennium, for example, who could claim to know where religion stops and politics begins in the troubled regions of the Middle East?

In the West, religion is no longer associated in any formal sense with secular power. Charging religion with violence today is no more reasonable than blaming science for those calamities made possible by scientific advance.

Standards of Truth

The last essay in *A Devil's Chaplain* is a letter addressed by Dawkins to his daughter Juliet on the occasion of her tenth birthday: "Good and Bad Reasons for Believing." The good reasons, not surprisingly, are those based on evidence, with many examples from science, and the bad reasons are those based on tradition, authority, and revelation, the reasons used by religion.

The letter to Juliet is eloquent and beautiful, showcasing Dawkins's considerable rhetorical skills. He explains the scientific method to Juliet in a few words, then moves quickly into his attack on religion. Children, he says, believe what they have been told, which means quite incompatible things in different religions. Tradition means that people believe something merely because people have believed it over centuries. Religious people, he tells Juliet, often go to war over their disagreements. Authority means that you believe something merely because some important person says it is true. Revelation is suspect because it is based on dubious personal experiences. Millions of people believe quite different things that cannot be true at the same time; they believe in the local religion because that is where they were born.[62]

Dawkins concedes no positive value to religion and implies that intelligent people cannot be religious, as religion is nothing but prejudice transmitted like an infection to children. Truth and evidence belong to science. As a "lover of truth," he writes in *The Devil's Chaplain*, "I am suspicious of strongly held beliefs that are unsupported by evidence: fairies, unicorns, werewolves."[63] Dawkins clearly holds no respect for his Oxford colleagues who somehow think that belief in God is different than belief in fairies.

This should not surprise us, however, for Dawkins's idea of God is about as well developed as his idea of fairies. In *Climbing Mount Improbable* he writes:

> Any Designer capable of constructing the dazzling array of living things would have to be intelligent and complicated beyond all imagining. And complicated is just another word for improbable—and therefore demanding of explanation. A theologian who proclaims that his god is sublimely simple has (not very) neatly evaded the issue, for a sufficiently simple god, whatever other virtues he might have, would be too simple to be capable of designing a universe (to say nothing of forgiving sins, answering prayers, blessing unions, transubstantiating wine, and the many other achievements variously expected of him). You cannot have it both ways. Either your god is capable of designing worlds and doing all the other godlike things, in which case he *needs* an explanation in his own right. Or he is not, in which case he cannot *provide* an explanation.[64]

Dawkins, proudly confirming his total lack of familiarity with theology, seems unaware that the God of the Abrahamic faiths has always been conceived as a being whose existence does not depend on other beings. God, by these lights, is the source of all created beings. Paul Tillich's immortal phrase for this aspect of God was that God is the Ground of Being. Dawkins's arguments against the religions of other people are indeed passionate, but simplistic and uninformed as well.

Three Arguments against Religion

H. Allen Orr has this to say about *A Devil's Chaplain*:

> Dawkins's passion for evolution is perhaps matched only by his hatred of religion. Indeed Dawkins has railed so often against religion

that his reputation as a God-basher may now nearly rival his reputation as a science-booster. *A Devil's Chaplain* leaves little doubt that the reputation is well deserved. Arguing that those who have masked their contempt for religion must speak out, Dawkins lets loose. He announces that religion is a "dangerous collective delusion" and a "malignant infection." Acknowledging that this position may seem "contemptuous or even hostile," he insists that "it is both." Asked why he is so hostile to organized religion, he answers that he's not particularly fond of disorganized religion either. Indeed: "I think a case can be made that *faith* is one of the world's great evils, comparable to the smallpox virus but harder to eradicate."[65]

Orr analyzes Dawkins's arguments against religion in three steps. The first argument is that "religion is just plain false." Why, then, do people believe in those falsities? We have already found Dawkins's answer: They are memes, *viruses of the mind* spread mainly by tradition into children's minds, and through the influence of powerful personalities in the case of adults. Instead, scientific ideas are supported by testability, precision, quantifiability, and other scientific standards. Orr comments,

> I confess that I find this argument astonishing. Why in the world should conformity to scientific criteria decide what counts as a "good, useful" meme? Why aren't good, useful memes the ones that make you happy, or give you a sense of belonging, or increase the odds of having cooperative friends about? If anything, these criteria would seem more natural than Dawkins'. But the deeper point is that there *are* no natural criteria. The whole point of memes is that a good meme is one that increases in frequency, period. Now we, as armchair memeticists, are free to partition successful memes into those that are "useful" vs. those that aren't, but someone has to decide: useful for what? For describing nature? Science is a useful meme. For building community? Religion is a useful meme. In the end, Dawkins's religion-is-a-virus argument comes perilously close to tautology.[66]

The caution raised by Orr is real. Dawkins does not examine the truth of religious claims: He merely takes their falseness for granted *because* they do not fit the standards of empirical science. But why should religious claims be measured against the standards of empirical science? Is there some obvious reason why we should accept a philosophically contradictory and ultimately self-defeating scientism? Surely we are right to ask for the reasons why religious claims are being put forth before accepting them, but this does not mean that such claims must align with criteria we use when we study natural phenomena. For starters, if a being like God exists, we will generally not find that God at the completion of a scientific investigation. And the more specific claims of religion are even less amenable to scientific investigation. No scientific experiment will lead to the conclusion that we are sons and daughters of God, that Christ is the Son of God, that we are morally obligated to love each other, and so on. These claims are not "scientific claims with no support"; they simply are not scientific claims at all.

Dawkins insists that religious claims should be evaluated with the methods of science because he thinks they are, in fact, scientific claims. His arguments on this point are, as we have seen, quite poor. The methods of science are more than adequate to refute ideas that can be stated and tested scientifically. The claim that the sun goes around the earth, or the moon is made of green cheese, can both be investigated scientifically and refuted to anyone's satisfaction. The power of science to do that so effectively is the reason it commands such respect in our society. But for science to refute the claims of religion, those claims must be scientific claims, and most of them are not.

The second argument made by the devil's chaplain is that religion is the root of much evil. Orr comments,

Dawkins' history seems curiously Victorian. In his drive to show that religion is the source of so much evil, he must obviously confront the awkward fact that the twentieth century was largely a chronicle of *secular* evil. Stalin, Mao, and Pol Pot were atheists and Hitler wasn't particularly pious. Dawkins deals with the problem in an especially simple way: he ignores it. Except for a mention of Hitler, he sidesteps what is arguably the key lesson of the twentieth century—that secular ideologies, including atheist ones, inspire atrocity and genocide as readily as any religious creed. And Dawkins' treatment of Hitler is remarkable: arguing "please don't trot out Hitler as a counter-example," he notes that Hitler never renounced his Roman Catholicism and quotes from an obscure speech in which the future Führer emphasized that he was a good Christian boy. Dawkins' normally robust skepticism seems to fail him here and he's silent on the obvious interpretation—that Hitler knew how to manipulate a Catholic crowd. The point is not that religious views don't sometimes lead, directly or indirectly, to evil. Of course they do. The point is that they have no monopoly: nationalist views (Italian fascism), economic views (child labor), and even scientific views (eugenics) have all had horrid consequences. Now in the last case Dawkins would surely argue that it was the *abuse* of science that led to acts of evil (forced sterilization, racist immigration policies). And I would agree. But if you allow this kind of move for science, it's a bit unclear why you don't allow it for religion too: Did Jesus really intend the Crusades?[67]

There is no need to say more.

Dawkins's third argument refers to the presumed historical opposition between science and religion. Orr speaks for recent scholarship[68] when he notes, "The popular impression of long warfare between Church and science—in which an ignorant institution fought to keep a fledgling science from escaping the Dark Ages—is nonsense, little more than Victorian propaganda." Orr concludes that "matters are considerably more complex—and considerably more subtle—than Dawkins's arguments admit."[69]

Is Dawkins obsessed with bashing religion, or is it simply one of many topics on his great canvas of inquiry? The charitable stance would be the latter, but the evidence points to the former. A case in point is his 2004 book *The Ancestor's Tale*, a massive 673-page description of forty steps leading from eubacteria to *Homo sapiens* subtitled *A Pilgrimage to the Dawn of Evolution*. The index registers four brief references to religion. A reader who has gone through the whole book will be surprised to find that the very last paragraphs are a gratuitous bashing of religion, unrelated to the rest of the book. In his characteristic sparkling prose, Dawkins praises the marvels of life across the whole book and then, all at once, antireligious rhetoric comes out of the blue. Referring to the title of the book, he writes, "'Pilgrimage' implies piety and reverence. I have not had occasion here to mention my impatience with traditional piety, and my disdain for reverence where the object is anything supernatural. But I make no secret of them. . . . My objection to supernatural beliefs is precisely that they miserably fail to do justice to the sublime grandeur of the real world. They represent a narrowing-down from reality, an impoverishment of what the real world has to offer."[70] This is an odd claim. Religious believers of many faiths have long reasoned from the astonishing power, efficiency, and beauty of the natural world to God as the creator of that world. Philosophers have long debated whether it is reasonable to claim that such a world contains within itself its reasons for existing. Paradoxically, Dawkins has said that the world is so filled with evil that it cannot be the creation of God. What, then, is Dawkins true view of the world? Is it marvelous or evil? How can it simultaneously be so evil that it refutes a loving creator, and so marvelous that religious creation stories seem impoverished?

Is Evolution a Secular Religion?

In the United States, Dawkins has become the poster child for those who charge that evolution is being promoted as a secular religion. Michael Ruse has written:

> With respect to my fellow scientists, especially with respect to my fellow Darwinians, the intensive study that I have done of evolutionary theory and its history reported at length in my *Monad to Man: The Concept of Progress in Evolutionary Biology*, and at less length in my *Mystery of Mysteries: Is Evolution a Social Construction?* has convinced me that in one major respect the creationists in their criticisms are absolutely right. They complain that Darwinism is no less a religion than is creationism (or intelligent design, to use the trendy modern equivalent). In many respects, I now think that this is true. People like Richard Dawkins use Darwinism as a skeleton on which to hang all sorts of ethical and other directives and have the theory as a kind of background metaphysic no less than the Archbishop of Canterbury has Christianity as his background metaphysic.[71]

Dawkins's readers may reasonably conclude that science in general, and Darwinism more specifically, are for Dawkins a metaphysical framework, an all-encompassing worldview, something that makes metaphysics or religion redundant (even though, to be fair, we should note that Dawkins separates the purviews of Darwinism and ethics). Ruse agrees with Dawkins on many issues, and is also a nonbeliever. But he rejects Dawkins's claim that Darwinism and religion are incompatible. Speaking of "the secular theology of Richard Dawkins," Ruse comments that "whatever the status of Christianity, secular religion is alive and well today at Oxford University."[72] Of course, as we have noted above, there are also several leading Christian thinkers in the faculty ranks at Oxford.

In *The Third Culture*, edited by his literary agent, John Brockman, Dawkins declares, "I'm a Darwinist because I believe the only alternatives are Lamarckism or God, neither of which does the job as an explanatory principle."[73] Why these seem so obviously exclusive to Dawkins is not clear, perhaps for the same reasons that most people can't see why Darwinism should be viewed as a religion.

Dawkins's challenges to religion are not entirely vacuous. But he possesses a visceral hatred of religion that expresses itself in ways that go far beyond rational critique. Perhaps it is related to his passion for science; perhaps it derives from his personal experience with religion; probably it comes from both. Whatever the origins, this passion leads him—an otherwise brilliant thinker—to simplify his analysis to the point where both he and his arguments become caricatures. Dawkins often reveals that he is aware of the answers to his objections, and he knows that he has not defended himself adequately against the charges of scientism. Nevertheless, he remains strangely untouched by these challenges. He defends his position with the same blinkered tenacity that characterizes the very fundamentalists he despises.

There is no doubt that Dawkins is a brilliant writer, one of the finest in the English-speaking world. He is not only, as a scientist, a Fellow of the Royal Society, but also a Fellow of the Royal Society of Literature. No one can doubt that his knowledge of biology is both wide and deep, especially in his own field of animal behavior. His books contain wonderful examples taken from the behavior of diverse animals and present them accurately and clearly. The overall presentation is seductive—an articulate and informed popular science exuding credibility. But Dawkins is not just telling stories. He is making sustained and elaborate arguments for controversial conclusions, something that is easy to overlook beneath the delightful tales of primate culture and bat radar.

Aggressive critiques of Dawkins now populate the antievolutionary literature, and he has become a walking argument for the incompatibility of evolution and religion, something that plays into the arguments of the creationists as they lobby Christians to reject evolution. Even those who share Dawkins's belief in the general adequacy of evolution to explain origins are often put off by the connections he makes with religion, as we saw above with Michael Ruse. Brown University biologist Kenneth Miller, another critic of creationism and Intelligent Design, actually compares Dawkins to the creationists: "Dawkins's personal skepticism no more disproves the existence of God than the creationists' incredulity is an argument against evolution."[74] Karl Giberson and Don Yerxa identify Dawkins as the leader of what they label "The Council of Despair," a group of science popularizers who argue for a world without meaning.[75]

More recently, the Oxford theologian Alister McGrath has produced a devastating book-length critique of Dawkins. McGrath pulls no punches:

> To put it bluntly, Dawkins' engagement with theology is superficial and inaccurate, often amounting to little more than cheap point scoring. My Oxford colleague Keith Ward has made this point repeatedly, noting in particular Dawkins' "systematic mockery and demonizing of competing views, which are always presented in the most naive light." His tendency to misrepresent the views of his

opponents is the least attractive aspect of his writings. It simply
reinforces the perception that he inhabits a hermetically sealed
conceptual world, impervious to a genuine engagement with
religion.[76]

McGrath notes Dawkins's idea of faith: "Blind trust, in the absence of
evidence, even in the teeth of evidence"[77] and he comments:

> But why should anyone accept this ludicrous definition? ... So what
> is the evidence that anyone—let alone religious people—defines
> "faith" in this absurd way? The simple fact is that Dawkins offers no
> defense of this definition, which bears little relation to any religious
> (or any other) sense of the word. ... I don't accept this idea of faith,
> and I have yet to meet a theologian who takes it seriously. It cannot
> be defended from any official declaration of faith from any Christian
> denomination. ... What is really worrying is that Dawkins genuinely
> seems to believe that faith actually is "blind trust," despite the fact
> that no major Christian writer adopts such a definition. This is a core
> belief for Dawkins, which determines more or less every aspect of his
> attitude to religion and religious people. ... Having set up his straw
> man, Dawkins knocks it down. It is not an unduly difficult or de-
> manding intellectual feat. Faith is infantile, we are told—just fine for
> cramming into the minds of impressionable young children, but
> outrageously immoral and intellectually risible in the case of adults.
> We've grown up now, and need to move on. Why should we believe
> things that can't be scientifically proved? Faith in God, Dawkins ar-
> gues, is just like believing in Santa Claus and the Tooth Fairy. When
> you grow up, you grow out of it. ... This is a schoolboy argument that
> has accidentally found its way into a grown-up discussion. It is as
> amateurish as it is unconvincing. There is no serious empirical evi-
> dence that people regard God, Santa Claus, and the Tooth Fairy as
> being in the same category.[78]

Like others who have looked closely at the celebrated author of *The Selfish
Gene*, McGrath finds Dawkins's reaction to religion naive, unfounded, and
puzzling in terms of both its ferocity and its origins. He comments: "Dawkins' insistence that atheism is the only legitimate worldview for a natural
scientist is an unsafe and unreliable judgment. Yet my anxiety is not limited
to the flawed intellectual case that Dawkins makes for his convictions; I am
troubled by the ferocity with which he asserts his atheism. One obvious potential answer is that the grounds of Dawkins' atheism lie elsewhere than his

science, so that there is perhaps a strongly emotive aspect to his beliefs at this point."[79]

That Dawkins would occasion a book-length response from a scholar of McGrath's stature is a testimony to the power, relevance, and controversial character of his ideas. A recent book celebrating Dawkins's cultural significance contains largely laudatory essays by more than 25 scholars on topics from biology to logic to popular writing. Several of them praise his public role as a critic of religion. The editors celebrate Dawkins from being "so exactingly logical in science, so patiently lucid in promoting the public understanding of science, and so outspoken and clear-headed in the public sphere.[80]

Dawkins remains active as an important cultural voice and will certainly be shaping public perceptions of science and upsetting religious believers for years to come, especially if he continues in the mode he used in "Opiate of the Masses." In that offensive 2005 essay he discussed the great dangers of the drug "Geriniol," an anagram of the letters in "religion." His putative efforts at cleverness were, unfortunately, deeply submerged beneath layers of vitriol.[81] His latest book, *The God Delusion*, continues in the same vein, and will certainly do nothing to undermine his position as the poster child for religious bigotry.[82] His vision of the science he loves and the religion he hates, however, is both inadequate and unsettling, strangely archaic in a postmodern world. Dawkins is beginning to resemble a museum piece that becomes ever more interesting because, while everything else moves forward and changes, it remains the same.

2

Rocks of Ages and the Ages of the Rocks

Stephen Jay Gould

The late Stephen Jay Gould was passionately interested in just about everything, from baseball, racism, and evolution to the relationship between science and religion, and he wrote with great vitality and eloquence. He produced a book-length argument that science and religion should be confined to completely separate spheres, a controversial scheme he called *non-overlapping magisteria*; in another book he argued that the sciences and the humanities are complementary. His last book contained profound and thoughtful meditations on baseball. A declared agnostic, he was particularly interested in showing that humans were a random and purely casual result of an unpredictable evolutionary process. Comfortable with controversy, Gould often found himself under fire. Religious people objected to his reduction of religion to morality and his insistence that human origins were random. His fellow evolutionists objected, not surprisingly, to his eloquent and withering critiques of some of their ideas, including evolutionary psychology, and the concept of the "selfish gene."

Gould's primary agenda became clear with his first book: The Darwinian revolution was a major upheaval with far-reaching consequences, and people should come to terms with its implications, no matter how threatening they appear. Gould's idiosyncratic interpretations of evolution often put him at odds with his colleagues. His critiques of evolutionary orthodoxy were even manipulated by creationists to look like arguments that evolutionary theory was in trouble, a development that enraged him. Evolution was the skeleton of Gould's worldview, and he believed firmly that his ideas embodied the true spirit of Darwin for his generation of scholars. He happily embraced his role as a public intellectual, writing about science for the general reader.

A Prolific New Yorker

Gould was proud to be a New Yorker; he was born in the city on September 10, 1941. His maternal grandfather, Joseph Rosenberg, was a young Hungarian immigrant, just thirteen years old when he arrived at Ellis Island on September 11, 1901. He arrived with his mother and two younger sisters. The family put down roots, and grandfather Rosenberg began his version of the great American story, rising "from poverty to solvency as a garment worker on the streets of New York City."[1]

"I grew up in an environment that seemed entirely conventional and uninteresting to me," notes Gould, "in a New York Jewish family following the standard pattern of generational rise: immigrant grandparents who started in the sweatshops, parents who reached the lower rank of the middle classes but had no advanced schooling, and my third generation, headed for a college education and a professional life to fulfill the postponed destiny." To highlight "the extreme parochiality" of his childhood in Queens, he adds that when his father told him that Protestantism was the most common religion in America, he didn't believe him, "because just about everyone in my neighborhood was either Catholic or Jewish—the composition of New York's rising Irish, Italian, and Eastern European working classes, the only world I knew." Of his religion Gould says, "I had no formal religious education. . . . I am not a believer. I am an agnostic in the wise sense of T. H. Huxley, who coined the word in identifying such open-minded skepticism as the only rational position because, truly, one cannot know."[2]

Gould earned a Ph.D. at Columbia University, New York, and spent the rest of his life teaching at Harvard University, where he was the curator of the invertebrate section in the Museum of Comparative Zoology. He spent part of his time living and teaching in New York. His scientific research centered on paleontology, the study of fossils, specializing in the snails of the Bermuda Islands. At age forty he was diagnosed with cancer and told he had just a few months to live. Heroically, he overcame the negative prognosis and lived twenty more full, productive years. A second cancer, however, led to his death on May 20, 2002, at age sixty.

Over the course of his extraordinary career, Gould was awarded many prizes, distinctions, and honorary degrees. He was probably America's best-known scientist and even appeared as a character in an episode of Fox Television's hit show *The Simpsons*.

From 1974 to 2001, Gould wrote three hundred articles for the monthly magazine *Natural History*. Many of them were collected in ten books published from 1977 to 2002. In the preface to his last book of essays he wrote:

> Thus, when I realized that my three-hundredth monthly essay for
> *Natural History* (written since January 1974, without a single inter-
> ruption for cancer, hell, high water, or the World Series) would fall
> fortuitously into the millennial issue of January 2001, the inception
> of a year that also marks the centenary of my family's arrival in the
> United States, I did choose to read this coincidence of numerological
> 'evenness' as a sign that this particular forum should now close at
> the equally portentous number of ten volumes (made worthy of men-
> tion only by the contingency of our decimal mathematics. Were
> I a Mayan prince, counting by twenties, I would not have been so
> impressed, but then I wouldn't have been writing scientific essays
> either).[3]

Gould was an astonishingly prolific author, publishing many books and countless articles. He wrote on a remarkably broad range of topics, including an extended and mathematically sophisticated baseball article analyzing the disappearance of .400 hitters. He appeared prominently in Ken Burns's PBS documentary on the sport, offering winsome reflections on enjoying games with his father, and even singing "Take Me Out to the Ball Game."[4] To the end Gould was passionate about baseball, and a collection of his published writings on the sport ran to almost 350 pages.[5] Gould's friend and colleague Alan Dershowitz, who shared much of Gould's passion for baseball and went to games with him, believes that "Gould's view of baseball informed his larger view of history."[6] Evolution, like baseball, is highly contingent. In baseball the difference between loss and victory often turns on the smallest of variations: A called strike, a stumble on the base-paths, a pitcher who gets tired, a heroic diving catch, and so on, can make all the difference in the world. Dershowitz was convinced that Gould's profound understanding of contingency in base-ball informed his view of evolution, helping him appreciate the relevance of tiny events in natural history.

Another of Gould's passions was singing in a choir: "I have been a choral singer all my active life," he wrote in one of his last books.[7] In *The Mismeasure of Man*, he offered a passionate and sobering look at how racism has tainted scientific research into human intelligence.[8] Gould's career and publications, however, centered primarily on biological evolution, and he was one of its leading voices for most of his life. Shortly before his death in 2002, he published his opus on evolution, a massive 1,433-page tome titled *The Structure of Evolutionary Theory*. His own research featured prominently in this work, as he was already famous in 1972 as the coauthor, with Niles Eldredge, of a controversial interpretation of evolution known as *punctuated equilibrium*.

Punctuated Equilibrium

Evolutionary theory states that organisms living today are the descendants of one or a few forms of life that existed some 3.5 billion years ago. Modification of the hereditary material of life-forms across these billions of years of natural history has resulted in the appearance of a steadily increasing number of species. Fossil remains of ancient but extinct life forms are the primary evidence for the long history of life on our planet. These links between ancient and modern organisms, however, as the historical record of evolution, pose difficulties because many presumed links between species are not represented in the fossil record.

The incompleteness of the fossil record has always been a controversial issue. Fossilization is a rare and complex process and occurs only under the most favorable of circumstances. Most organisms and even species disappear without leaving any fossil record whatsoever. Furthermore, fossilization preserves only the hard parts of the organisms, leaving questions about soft tissues like eyes and muscles largely unanswered. Finding and interpreting fossils is very, very difficult.

How we evaluate the fossil record depends to a large degree on how we interpret evolution. According to the standard Darwinian formulation, evolution is a gradual process, the result of the steady accumulation of small changes. We should thus expect to find many fossils showing the gradual transformation of organisms from one species into another. But this is not what we find. What we find is an incomplete fossil record, indicating that many of these fossils have not been preserved or that we haven't found them yet. What is going on here? Why doesn't the fossil record speak clearly about the gradual transitions demanded by evolution? Is it really a simple matter of "missing fossils"?

This was the question posed by Gould and Eldredge, both professional paleontologists. The two were convinced that the fossil record implied that species did *not* change gradually over long periods of time. The stability of species in the fossil record, they argued, was a fact of history, not an artifact of incomplete data. They did not, of course, challenge the *fact* of evolution, although the creationists used their work to this end.[9] They challenged the prevailing evolutionary paradigm of *gradualism*. The continuous chain of fossils postulated by gradualism would never be found, the two argued, because they did not exist. As Gould put it in his last book on evolution, "Abrupt appearance may record an absence of information, but *stasis is data*. Eldredge and I became so frustrated by the failure of many colleagues to grasp this evident point...that we urged the incorporation of this little phrase as a mantra or motto. Say it ten times before breakfast every day for a week, and the argument will surely seep in by osmosis: 'stasis is data; stasis is data.'"[10]

The simple fact of stasis, however, was not easily accepted. According to Gould, a curious situation emerged:

> Paleontology therefore fell into a literally absurd vicious circle. No one ventured to document or quantify—indeed, hardly anyone even bothered to mention or publish at all—the most common pattern in the fossil record: the stasis of most morpho-species throughout their geological duration. All paleontologists recognized the phenomenon, but few scientists write papers about failure to document a desired result. As a consequence, most nonpaleontologists never learned about the predominance of stasis, and simply assumed that gradualism must prevail.... Eldredge and I proposed punctuated equilibrium in this explicit context—as a framework and different theory that, if true, could validate the primary signal of the fossil record as valuable information rather than frustrating failure.[11]

Eldredge and Gould published their original paper on punctuated equilibrium in 1972,[12] stressing that *stasis is data* and that stability of species is the rule. The equilibrium of species is *punctuated* by episodes of change that are relatively rapid in geological time. The changes, of course, are not instantaneous, as some critics oddly (mis)inferred. The changes are long compared to our sense of time, but rapid compared to the hundreds of millions of years involved in paleontology.

Whatever the ambiguous message of the fossil record, the central problem remains: How do species originate? It has been said that Charles Darwin's *The Origin of the Species* explains everything except the origin of the species. The late Ernst Mayr, longtime Harvard professor born in 1904, was the main representative of orthodox Darwinism still alive at the beginning of the twenty-first century. In 2001, at age ninety-seven, he wrote, "Darwin himself failed to solve the problem of speciation."[13] Darwin, of course, cannot be blamed for this failure, for neither he nor his generation knew much about the critically important science of genetics.[14] The development of genetics in the twentieth century led to the formulation, in the 1930s and 1940s, of the *modern synthesis* of Darwinism and genetics known as *neo-Darwinism*, the prevailing contemporary understanding of evolution.

Mayr was one of the architects of neo-Darwinism. To explain *speciation* (the origin of new species) he extended the existing theory of *geographical* or *allopatric speciation* (*allopatric* comes from the Greek: *allos* means "other," "different," and *patra* means "fatherland"). According to this theory, a new species may evolve when a group splits off from a "parent" population and becomes geographically isolated. Genetic modifications in this isolated group eventually give rise to a new species unable to breed with the original parent population. This leads to *reproductive isolation*, the main characteristic of new species. In his 1942 book *Systematics and the Origin of Species*, Mayr argued that allopatric speciation was the *exclusive* mechanism of speciation in mammals and birds. In his 2001 book, however, he admitted the existence of *sympatric speciation*, where new species emerge alongside the old ones; he also conceded other processes of speciation such as changes in chromosomes.[15]

Mayr's ideas on allopatric speciation influenced Gould's and Eldredge's interpretation of the fossil record. At the beginning of their 1972 paper they wrote:

> Paleontology's view of speciation has been dominated by the picture of "phyletic gradualism." It holds that new species arise from the slow and steady transformation of entire populations. Under its influence, we seek unbroken fossils series linking two forms by insensible gradation as the only complete mirror of Darwinian processes; we ascribe all breaks to imperfections in the record. The theory of allopatric (or geographic) speciation suggests a different interpretation of paleontological data. If new species arise very rapidly in small, peripherally isolated local populations, then the great expectation of insensibly graded fossil sequences is a chimera. A new species does not evolve in the area of its ancestors; it does not arise from the slow transformation of all its forbears. Many breaks in the fossil record are real. The history of life is more adequately represented by a picture of "punctuated equilibria" than by the notion of phyletic gradualism. The history of evolution is not one of stately unfolding, but a history of homeostatic equilibria, disturbed only "rarely" (i.e., rather often in the fullness of time) by rapid and episodic events of speciation.[16]

Punctuated equilibrium has been used by creationists to argue that evolutionists disagree on basic issues. But Gould and Eldredge are as evolutionary as anyone, and it is generally recognized that punctuated equilibrium is fully compatible with Darwinism. Mayr is explicit on this.[17] In a 1993 paper, Gould and Eldredge reviewed punctuated equilibrium on the occasion of its coming of age (twenty-one years). They analyzed the theory, its empirical support, and its fertility for research. They left the issue unresolved, concluding: "Punctuated equilibrium, in this light, is only paleontology's contribution to a *Zeitgeist* [the *spirit of the time*], and *Zeitgeists*, as (literally) transient ghosts of time, should never be trusted. Thus, in developing punctuated equilibrium, we have either been toadies and panderers to fashion, and therefore destined for history's ash heap, or we had a spark of insight about nature's constitution. Only the punctuational and unpredictable future can tell."[18]

Gould highlights the complexity of the many problems in evolution, and the necessity of multiple explanations. Nobody doubts that genetic mutations happen, that natural selection plays a role, that isolation is important, that gradualism is real, and so on. But there are also many things we don't know. We are just beginning to learn how genes act at different levels in combination. After years of believing much of the genome was junk DNA, we are now told that this "useless" DNA could be key in understanding regulatory processes playing important roles in development.[19] Evolution, as Gould argued, is a big, complex topic, and we should be wary of oversimplified explanatory schemes.

This View of Life

In 1977 Gould published his first two books. The first was a specialized work titled *Ontogeny and Phylogeny*[20] and dealt with the famous law that ontogeny recapitulates phylogeny, that is, that embryos, in their individual development (*ontogeny*), pass through the stages of the previous evolution of their species (*phylogeny*). Gould analyzed the history and utility of the idea. The other book, *Ever Since Darwin*, was the first collection of essays published by Gould in the magazine *Natural History* under the title "This View of Life."[21]

Gould's intellectual life orbited about the central sun of evolutionary theory, which illuminated his professional work and his worldview. In the prologue to *Ever Since Darwin*, Gould explains that he wants to spread Darwin's message. He thinks we are far from having accepted it completely, not for scientific reasons, but because of the philosophy associated with it:

> Nonetheless, I believe that the stumbling block to its acceptance [of
> Darwin's message] does not lie in any scientific difficulty, but rather

in the radical philosophical content of Darwin's message—in its challenge to a set of entrenched Western attitudes that we are not yet ready to abandon. First, Darwin argues that *evolution has no purpose*. Individuals struggle to increase the representation of their genes in future generations, and that is all. If the world displays any harmony and order, it arises only as an incidental result of individuals seeking their own advantage—the economy of Adam Smith transferred to nature. Second, Darwin maintained that *evolution has no direction*; it does not lead inevitably to higher things. Organisms become better adapted to their local environments, and that is all. The "degeneracy" of a parasite is as perfect as the gait of a gazelle. Third, Darwin applied a consistent *philosophy of materialism* to his interpretation of nature. Matter is the ground of all existence; mind, spirit, and God as well, are just words that express the wondrous results of neuronal complexity.[22]

Gould is right to note that Darwin's theory carries unattractive philosophical baggage. We ask, however, if this baggage really belongs to Darwin. Do the three gloomy claims listed above really belong to evolution? Are they really scientific claims resting on the same empirical foundations as the theory of evolution? Or are they philosophical claims that originate outside science?

Gould borrowed the title for his monthly essays, "This View of Life," from the last paragraph of Darwin's *Origin of Species*: "There is grandeur in this view of life."[23] Gould's *view of life* extends beyond biological evolution to a worldview encompassing science, philosophy, and even religion. Evolution, says Gould, rules out purpose and plan in the natural world and implies a *materialism* that eliminates God and any other form of spiritual reality.

Nevertheless, and perhaps surprisingly, Gould holds that science and religion belong to different realms, and he acknowledges the limits of science. In December 1981 he testified on the nature of science, specifically evolution, in *McLean versus the Arkansas Board of Education*. This landmark trial overturned the Arkansas decision that evolution and "creation science" should be given a "balanced" treatment in school. Based on the testimony of Gould and others,[24] judge William R. Overton decided against the balanced treatment.[25] On November 27, 1981, before the trial started, attorney David L. Williams examined Gould in New York City. When asked, "Do you think that a religious person can be a competent scientist?" Gould answered, "Of course. The empirical record proves it. There are thousands upon thousands of religious people who are competent scientists."[26] When Williams asked, "Where did the matter, the nonlife come from?" Gould responded: "Oh, that's not even a scientific question.... Science itself doesn't deal in ultimate origins. I am sorry, I thought you were giving me the chemical constituents of the earth. You asked me where matter came from, how can science deal with that question. I have no opinion on that. That is the mystery of mysteries."[27]

In June 1987 the Supreme Court ruled 7–2 against allowing creation science in the public schools. Gould analyzed Justice Scalia's contrary vote, suggesting that it relied "crucially upon a false concept of science." Scalia's mistake, said Gould, was to presume that science dealt with ultimate questions:

> Let theology deal with ultimate origins, and let science be the art
> of the empirically soluble.... Scientists can also spin out ideas
> about ultimates. We don't (or, rather, we confine them to our private
> thoughts) because we cannot devise ways to test them, to decide
> whether they are right or wrong.... Evolution is not the study of life's
> ultimate origin as a path towards discerning its deepest meaning....
> They [fundamentalist groups] ignored what evolutionists actually
> do and misrepresented our science as the study of life's ultimate
> origin.[28]

We have to agree with Gould on these points and applaud his clear-headed distinction between ultimate and proximate theories of origins. But we wonder what has happened to the philosophical baggage that a much younger Gould claimed went with evolution.

A Wonderful Life

Gould's most consistently developed idea is the unpredictability and contingency of evolution. Evolution, he argued, must not be viewed as a ladder of increasing perfection leading to humanity. If we view evolution as a movie that can be replayed at will from the beginning, the probability that it would lead again to us is negligible. The contingency of evolution implies that its results are unpredictable. Accordingly, humans are a casual by-product of evolution, not the result of a plan. There is, says Gould, nothing special about our origins.

Gould consistently championed this view. A few months before his death, at the end of his last big book, he wrote: "I have championed the cause, and equal claim, of contingency (particularly in *Wonderful Life* and *Full House*) to the point of my ready identification as a proponent of this position (and with no complaint on my part, and no feeling that my critics have been unfair in any oversimplification)."[29]

In fact, Gould's aim in *Wonderful Life* (1989) and *Full House* (1996) was to highlight the contingency of the path that has led to our existence. The title *Wonderful Life* was borrowed from Frank Capra's film *It's a Wonderful Life*. In the preface we read that the theme of contingency in history "is central to the most memorable scene in America's most beloved film—Jimmy Stewart's guardian angel replaying life's tape without him, and demonstrating the awesome power of apparent insignificance in history. Science has dealt poorly with the concept of contingency, but film and literature have always found it fascinating."[30]

Gould develops these ideas with concrete examples from natural history. *Wonderful Life* tells the story of the paleontologists' beloved Burgess Shale, a rich fossil bed discovered in 1909 by Charles Doolittle Walcott. The fossils were interpreted as primitive stages of organisms that later developed into more complex organisms, a conventional interpretation very much in accordance with ideas prevalent at the time. Gould the paleontologist calls the Burgess Shale "the most precious and important of all fossil localities"[31] and explains why:

> I state that the invertebrates of the Burgess Shale, found high in the Canadian Rockies in Yoho National Park, on the eastern border of British Columbia, are the world's most important animal fossils. Modern multicellular animals make their first uncontested appearance in the fossil record some 570 million years ago—and with a bang, not a protracted crescendo. This "Cambrian explosion" marks the advent (at least into direct evidence) of virtually all major groups of modern animals—and all within the minuscule span, geologically speaking, of a few million years. The Burgess Shale represents a period just after this explosion, a time when the full range of its products inhabited our seas. These Canadian fossils are precious because they preserve in exquisite detail, down to the last filament of a trilobite's gill, or the components of a last meal in a worm's gut, the soft anatomy of organisms. Our fossil record is almost exclusively the story of hard parts. But most animals have none, and those that do often reveal very little about their anatomies in their outer coverings (what could you infer about a clam from its shell alone?). Hence, the rare soft-bodied faunas of the fossil record are precious windows into the true range and diversity of ancient life. The Burgess Shale is our only extensive, well-documented window upon that most crucial event in the history of animal life, the first flowering of the Cambrian explosion.[32]

Walcott's interpretation of the Burgess Shale fossils followed the usual pattern, viewing evolution as progress from the simple to the complex. Years later, starting in 1971, Professor Harry Whittington of Cambridge University published studies on the Burgess Shale fossils that suggested a different interpretation.

In the Burgess Shale we find designs of invertebrates that have not survived, rich body plans with no contemporary counterparts. Therefore, most of these fossils were *not* primitive stages of simple organisms that eventually evolved into more complex ones. Gould concludes, "The history of life is a story of massive removal followed by differentiation within a few surviving stocks, not the conventional tale of steadily increasing excellence, complexity, and diversity."[33]

Gould insists that evolution is not a ladder leading to increasing complexity and perfection. It is, rather, like a bush with branches. Each branch is a species, most of which became extinct, not because they were replaced by other, more perfect species, but simply because they were not adapted to changing circumstances, or died in mass extinctions. "Life," says Gould, "is a copiously branching bush, continually pruned by the grim reaper of extinction, not a ladder of predictable progress."[34]

Gould's "grim reaper of extinction" was no friend to *adaptationism*, the orthodox view. Neo-Darwinians like Richard Dawkins and John Maynard Smith view evolution as the accumulation of small changes, a process of adaptation to diverse circumstances guided by natural selection. Gould labels the adherents of this view *ultra-Darwinists*. Gould claims he is more faithful to Darwin in one crucial aspect, namely Darwin's idea that it is meaningless to speak of more or less perfect. Gould wants a *paradigm shift* in our view of evolution, discarding the ladder for the bush. This shift is surely related to his theory of punctuated equilibrium. In both cases Gould insists that new emerging forms cannot be viewed as a progressive continuum. Consistent with the fossil record, new forms appear quite suddenly, not as the accumulation of many small adaptive changes.

Philosopher Michael Ruse has identified three factors that shaped Gould's ideas. First, while working on *Ontogeny and Phylogeny*, Gould was influenced by the German approach to biology, which emphasized the general plans of organisms. Second, Gould was influenced by his father's Marxism, even acknowledging that punctuated equilibrium had a revolutionary flavor of the sort that Marxists like. Third, Gould's ideas promoted paleontology over genetics, which certainly served his interests as a paleontologist. Whatever we may make of Ruse's provocative analysis of extra-scientific influences on Gould, and exactly why Gould championed his various causes, we must note the enthusiasm he brought to his emphasis on humanity's unpredictable, contingent origins. Gould spent most of his career on a soapbox, preaching that humanity needed to get over its tendency to see itself as the culmination of a marvelous process, rather than the by-product of a long series of accidents.[35]

A Cosmic Redefinition

Gould opens *Wonderful Life* with an attack on representations of evolution as a ladder or cone of progressing complexity, and he explains the enduring popularity of these images: "I don't think that any particular secret, mystery, or inordinate subtlety underlies the reasons for our allegiance to these false iconographies of ladder and cone. They are adopted because they nurture our hopes for a universe of intrinsic meaning defined in our terms."[36]

The natural world, he argues, cannot provide the desired clues for the all-important meaning of human life, nor can it be a source for morality:

> But, as Freud observed, our relationship with science must be para-doxical because we are forced to pay an almost intolerable price for each major gain in knowledge and power—the psychological cost of progressive dethronement from the center of things, and increas-ing marginality in an uncaring universe. Thus, physics and astron-omy relegated our world to a corner of the cosmos, and biology shifted our status from a simulacrum of God to a naked, upright ape. To this cosmic redefinition, my profession contributed its own special shock—geology's most frightening fact, we may say. By the turn of the last century, we knew that the earth had endured for millions of years, and that human existence occupied but the last geological milli-microsecond of this history—the last inch of the cosmic mile, or the last second of the geological year, in our standard pedagogical meta-phors. We cannot bear the central implication of this brave new world. If humanity arose just yesterday as a small twig on one branch of a flourishing tree, then life may not, in any genuine sense, exist for us or because of us. Perhaps we are only an afterthought, a kind of cos-mic accident, just one bauble on the Christmas tree of evolution.[37]

The Freud reference connects *Wonderful Life* (1989) to *Ever Since Darwin* (1977), where Gould defended "the radical philosophical content of Darwin's message." There we read:

> Sigmund Freud expressed as well as anyone the ineradicable impact of evolution upon human life and thought when he wrote: "Humanity

has in course of time had to endure from the hands of science two great outrages upon its naive self-love. The first was when it realized that our earth was not the center of the universe, but only a speck in a world-system of a magnitude hardly conceivable. . . . The second was when biological research robbed man of his particular privilege of having been specially created, and relegated him to a descent from the animal world." I submit that the knowledge of this relegation is also our greatest hope for continuity on a fragile earth. May "this view of life" flower during its second century and help us to comprehend both the limits and the lessons of scientific understanding—as we, like Hardy's fields and trees, continue to wonder why we find us here.[38]

We must accept that our place in the world is neither central nor privileged. This, says Gould, is the necessary consequence of "geology's most frightening fact":

What options are left in the face of geology's most frightening fact? Only two, really. We may, as this book advocates, accept the implications and learn to seek the meaning of human life, including the source of morality, in other, more appropriate, domains—either stoically with a sense of loss, or with joy in the challenge if our temperament be optimistic. Or we may continue to seek cosmic comfort in nature by reading life's history in a distorted light. If we elect the second strategy, our maneuvers are severely restricted by our geological history. When we infested all but the first five days of time, the history of life could easily be rendered in our terms. But if we wish to assert human centrality in a world that functioned without us until the last moment, we must somehow grasp all that came before as a grand preparation, a foreshadowing of our eventual origin. . . . In short, I cannot understand our continued allegiance to the manifestly false iconographies of ladder and cone except as a desperate finger in the dike of cosmically justified hope and arrogance.[39]

Completing the Revolution

Darwin's great revolution, Gould insists, remains tragically incomplete until we embrace its philosophical implications: We must not conceptualize evolution as a planned process, gloriously unfolding across natural history, moving inexorably toward our appearance as the apex of the creation. Gould's enthusiasm for dethroning humanity inspires his whole program; he returned to this theme regularly over the decades of his professional life. In a 1994 issue of *Scientific American* devoted to evolution, Gould contributed an article on the evolution of life on earth in which he elected to emphasize this point: "*Homo sapiens* did not appear on the earth, just a geologic second ago, because evolutionary theory predicts such an outcome based on themes of progress and increasing neural complexity. Humans arose, rather, as a fortuitous and contingent outcome of thousands of linked events, any one of which could have occurred differently and sent history on an alternative pathway that would not have led to consciousness."[40]

Gould critiques once more the traditional textbook representation of evolution as a progressive process of complexification represented as an "age of invertebrates" followed by an "age of fishes," an "age of reptiles," an "age of mammals," and an "age of man." Gould agrees, of course, that life on this planet has become more complex since it began. And this history seduces us into thinking that the process of evolution has some built-in drive to produce ever more complex forms of life. The reality, however, is that life begins in such a simple state of "minimal complexity" that it cannot help but move away from this initial simplicity to greater complexity. Gould compares this to a famous statistics problem known as the "drunkard's walk." A drunkard, placed initially at some point (0,0) will stagger randomly in such a way that he will gradually move farther and farther from this point. Yet we cannot claim that the drunkard is *deliberately* trying to move from this point, as if he intends to get farther from his starting location. In the same way, evolution moves life randomly from simple beginnings to great complexity. We must avoid the temptation to see this trajectory toward complexity as if it is somehow central to the evolutionary process: "Our conventional desire to view history as progressive, and to see humans as predictably dominant, has grossly distorted our interpretation of life's pathway by falsely placing in the center of things a relatively minor phenomenon that arises only as a side consequence of a physically constrained starting point."[41]

Gould refers again to Freud's claim that scientific progress has dethroned humanity from its special status at the apex of creation:

> Sigmund Freud often remarked that great revolutions in the history of science have but one common, and ironic, feature: they knock human arrogance off one pedestal after another of our previous conviction about our own self-importance. In Freud's three examples, Copernicus moved our home from center to periphery; Darwin then relegated us to "descent from an animal world"; and finally (in one of the least modest statements of intellectual history), Freud himself

discovered the unconscious and exploded the myth of a fully rational mind. In this wise and crucial sense, the Darwinian revolution remains woefully incomplete because, even though thinking humanity accepts the fact of evolution, most of us are still unwilling to abandon the comforting view that evolution means (or at least embodies a central principle of) progress defined to render the appearance of something like human consciousness either virtually inevitable or at least predictable. The pedestal is not smashed until we abandon progress or complexification as a central principle and come to entertain the strong possibility that *H. sapiens* is but a tiny, late-arising twig on life's enormously arborescent bush—a small bud that would almost surely not appear a second time if we could replant the bush from seed and let it grow again.[42]

Elsewhere Gould refers to "an all too common tendency among natural historians—the erection of a picket fence around their own species."[43] He adds, "The picket fence around *homo sapiens* rests on several supports: the most important posts embody claims for *preparation* and *transcendence*. Humans have not only transcended the ordinary forces of nature, but all that came before was, in some important sense, a preparation for our eventual appearance."[44] Gould cites Alfred Russel Wallace, the codiscoverer with Darwin of natural selection as an explanation for the origin of species, as a primary example of *preparation*. Wallace saw the material world as foreordained for the existence of human beings. According to Gould, "all evolutionists would now reject Wallace's version of the argument for preparation,"[45] and the new version of *preparation* centers on an untenable inference of predictability:

> The modern version chucks foreordination in favor of predictability. It abandons the idea that the germ of Homo sapiens lay embedded in the primordial bacterium, or that some spiritual force superintended organic evolution, waiting to infuse mind into the first body worthy of receiving it. Instead, it holds that the fully natural process of organic evolution follows certain paths because its primary agent, natural selection, constructs ever more successful designs that prevail in competition against earlier models. . . . We are here for a reason after all, even though that reason lies in the mechanics of engineering rather than in the volition of a deity. But if evolution proceeded as a lock step, then the fossil record should display a pattern of gradual and sequential advance in organization. It does not, and I regard this failure as the most telling argument against an evolutionary ratchet.[46]

Freud and Gould

Gould's use of Freud is not fortuitous. He returns to it several times in his publications, always using it in exactly the same way. Gould, as we have noted, was an excellent writer, a powerful public intellectual, and he knew—and acknowledged—exactly what he was doing. He wanted to impress upon his many readers the core notion that Freud was right in stating that humanity had been repeatedly and definitively dethroned, first by Copernicus, then by Darwin, and finally by Freud himself.

Examining this idea, as Freud himself articulated it, turns up some interesting insights. Freud (1856–1939) delivered a series of twenty-eight lectures between 1915 and 1917 at the University of Vienna, introducing psychoanalysis to the general public. Published immediately in German in 1917, the first English edition of the lectures appeared in 1920.[47] It would be natural to suppose that Freud's message on the significance of great scientific revolutions would be contained in a historical study, but this is not the case. Freud invoked the history of science to defend psychoanalysis from the hostility it had provoked.

In his first lecture, Freud notes that when a neurotic is beginning a psychoanalytic treatment, the patient is informed of the difficulties of the method. Then he goes on: "Now forgive me if I begin by treating you in the same way as I do to my neurotic patients, for I shall positively advise you against coming to hear me a second time.... For I shall show you how the whole trend of your training and your accustomed modes of thought must inevitably have made you hostile to psycho-analysis."[48]

We find the passage used so often by Gould (he never provides the specific reference) in the eighteenth lecture, where Freud's tone is both negative and defensive: "By thus emphasizing the unconscious in mental life we have called forth all the malevolence in humanity in opposition to psycho-analysis."[49] Immediately he argues that his audience should not be astonished by the widespread hostility to psychoanalysis. The opposition, however, does not derive from the difficulty of conceiving the unconscious or from the fragility of the evidence supporting it. The opposition has a deeper source, and it is here that Gould embraces Freud's conclusions about the Copernican, Darwinian, and now Freudian revolutions. Freud has a simple explanation for this opposition. Just as the revolutions of Copernicus and Darwin were difficult to accept because they implied a dethroning of humanity from a pedestal built by ourselves, so do we oppose yet another dethronement by Freud's revolutionary ideas:

Humanity in the course of time had to endure from the hands of science two great outrages upon its naïve self-love. The first was when it realized that our earth was not the centre of the universe, but only a tiny speck in a world-system of a magnitude hardly conceivable; this is associated in our minds with the name of Copernicus, although Alexandrian doctrines taught something very similar. The second was when biological research robbed man of his peculiar privilege of having been specially created, and relegated him to a descent from the animal world, implying an ineradicable animal nature in him: this transvaluation has been accomplished in our own time upon the instigation of Charles Darwin, Wallace, and their predecessors, and not without the most violent opposition from their contemporaries. But man's craving for grandiosity is now suffering the third and most bitter blow from present-day psychological research which is en-deavouring to prove to the *ego* of each one of us that he is not even master in his own house, but that he must remain content with the veriest scraps of information about what is going on unconsciously in his own mind.[50]

Gould refers to this quotation at least ten times in his books, and even enlarges Freud's trio of insults into a quartet, suggesting a fourth revolution in the same line: the discovery of deep time. Gould's own field of paleontology reveals humanity to be but a newcomer to the world. We have arrived at the very last moment; we occupy but a tiny fragment of the great timeline of life on the earth; we look, for all the world, like an afterthought.[51] Natural his-tory does little to dispel this view. The age of the earth is estimated at 4.5 bil-lion years, primates appeared about 60 million years ago, hominids 4 million years ago, and modern humans have existed on earth for just the last 200,000 years. If there were an argument that natural history had humans as its target, this would be less sobering. After all, there are many great things on the earth, from the ancient pyramids to the latest laptop computer, that had vast periods of planning and preparation precede their actual physical appearance. But Gould has rejected this possibility, arguing that the very existence of primates is a contingent fact of history. Had the dinosaurs not had the misfortune to be occupying the earth when a great asteroid collided with the planet, they might never have gone extinct. Had this bizarre and seemingly random catastrophe not occurred, there might never have been enough ecological space for the first small primates to evolve into our immediate predecessors, and we would not be here, celebrating our good fortune and lamenting the fate of the dinosaurs.

Gould uses the sheer improbability of the dinosaur extinction to argue that our existence is not only contingent, but utterly improbable. We are the end result of a long series of cosmic rolls of the dice, each roll turning up a purely random number, and the sequence of rolls making a mockery of any overall trajectory to the game. Gould's image of a videotape summarizes this point: If we replay the tape of the history of life on this planet again from the beginning, the story and its conclusion will be completely different.

A Matter of Degree

A second argument used in favor of the centrality of humanity relates to *transcendence*, the capacity of human beings to rise above or go beyond their purely physical composition and entirely natural origins. Do human beings really transcend the rest of the natural world?

Not surprisingly, Gould sides with the materialists in answering no. In *A Matter of Degree*, from his first collection of essays, he repeats a favorite theme: "The Western world has yet to make its peace with Darwin and the implications of evolutionary theory." He refers to "the greatest impediment to this reconciliation—our unwillingness to accept continuity between ourselves and nature, our ardent search for a criterion to assert our uniqueness."[52] Developing this argument, he writes:

> Chimps and gorillas have long been the battleground of our search for uniqueness; for if we could establish an unambiguous distinction— of kind rather than of degree—between ourselves and our closest relatives, we might gain the justification long sought for our cosmic arrogance. The battle shifted long ago from a simple debate about evolution: educated people now accept the evolutionary continuity between humans and apes. But we are so tied to our philosophical and religious heritage that we still seek a criterion for strict division between our abilities and those of chimpanzees.... Many criteria have been tried, and one by one they have failed. The only honest alternative is to admit the strict continuity in kind between ourselves and chimpanzees. And what do we lose thereby? Only an antiquated concept of soul to gain a more humble, even exalting vision of our oneness with nature.[53]

In another essay titled "Darwin's Delay," Gould poses the question: "Charles Darwin developed a radical theory of evolution in 1838 and published it twenty-one years later.... Why then did he wait for more than twenty years to publish his theory?" Gould outlines the standard explanation: "Darwin waited twenty years—so the usual argument runs—simply because he had not completed his work. . . . He was determined not to publish until he had amassed an overwhelming dossier of data in its support, and this took time." Gould rejects this version, noting that Darwin spent much of his time in those years in activities that had little to do with these data. He goes on: "I feel sure of one thing: the negative effect of fear must have played at least as great a role as the positive need for additional documentation. Of what, then, was Darwin afraid?"[54] Gould finds the answer in Darwin's so-called M and N notebooks, written in 1838 and 1839, where Darwin recorded his thoughts on philosophy, esthetics, psychology, and anthropology: "On rereading them in 1856, Darwin described them as 'full of metaphysics on morals.' They include many statements showing that he espoused but feared to expose something he perceived as far more heretical than evolution itself: philosophical materialism—the postulate that matter is the stuff of all existence and that all mental and spiritual phenomena are its by-products. No notion could be more upsetting to the deepest traditions of Western thought than the statement that mind—however complex and powerful—is simply a product of brain."[55]

As is typical, Gould makes his case with passion, enthusiastic to show that Darwin accepted a philosophy of materialism:

> The notebooks prove that Darwin was interested in philosophy and aware of its implications. He knew that the primary feature distinguishing his theory from all other evolutionary doctrines was its uncompromising philosophical materialism. Other evolutionists spoke of vital forces, directed history, organic striving, and the essential irreducibility of mind—a panoply of concepts that traditional Christianity could accept in compromise, for they permitted a Christian God to work by evolution instead of creation. Darwin spoke only of random variation and natural selection. In the notebooks Darwin resolutely applied his materialistic theory of evolution to all phenomena of life, including what he termed "the citadel itself"—the human mind. And if mind has no real existence beyond the brain, can God be anything more than an illusion invented by an illusion? . . . Darwin cut through 2,000 years of philosophy and religion in the most remarkable epigram of the M notebook: "Plato says in *Phaedo* that our imaginary ideas arise from the preexistence of the soul, are not derivable from experience—read monkeys for preexistence."[56]

Gould embraces the materialism he finds in Darwin, arguing that this is the only option for educated people. He did not write much about materialism, however, perhaps because he wanted to remain, as did Darwin, "a gentle revolutionary." No doubt Gould believes, also with Darwin, that scientific progress is a solid ally of materialism:

> Darwin was, indeed, a gentle revolutionary. Not only did he delay his work for so long, but he also assiduously avoided any public statement about the philosophical implications of his theory. In 1880, he wrote: "It seems to me (rightly or wrongly) that direct arguments against Christianity and Theism hardly have any effect on the public; and that freedom of thought will best be promoted by that gradual enlightening of human understanding which follows the progress of science. I have therefore always avoided writing about religion and have confined myself to science." Yet the content of his work was so disruptive to traditional Western thought that we have yet to encompass it all. Arthur Koestler's campaign against Darwin, for example, rests upon a reluctance to accept Darwin's materialism and an ardent desire once again to invest living matter with some special property (see *The Ghost in the Machine* or *The Case of the Midwife Toad*). This, I confess, I do not understand. Wonder and knowledge are both to be cherished. Shall we appreciate any less the beauty of nature because its harmony is unplanned? And shall the potential of mind cease to inspire our awe and fear because several billion neurons reside in our skulls?[57]

Gould was not inclined to develop elaborate arguments in defense of materialism. This was not his style, and he did not see himself as even capable of doing so:

> I am not a modest man, but I do know my great weaknesses amidst one lucky strength. . . . I am not illogical, but how I yearn for the awesome ability I note in many colleagues to identify, develop, and test the linear implications of an argument. . . . I cannot forget or expunge any item that enters my head, and I can always find legitimate and unforced connections among the disparate details. In this sense, I am an essay machine; cite me a generality, and I will give you six tidbits of genuine illustration. A detail, by itself, is blind; a concept without a concrete illustration is empty. The conjunction defines the essay as a genre, and I draw connections in a manner that feels automatic to me.[58]

One could hardly find a better description of the style of America's best-known science essayist.

While Gould may have chosen not to enter into a complex defense of philosophical materialism, there can be no doubt that he both embraced and promoted materialism. In a short essay about his triumph over his first cancer at age forty, he writes: "Attitude clearly matters in fighting cancer. We don't know why (from my old-style materialistic perspective, I suspect that mental states feed back upon the immune system)."[59]

This is hardly a throw-down-the-gauntlet declaration of philosophical materialism, but it does raise the question of how well Gould articulated his personal philosophy.

Gould's Personal Agenda

Gould's agenda might possibly be construed as simply excluding spiritual realities from the purview of science. God, the human soul, human beings as the image of God, divine providence, and so on could have their proper place in metaphysics or theology, without being the subject of empirical science. Almost everyone would agree on this. Is this what Gould is after?

Gould's agenda is more ambitious. As we have seen, he set forth his agenda in his first book, *Ever Since Darwin*: "Mind, spirit, and God as well, are just words that express the wondrous results of neuronal complexity." In his last book of essays, twenty-five years later, he returned to this topic, using the same quotation by Freud but with a stronger emphasis:

> In a wise statement that will endure beyond the fading basis of his
> general celebrity, Sigmund Freud argued that all great scientific
> revolutions feature two components: an intellectual reformulation of
> physical reality and a visceral demotion of *Homo sapiens* from arro-
> gant domination atop a presumed pinnacle to a particular and con-
> tingent result, however interesting and unusual, of natural processes.
> Freud designated two such revolutions as paramount: the Copernican
> banishment of Earth from center to periphery and the Darwinian
> "relegation" (Freud's word) of our species from God's incarnated im-
> age to "descent from an animal world." . . . The biblical Psalmist evoked
> our deepest fear by comparing our bodily insignificance with cosmic
> immensity and crying out: "What is man, that thou art mindful of
> him?" (Psalm 8). But he then vanquished this spatial anxiety with
> a constitutional balm: "Thou hast made him a little lower than the
> angels . . . thou madest him to have dominion . . . thou hast put all
> things under his feet." Darwin removed this keystone of false comfort

more than a century ago, but many people still believe that they cannot navigate our earthly vale of tears without such a crutch.[60]

Comments like this are sprinkled liberally throughout Gould's work, suggesting that evolution has eliminated spiritual realities. However, we can also find Gould explicitly affirming the compatibility of evolution and religion: "A man may be both an evolutionist and a devout Christian," he writes. "Millions successfully juxtapose these two independent viewpoints."[61]

There is thus a certain ambiguity in Gould. On the one hand, he seems a staunch agnostic with no place for God. On the other, he affirms that evolution is compatible not only with a generic idea of God, but specifically with Christianity.

Gould's treatment of the famous Jesuit father Pierre Teilhard de Chardin (1881–1955) is particularly illuminating in this respect. Gould is insistent that evolution is unpredictable and humans are not the result of a plan, in complete opposition to Teilhard, a colleague and fellow paleontologist. Teilhard published several books integrating evolution and Christianity, treating evolution as a process directed by God. Humans were the result of a tendency toward increasing complexification of matter accompanied by a corresponding increase in consciousness, arriving finally at the human capacity for spirituality.

Gould, of course, comes down quite hard on Teilhard. He even published an article implicating Teilhard in the infamous "Piltdown Man" fraud,[62] an accusation that provoked a controversy to which Gould had to respond.[63] But the attack on Teilhard's character was not simply an ad hominem attack on his ideas. Quite the contrary, in fact, for when Gould deals with Teilhard's ideas, he is quite polite. He disagrees, of course, with Teilhard's reading of evolution as a process leading in a predictable way to humans, but he respects Teilhard's concern about human uniqueness and even acknowledges his own perplexities on the matter:

> We live in an essential and unresolvable tension between our unity with nature and our dangerous uniqueness. Systems that attempt to place and make sense of us by focusing exclusively either on the uniqueness or the unity are doomed to failure. But we must not stop asking and questing because the answers are complex and ambiguous. We can do no better than to follow Linnaeus's advice, embodied in his description of *homo sapiens* within his system. He described other species by the numbers of their fingers and toes, their size and their color. For us, in place of anatomy, he simply wrote the Socratic injunction: Know thyself.[64]

Encapsulating Gould's rich personality and wide-ranging ideas is impossible. He was not a religious believer, of course, and his worldview was that of an agnostic. But Gould had no desire to bash religion with the club of science. He rejected scientism and all forms of scientific imperialism. He opposed extrapolations of science outside its own fences; he wrote essays about people marginalized in the official records of scientific progress. He defended the Church against the widespread but false belief that it rejected the roundness of the earth during the so-called Dark Ages. He sang oratories in a choir, referred respectfully to God, and displayed an impressive knowledge of both the Old and New Testaments. His relationship to religion was very complex and merits further consideration.

Contingency versus Providence

Gould, as we have seen, was a champion of contingency and unpredictability, treating humanity as an insignificant and casual by-product of evolution: "The world wasn't made for us," he says simply.[65] Typically Gould believes that natural history rules out the possibility of a divine plan, a conclusion drawn by many, but not all, thinkers who have reflected on the meaning of Darwin's revolution.

When evolution emerged in the second half of the nineteenth century, many Christian thinkers argued that evolution was not incompatible with divine providence. For example, the Catholic American priest John Zahm, a professor of sciences at the University of Notre Dame, argued as long ago as 1896 that evolution could be viewed as a "derived creation." By these lights, God acts through secondary causes, through the very natural laws that He created and sustains with his providence. Zahm noted that this view was entirely consistent with Church tradition and could be found in the writings of thinkers like Augustine and Thomas Aquinas. They, of course, did not think of evolution as we now understand it, "for the simple reason that the subject had not even been broached in its present form, and because its formulation as a theory, under its present aspect, was impossible before men of science had in their possession the accumulated results of the observation and research of these latter times. But they did all that was necessary fully to justify my present contention; they laid down principles which are perfectly compatible with theistic Evolution."[66]

In the thirteenth century, of course, Aquinas could not speak of genetic mutations, and how their randomness highlights the role of chance in evolution. But he (and many others) spoke abundantly about the compatibility of chance and divine providence in the world. In the *Summa Theologica*, for instance, Aquinas poses the question: "Whether the will of God imposes necessity on the things willed?"[67] He asks, "Whether everything is subject to the providence of God?" "Whether God has immediate providence over everything?" and "Whether providence imposes any necessity on things foreseen?"[68] In the *Summa contra Gentiles*, Aquinas examines the same questions, concluding, "The divine will does not remove contingency from things, nor does it impose absolute necessity on them."[69]

Again in the same work Aquinas defends theses relevant to the present discussion. He asks "How the same effect is from God and from a natural agent?" He articulates God as the First Cause on which all other created causes depend. The created secondary causes produce effects but are themselves dependent on God's primary causality. Aquinas also argues "That divine providence does not entirely exclude evil from things," "That divine providence does not exclude contingency from things," "That divine providence does not exclude fortune and chance," and other related issues germane to our discussion.[70]

These surprisingly traditional ideas show that evolution is indeed compatible with divine providence. Our primary challenge arises from our tendency to view God as a super-being, controlling the world but acting in the same sort of ways that we would act. Our "divine" plan to produce humans as the pinnacle of the world would surely reveal the existence of a predictable direction in the evolutionary process. Gould makes it clear that natural history discloses no such plan: "Yet history, with its quirky pathways and quixotic reorganizations, teaches a hard lesson. Unless God is even more inscrutable than we ever dared to imagine (or unless He explicitly designed our modes of thought so that we would never grasp His own), the history of life confers no special or preordained status upon human intelligence."[71]

The Christian tradition, however, has always attributed exactly this sort of ineffability to God. Theology affirms that God exists and that we can have an idea of his attributes, but God's perfection and power transcend comprehension. We may know what "omnipotence" and "omniscience" mean, but theologians speak with greater confidence about what God is *not* than what God *is*. Knowing God's providence in general, however, has little to do with knowing in detail the way of God's action in the world.

No irrationalism is entailed by this belief. Christian doctrine affirms God created a rational world, governed by created natural laws. Human beings are created in God's image and endowed with the capacity to know the natural order. None of this denies space for random events, and we must not suppose that the presence of chance implies the absence of law. The world contains a confluence of independent causal chains; effects occur that could not be predicted on the basis of natural law. This poses no limit on God's knowledge of the world or action within it.

Gould notes that his rejection of a divine plan is compelling "unless God is even more inscrutable than we ever dared to imagine." Unfortunately for Gould, Christianity has long insisted that God is most definitely more inscrutable than anything we can ever imagine. But this does not mean that God "explicitly designed our modes of thought so that we would never grasp His own," as if God were trying to deceive us. It simply means that our knowledge of evolution, with its unpredictability, contingency, and randomness, is, after all, human—not divine—knowledge.

This does not establish, of course, that there is divine plan, or even that there is an argument for a divine plan. But it does deny the basis for Gould's confident assertion that the facts rule out the possibility that evolution unfolds according to a divine plan.

Human Uniqueness

We now turn our attention to humanity's alleged "dethroning" by the great scientific revolutions. We start by noting that the progress of science, including Freud's revolutions, has actually had the opposite effect, consistently showcasing the extraordinary, unique, and surprising power of the human mind. Indeed, the first of the great revolutions, inaugurated by Copernicus and completed by Newton, so enlarged the perceived capacities of the human mind that knowledge began an exponential growth that continues to this day.

Gould is certainly no pessimist when it comes to evaluating human potential, but he has also written eloquently about our all-too-human tendency to read our personal agendas into our science. His analysis of scientific racism is particularly sobering on this point, showing how subjective preconceptions influenced what should have been the objective gathering of numerical data.[72]

Science is a very human enterprise. Creativity, argument, and interpretation all play important, even critical, roles in science, but each provides an opening through which subjectivity can enter the scientific process. To take one example, science requires that we represent the world as an object, substituting partially idealized and oversimplified models for an unmanageably complicated "real" world. This abstraction is a highly imaginative act deeply dependent on the scientist's ability to intuit the essential features of the phenomena under consideration. When Newton imagined the earth reaching across space to pull on the moon, he had to envision both the earth and the moon as nothing but abstract points of mass. While doing science, we must note that we are located in the natural world but, at the same time, transcend it: Our models represent the natural world to varying degrees; we investigate its structures and the interrelationship of its parts, but never completely. Combining our intellectual and empirical skills, we pose all sorts of questions about the composition of the world, about the laws that govern its behavior, origins, and evolution. All this requires that we transcend our immediate experience. And this often demands the exercise of a most robust and informed imagination.

Scientific achievement demands imagination and creativity. We must go beyond the "given" facts to conceptualize new possibilities; we must create novel hypotheses to explain mysterious phenomena; we must design ingenious experiments to test our hypotheses; and then we must revise our hypotheses in light of the data we gather. We must make judgments about the congruence between nature and our models, deciding when the hand of nature fits adequately within the glove of explanation. Absent creativity, this remarkable process grinds to a halt.

Interpretation and argument also figure prominently. Data never speak for themselves but always require interpretation, which demands wisdom and judgment. Data must be interpreted in light of current theories, but current theories must not dictate what the data has to say. A careful balance is required. Arguments must be developed to establish logical connections between known data and unknown explanations. Skeptical colleagues must be brought on board if a new theory is to become established. Scientific conclusions are more often the end product of animated discussion than the immediate inference from "facts."

Creativity, imagination, argument, and interpretation are uniquely and profoundly human attributes, remarkable in their power to forge new understandings of the world. The extraordinary achievement we call science testifies to this power and lifts the human mind onto an exalted plane, independently of whether that mind resides at the center of the universe or evolved from simpler forms of life.

The alleged "dethronings" of humanity take on a rather different hue when viewed by these lights. The Copernican revolution, for starters, inaugurated modern science as a self-sustained enterprise and is usually seen as something of a triumph of human reason. And the Darwinian revolution was hardly the first hint that we were animals. In fact, the theological claim that humans were in the "image of God" was often made in the light of a recognition that we were not all that different from the animals. And as for the self-proclaimed "Freudian" revolution, many scientists and philosophers don't consider it a revolution at all. Finally, Gould's paleontological revolution of deep time has no obvious philosophical or theological implications. We could argue, for example, that it highlights the extraordinary uniqueness of humanity by calling attention to the long and complex route by which we arrived. So much for our scientifically inspired "dethronings."

Finally, the contingency of our existence highlighted by Gould is really no novelty at all for a religious thinker. Christian doctrine affirms that God freely created the world and everything in it. *Everything* is thus contingent, including the universe itself. We could have not existed; thus our existence is completely contingent. And this was known long before evolution.

These brief reflections suggest that Gould's examples can be used to either dethrone or "enthrone" humanity. Gould, like Freud before him, is putting his own personal spin on a complex history capable of multiple interpretations.

Gould on Science and Religion: Non-Overlapping Magisteria

In 1999, Gould published *Rocks of Ages,* a sustained and provocative analysis of the "relationship" between science and religion, which he suggested should be a cordial nonrelationship:

> I do not see how science and religion could be unified, or even synthesized, under any common scheme of explanation or analysis; but I also do not understand why the two enterprises should experience any conflict. Science tries to document the factual character of the natural world, and to develop theories that coordinate and explain these facts. Religion, on the other hand, operates in the equally important, but utterly different, realm of human purposes, meanings, and values—subjects that the factual domain of science might illuminate, but can never resolve.[73]

Gould called this scheme of cordial coexistence *non-overlapping magisteria,* or NOMA: "I propose that we encapsulate this central principle of respectful noninterference—accompanied by intense dialogue between the two distinct subjects, each covering a central facet of human existence—by enunciating the principle of NOMA, or Non-Overlapping Magisteria. I trust that my Catholic colleagues will not begrudge this appropriation of a common term from their discourse—for a magisterium (from the Latin *magister,* or teacher) represents a domain of authority in teaching."[74] Gould's peacemaking efforts have not met with widespread approval and, in fact, have been widely criticized. Supporters of religion find that the space Gould allocates to religion is simply too small for their religion to fit. On the other hand, opponents of religion want scientific warrant to challenge the truth-claims of religion.

Despite these legitimate criticisms, Gould has correctly noted that science and religion do occupy two very different spheres of human experience. We should also note that Gould conceives of science as the pursuit of knowledge of "the factual character of the natural world," specifically excluding problems such as the existence of God and God's action in the world. He also does not reduce religion *merely* to ethics, as some of his critics have charged,[75] but includes in its purview "human purposes, meanings, and values." Gould has a personal appreciation for religion, clearly in evidence from his knowledge of religious people, his regular use of biblical texts, his participation in a choir singing oratories, and his frequent focus on specific religious problems.

In a work published posthumously, Gould returned to science and religion, in the wider context of the harmony between science and the humanities. There he refers to NOMA, adding a slight but important difference:

> I have made the general argument in my book *Rocks of Ages* (Ballantine, 1999), a book that expresses the consensus of a great majority of professional scientists and theologians, not an original formulation from my pen. In briefest summary, no dichotomous opposition can exist in logic because science and religion treat such different (and equally important) aspects of human life—the principle that I have called NOMA as an acronym for the "non-overlapping magisteria," or teaching authorities, of science and religion. Science tries to record and explain the factual character of the natural world, whereas religion struggles with spiritual and ethical questions about the meaning and proper conduct of our lives. The facts of nature simply cannot dictate correct moral behavior or spiritual meaning.[76]

This text is something of an *authorized* interpretation of NOMA, offered by Gould himself. He reiterates that science refers to "the factual character of the natural world," but reformulates the scope of religion. Instead of saying that religion deals with "human purposes, meanings, and values," he speaks of "spiritual and ethical questions about the meaning and proper conduct of our lives." This certainly seems like more than just ethics, especially if we note that Gould lists both "spiritual" and "ethical" questions; he also speaks of the "meaning" of our lives. His view of religion is indeed personal and perhaps even idiosyncratic, but it is more than simply ethics.

Gould's Notion of Religion

H. Allen Orr, an outspoken critic of the science-and-religion dialogue, offers a most interesting perspective on Gould's NOMA proposal in a review of *Rocks of Ages*:[77]

> When I heard that Stephen Jay Gould had written a book on science and religion, I got worried. Not that I usually disagree with Gould. On the contrary, I find that I often side with him on larger social or intellectual issues.... I got worried because of a peculiar property of the topic. Talk of the relationship between science and religion routinely reduces normally sensible people, as if by magic, to idiots. Or if not idiots, charlatans.... the discussion suffers from an unusual amount of intellectual dishonesty. The good news is that Gould avoids most of the usual dishonesties in *Rocks of Ages*. The bad news is that he invents a few of his own.

Gould's idea, says Orr, seems "fairly sensible," as "his cardinal claim is that the two enterprises, rightly understood, are compatible. Science has its subject—the material world—and religion its—moral discourse—and each leaves the other plenty of elbow room." Nevertheless, Orr criticizes Gould's concept of religion as too narrow, offering reconciliation by redefining religion in a way that would not be recognized by religious believers.

Gould, notes Orr, avoids two widespread misunderstandings about science and religion. The first is that of scientists who not only deny conflict between science and religion, but even argue that science vindicates religion. The John Templeton Foundation and its many projects fall under this part of Orr's indictment, shared by Gould, who calls it "syncretist."[78] The second, more popular, view is that of "warfare," which views science and religion as implacably hostile to each other. Gould references the two classic nineteenth-century "warfare" works, the *History of the Conflict between Religion and Science*, by John William Draper (1874), and *A History of the Warfare of Science with Theology in Christendom*, by Andrew Dickson White (1896): "I cannot emphasize too strongly that the old model of all-out warfare between science and religion—the 'standard' view of my secular education . . . simply does not fit this issue, and represents an absurdly false and caricatured dichotomy that can only disrespect both supposed sides of this nonexistent conflict. 'Religion,' as a coherent entity, never opposed 'science' in any general or comprehensive way."[79]

Orr agrees with Gould and presents a convincing explanation of the alleged historical conflict: "As Gould notes, the facts are right but the pattern misinterpreted. In reality, the trend reflects a near historical necessity. Because religion arrived on the scene first and was more or less all there was—the Church was the religious, secular, and intellectual authority in much of the West—it's inevitably the Institution that must cede turf. When you start as a monopoly, there is, over the long haul, only one possible direction of change."

Orr agrees with Gould that the history of religion is not a history of bloodshed. "It is a law of nature," Orr writes, "that scientists must bring up the Crusades within five minutes of mention of religion." Gould argues that these misfortunes emerged because, in some epochs, the Church was a secular and not merely religious institution. Orr agrees: "When the Church was a powerful state, it, not surprisingly, acted like a powerful state. It is also worth noting (and Gould doesn't) that when avowedly atheist governments called the shots their ethical track record was less than awe-inspiring. Stalin, Mao, and Pol Pot are not, so far as I know, in line for sainthood. The point isn't that godless commies are bad. The point is that it is dishonest to pretend that the Crusades count against theism but that Stalin doesn't count against atheism."

Last but not least, Orr sees in Gould's attempted reconciliation of science and religion one more manifestation of Gould's consistent concern about the imperialism of science:

> In different ways at different times, Gould has battled what he considers the excesses of science. Gould has doubtlessly been *the* most outspoken and effective voice for humanism among living scientists. . . . Gould's career can, I think, be seen as part of a larger intellectual move against scientism, the view that all truths are ultimately scientific. . . . Gould has, all along, been on the right side of this skirmish. Scientism is naive and it is hubristic. But, most of all, it's just plain wrong.

Despite these points of agreement, Orr sharply criticizes aspects of Gould's NOMA proposal. One is Gould's use of Aristotle's doctrine of the "mean." This doctrine argues that moral virtue requires avoiding extremes, but this is not obviously relevant to truth and falsehood, which are not the "extremes" of some epistemological spectrum. Orr's primary criticism is of Gould's definition of religion as essentially "moral discourse." As we have noted above, this poses a host of problems. Most atheists, for example, would not consent to being shut out of ethical discourse. And religious people are generally quite attached to their beliefs, which include many things besides moral precepts. Gould rightly notes that we cannot extract ethical directives from nature; but if we reduce religion to ethics and insist that we must find these ethical values within ourselves, we reduce religion to a personalized individual search for meaning. This is very different from the kind of tradition-driven communities at the center of most people's religion.

Orr concludes that Gould has transformed the concept of religion to fit his explanatory scheme, which is close to both materialism and secular humanism:

> In the end it is hard to resist the conclusion that Gould has lifted the word "religion" and grafted it onto a toothless, hobbled beast incapable of scaring the materialists.... it is obvious that Gould's religion is a close cousin to secular humanism.... Gould's view of religion is itself arrived at via science.... Gould's position is not therefore so much, "Render to Caesar the things that are Caesar's, and to God the things that are God's," as "Render to Caesar the things that are Caesar's, and to God the things that Caesar says he can have." Gould's view of religion follows fairly naturally, though not necessarily, given a prior commitment to materialism. But this is precisely the commitment many religious people do not make.

Gould is very close to being a materialist: "Speaking personally," he says, "I suspect that no world other than the material can muster any strong claim for factual existence."[80] But he was certainly aware that religion is essentially spiritual, and he defends its legitimacy.

Orr's conclusions about Gould depend to a large degree on Gould's presumed reduction of religion to ethics. But, as we noted above, Gould views religion as an arena of both ethics and spirituality. He thus defends the right of religious spokespersons on the grounds that "no aspect of empirical nature can challenge the legitimate role of religion in ethical and spiritual domains outside the logic and authority of science."[81]

Personal Conundrums

Gould's style, unfortunately, does not follow a straightforward logical path. In dealing with science and religion he offers his usual roster of interesting particular examples, each with something to say, but overall there is no carefully articulated logical argument. Moreover, Gould's affinity for agnosticism and materialism is always present. All this makes it hard to evaluate his NOMA proposal.

Gould is probably right when he suggests that the majority of scientists and theologians would agree with the broad outlines of his proposal. Science and religion do have quite different goals, and rarely need to overlap. Their perspectives and methods are also very different, as, of course, is their content. Science, qua science, is thus neither theistic nor atheistic.

Nevertheless, we would argue that, while NOMA may work in general, there are cases where *particular overlappings* of science and religion occur. Christianity, for example, makes claims about the natural world, something Gould barely notes. To be sure, most Christians no longer impose a literal reading of biblical texts on nature, but some central Christian beliefs, like the resurrection of Jesus, are affirmed as real, historical events. Nonetheless, given the nature of these sorts of claims, it is hard to see how purely scientific arguments would be capable of proving or disproving them.

Gould's NOMA is a sincere proposal advanced by a prestigious practicing scientist with wide humanistic interests, but one whose worldview has an agnostic and materialist tone. Using the metaphor of the endurance of the hedgehog (for deepest wisdom) and the varied and particular capacities of the fox, Gould claims: "We must firmly reject the common, yet utterly false, inference that science itself, by its very nature, must be irreligious, immoral, or inherently opposed to aesthetic urges and sensibilities. Science operates in the different domain of factual understanding. Any full human life (the hedgehog's one true way of wisdom) must be enriched by all these independent dimensions, and their fecund interactions: ethical, aesthetic, spiritual, and scientific (the fox's range of independent and necessary contributions)."[82]

If we extend Gould's view of religion to include spiritual dimensions, such as the existence of God or God's action on the world, NOMA is a solid place to begin. We wonder, however, why Gould sometimes seems to reduce religion to ethics and is not more explicit about the spiritual dimensions he is prepared to include in religion. The answer may have to do with the practical significance of NOMA.

One of the main reasons Gould favors NOMA derives from the particularities of American culture. He says that, for reasons quite mysterious to him, America is preeminent in the Western world in that an overwhelming majority of citizens believe in God, and this belief occupies a central position in their lives. Though he notes that he sees little practical significance in this conviction, he adds: "But I do not doubt the sincerity of the stated conviction for an instant. If people insist that such a belief occupies a central position in their lives, then, by God, it does."[83]

Gould then arrives at an important consequence of his NOMA proposal: "Given this firm sociological fact, if religious people then come to believe that science stands in intrinsic opposition to their spiritual convictions, then, if I may lapse into the vernacular, science is screwed. Our best strategy—and the intellectually soundest and most honest position in any case...—therefore requires genuine respect for these religious convictions (which a high percentage of scientists also share), and continual insistence that science cannot pose any threat to these central pillars of life's emotional support."[84]

We applaud Gould's sincerity and see no reason to doubt that NOMA is a honest proposal. On the practical side, Gould was involved in the Arkansas trial on evolution versus creation in 1981–82 and he saw up close what was at stake. He realized, to his credit, that "scientific creationists," despite their public relevance, were a minority within larger Christian communities that had made their peace with evolution and were opposed to a fundamentalist hermeneutic that turned the Bible into a source for biological science. He saw the sciences, the humanities, and religion coexisting and even cooperating under the banner of America's national motto, *e pluribus unum*:

> Fortunately, and in the most parochial American sense, we know a model of long persistence and proven utility for the virtues in fruitful union of apparent opposites. This model has sustained us through the worst fires of challenge.... We have even embodied this ideal in our national motto, *e pluribus unum*, "one from many."...Never before in human history has the experiment of democracy been tried across such a vast range of geographies, climates, ecologies, economies, languages, ethnicities, and capabilities. Lord knows we have suffered our troubles, and imposed horrendous and enduring persecutions upon sectors of the enterprise, thus sullying the great goal in the most shameful way imaginable. Yet, on balance, and by comparison to all other efforts of similar scale in human history, the experiment has worked, and has been showing substantial improvement in the course and memories of my lifetime at least. I offer the same basic prescription for peace, and mutual growth in strength, of the sciences and humanities.[85]

Gould is paradoxical in that he offers himself as the champion of the pacific coexistence of science and religion, while many believers see him as an adversary. This paradox arises from Gould's tendency to identify science with materialism. He was a brilliant essayist and he usually advanced interesting proposals, but, as he acknowledged, logical coherence was not his main strength. His agenda demanded the peaceful coexistence of materialism and religion, a noble, albeit impossible, task.

3

Reading the Mind of God

Stephen Hawking

Stephen Hawking is in a restaurant near the center of Cambridge.
Twelve students sit around his table. As usual, he is in his wheelchair,
and a nurse takes care of him. It is December 1988, and the actress
Shirley MacLaine joins the group. After the meal she spends two hours
asking Hawking about metaphysics and spirituality. She wants to
know "if he believes that there is a God who created the universe and
guides His creation. He smiles momentarily, and the machine voice
says, 'No.' The professor is neither rude nor condescending; brevity
is simply his way. Each word has to be painstakingly spelt out on a
computer attached to his wheelchair and operated by tiny movements
of two of the fingers of one hand, almost the last vestige of bodily
freedom he has."[1] But Hawking dislikes the label "atheist," for his
views on God are quite mysterious and he has written of his quest to
"know the mind of God."[2]

Hawking is widely admired as one of the greatest scientists in
history. *A Brief History of Time* introduced him to millions of readers,
and countless more have encountered him on television. After Einstein he is probably the most popular scientist ever, lecturing in
his computer-generated voice to packed houses of hushed and awe-
struck fans. He is a heroic, glorious, yet tragic figure. The image of a
mind soaring through the vast cosmos while trapped in a steadily
deteriorating physical body is compelling and invests his brief and
often cryptic pronouncements with a transcendent quality.

Almost completely paralyzed and attached to his wheelchair, Hawking addresses the big questions of our origins as if God is whispering answers into his ear. Critics accuse him of superficiality and philosophical ignorance, but he doesn't care. When he speaks, the world listens.

Hawking studied physics at Oxford University. In 1962, at twenty-one, he went to Cambridge University to do postgraduate research. At this time he was diagnosed with ALS, a motor neuron disease that doctors told him would take his life within two years. The disease progressed, and in a few years he could move almost none of his muscles. Nevertheless, he earned his Ph.D. and soon did some remarkable work in mathematical physics, becoming a widely respected physicist. In 1988 he emerged as a major cultural phenomenon with the publication of *A Brief History of Time*. He maintains his professorship at Cambridge University and travels the world, a media star who gives physics lectures.

Hawking's courage in facing his physical condition accounts for much of his fame. There is no doubt, however, that he is an important scientist. Sir Martin Rees, the Royal Astronomer who was close to Hawking when they were young postgraduate students at Cambridge, has written: "Hawking was, by the early 1970s, acknowledged as one of the leaders in relativity. He was already physically frail. None of us then predicted the astonishing later phases of his career. His most remarkable single discovery, black-hole evaporation, came in 1974. But that was itself just the impetus for a crescendo of achievement that continues to this day. Nobody else since Einstein (except perhaps Penrose) has contributed more to our understanding of gravity. And no physicist since Einstein has achieved such worldwide fame."[3]

Hawking likes to connect physics with God, which is why the crowds that pack his lectures, and people like Shirley MacLaine, seek him out. Rees, however, is not impressed: "My Cambridge colleague, Stephen Hawking, claimed in *A Brief History of Time* that each equation he included would have halved the book's sales. He followed that injunction, and so have I. But he (or maybe his editor) judged that each mention of God would double the sales.... Scientists' incursions into theology or philosophy can be embarrassingly naïve or dogmatic. The implications of cosmology for these realms of thought may be profound, but diffidence prevents me from venturing into them."[4] Regarding the astonishing success of *A Brief History of Time* he adds: "This success had one negative consequence: the book came to the attention of philosophers and theologians, and received more scrutiny than it could really bear."[5]

A Genius in the Making

Stephen William Hawking was born on January 8, 1942,[6] a date he likes to highlight as coincident with the three hundredth anniversary of Galileo's death. His parents, Frank and Isobel, lived in London but went to Oxford for his birth to avoid the London of World War II. Oxford was safer because the British and German governments had agreed not to bomb four famous university cities, Oxford and Cambridge in Britain, Heidelberg and Göttingen in Germany. Two weeks after the birth they returned to London; two years later their building was damaged in a bomb raid.

Both Frank and Isobel Hawking had studied at Oxford University. Frank studied medicine and became a specialist in tropical diseases. When the war broke out, he was in East Africa. He returned to volunteer for military service and was assigned to medical research. Isobel became a secretary and met Frank, and they married in the early days of the war. After the war, Frank headed the Division of Parasitology at the National Institute of Medical Research. The family stayed in London until 1950, when they moved twenty miles north to St. Albans in Hertfordshire. Stephen went to the private St. Albans School, beginning his studies in September 1952. He had two younger sisters, Mary and Philippa, and a brother, Edward.

Stephen soon discovered his great gift for mathematics and an intuitive capacity for good ideas. Nevertheless, he did not excel as an undergraduate at Oxford University. He got a scholarship to University College, founded in 1249, which had also been his father's college. He liked rowing but little else. His studies came easily and required little work, a handicap for his last exams, as he needed a strong performance to be accepted at Cambridge. He got it, though, and arrived at Cambridge with his B.A. in October 1962. He was twenty-one.

During his last year at Oxford, physical difficulties emerged. He did nothing about it, but when he went home for Christmas his mother had him examined in the hospital. He soon got the report that he had ALS, or amyotrophic lateral sclerosis, also known as motor neuron disease (in Great Britain) and Lou Gehrig's disease (in the United States). ALS affects the nerves of the spinal cord and the parts of the brain producing voluntary motor functions. This atrophies the muscles, interfering with movement and speech. After two or three years the respiratory muscles fail, leading to death from pneumonia or suffocation. Curiously, the brain can remain unaffected, with no impairment of thinking.

Hawking became depressed. At Cambridge his health deteriorated, requiring him to use a walking stick, which just barely enabled him to walk.

His friends had to help him. His speech was also affected. While home for Christmas in 1963, he met Jane Wilde, whom he later married. Jane energized Stephen and got him going again. In an interview broadcast on Christmas Day 1992, Sue Lawley asked Hawking: "How much of your success, would you say, do you owe to her, Jane?" The answer was: "I certainly wouldn't have managed it without her. Being engaged to her lifted me out of the slough of despond I was in. And if we were to get married, I had to get a job and I had to finish my Ph.D. I began to work hard and found I enjoyed it. Jane looked after me single-handedly as my condition got worse. At that stage, no one was offering to help us, and we certainly couldn't afford to pay for help."[7]

At Cambridge Hawking was a student at Trinity Hall. He intended to work under Fred Hoyle, but the famous astronomer was somewhat unapproachable, so he worked under a younger astronomer named Denis Sciama. Sciama had several students who became famous in addition to Hawking, including George Ellis, Brandon Carter, and Martin Rees. In the early 1960s a Department of Applied Mathematics and Theoretical Physics was created; it would be the permanent home for Hawking's work.

Hawking's fame began with work developed by Hoyle, well known for working with Hermann Bondi and Thomas Gold on the "steady-state" theory of the universe. They formulated this theory in 1948 because they were dis-satisfied with the "big bang" theory proposed in 1930 by Georges Lemaître, a Belgian astronomer and Catholic priest and developed by other physicists, including George Gamow. The big-bang theory implied that the universe had a definite beginning and a finite age, having originated from some primordial event. Lemaître suggested that the disintegration of some sort of "primordial atom" might be a way to think about the mysterious creative event that gave birth to our universe.

Hoyle objected to Lemaître's smuggling what he viewed as a self-serving "supernatural" origin for the universe into science, but there was no disputing that key observations were effectively explained by the new theory, to which Hoyle had dismissively assigned the silly name "big bang." The steady-state theory was developed to explain these same observations without invoking a mysterious creation event. By postulating the steady creation of new matter, this theory could accommodate an infinitely old and unchanging universe without invoking a "beginning."

Jayant Narlikar, Hoyle's collaborator, was next door to Hawking at Cam-bridge and kept him informed about Hoyle's mathematical work. So when Hoyle audaciously presented his findings at the Royal Society in London, Hawking surprised everyone, in the discussion after the talk, by correctly not-ing an error in Hoyle's mathematics. Hawking summarized his argument in a paper that his biographers Michael White and John Gribbin note "was well received by his peers and established him as a promising young researcher."[8]

Hawking the lazy Oxford undergraduate had shown little promise of becoming a great genius. But when the devastating consequences of his disease appeared in Cambridge, he began to shine with his own light, like a new star igniting into a bright nova.

Cosmic Singularities

Sir Roger Penrose, before being knighted for contributions to mathematics, played a critical role in Hawking's work. Penrose, then at Birkbeck College in London, was a prodigious mathematician who in the early 1960s worked on singularity theory, which would later engage Hawking.

Singularities occur in physics when infinite quantities appear; generally this results from something getting divided by zero. In principle, singularities are bad because nobody knows what to do with infinite quantities. Sometimes they can be cancelled using specialized techniques such as the so-called "renormalization." Some singularities, like the gravitational force at the center of a black hole, refer to actual physical quantities that cannot really be infinite (everything in the universe, as far as we know, is finite). Scientists consider that the relevant scientific laws no longer apply in these cases. Though they may work everywhere else, the laws "break down" at singularities and give nonsense results.

Two related singularities were important in Hawking's work: singularities associated with black holes, and the singularity existing in the big bang theory at the beginning of the universe. The gravitational force at each of these singularities is infinite, creating conceptual challenges for understanding what is going on.

The original theory of gravity was developed by Isaac Newton, who understood gravity as an attractive force between bodies that depends only on their masses and the distance between them. Newton's theory was supplanted by Einstein's Theory of General Relativity at the beginning of the twentieth century. The new theory, which worked much better, treated gravity as a distortion of space rather than a force between bodies. In both Newton's and Einstein's theories, large masses like stars have large effects; small masses like electrons, by contrast, have small effects that are generally insignificant compared to other forces, such as electromagnetism or the nuclear forces. Physical phenomena typically fell into two categories—large masses and great distances effectively treated by general relativity, and small masses and tiny distances where quantum mechanics was needed for explanation. The former theory described solar systems and galaxies, the latter described atoms and molecules, and there was rarely any need to apply both of these very successful theories at the same time. But black holes were an exception.

Black holes form when stars exhaust their fuel. Stars, composed primarily of hydrogen, shine by fusing atoms in a vast ongoing nuclear reaction that releases great energy. Hydrogen fuses into helium and helium fuses into heavier atoms and so on, with each fusion releasing energy. The process of combining light atoms into heavier ones uses up the fuel and makes the star increasingly dense. Eventually the nuclear reactions stop and the remaining matter collapses under the force of gravity. This collapse compresses the atoms into dramatically smaller volumes, forcing electrons that normally take up a lot of space into the nuclei. If the star is large enough, its matter compresses to such a degree that its nearby gravitational force can actually pull light into it, and then the light cannot escape. Such a star appears as a "black hole," unable to reflect or emit light, and detectable only by its gravitational effects on other bodies.

Black holes were not taken very seriously until the discovery in the 1960s of quasars and pulsars, mysterious and superdense astronomical objects. Hawking began attending talks at King's College in London, where Hermann Bondi, cocreator of the steady-state theory, was a professor. Penrose had recently proven that black holes have a central point of infinite density—a notorious singularity. Hawking imagined stellar collapse in reverse as a possible model of the big bang. As we go back in time, the matter of the universe compresses until we reach a time when all the matter was concentrated in a point, just like in a black hole. This could be the big-bang theory's first stage of the universe, a "primeval atom" with all matter and energy concentrated at very high density and temperature. Hawking calculated that this initial state would be a singularity, with density and temperature actually being infinite.

Gribbin and White connect Hawking's idea to the meetings at King's College.

> Over the course of the talks at King's, Roger Penrose had introduced his colleagues to the idea of a space-time singularity at the center of a black hole, and naturally the group from Cambridge was tremendously excited by this. One night, on the way back to Cambridge . . . an idea struck [Hawking]. . . . Turning to Sciama sitting across from him, he said, "I wonder what would happen if you applied Roger's singularity theory to the entire Universe." In the event it was that single idea that saved Hawking's Ph.D. and set him on the road

to science superstardom. Penrose published his ideas in January 1965.... Within months Sciama was beginning to realize that his young Ph.D. student was doing something truly exceptional. For Hawking this was the first time he had really applied himself to anything. As he says: "I ... started working hard for the first time in my life." ... The final chapter of Hawking's thesis was a brilliant piece of work."[9]

Thus, at the unusually young age of twenty-three, Hawking received his Ph.D.

Around this time, the Bell Labs scientists Arno Penzias and Robert Wilson discovered the background radiation that Gamow had predicted would be present if the big bang theory were correct. The 1965 discovery of this predicted radiation, a relic of the early universe, provided such strong confirmation for the big bang that the steady-state theory disappeared as a serious competitor.

Fascinating questions emerged in the aftermath of the big bang's confirmation: Can we explore the big bang itself? What happened before the big bang? Did the universe actually begin with the big bang?

Hawking's idea implied that the universe began at a singularity where the known laws of physics did not apply. Were there, then, other laws to be found? Hawking went to work on this question.

In 1970 Hawking and Penrose collaborated on a technical paper showing that a singularity existed at the big bang.[10] Years later, in 1987, a conference took place at Trinity College, Cambridge, where Newton lived from 1661 to 1696. While there, in 1687, Newton published the first scientific theory of gravitation. The 1987 conference gathered distinguished scholars, including Hawking, to present papers celebrating the third centennial of that historic event. Hawking recalled his early work:

If one traces the expansion [of the universe] back in time, one finds that all the galaxies would have been on top of each other about 15 thousand million years ago. At first it was thought that there was an earlier contracting phase and that the particles in the universe would come very close to each other but would miss each other. The universe would reach a high but finite density and would then re-expand. However, a series of theorems showed that if classical general relativity were correct, there would inevitably be a singularity at which all physical laws would break down. Thus classical cosmology predicts its own downfall. In order to determine how the classical evolution of the universe began one has to appeal to quantum cosmology and study the early quantum era.[11]

Hawking's pioneering proposal required merging gravitation and quantum theory into a much-sought-after but still-undiscovered theory of "quantum gravity." In *A Brief History of Time* he reviews his first contribution to this ambitious project:

> We have seen in this chapter how, in less than half a century, man's view of the universe, formed over millennia, has been transformed. Hubble's discovery that the universe was expanding, and the realization of the insignificance of our own planet in the vastness of the universe, were just the starting point. As experimental and theoretical evidence mounted, it became more and more clear that the universe must have had a beginning in time, until in 1970 this was finally proved by Penrose and myself, on the basis of Einstein's general theory of relativity. That proof showed that general relativity is only an incomplete theory. It cannot tell us how the universe started off, because it predicts that all physical theories, including itself, break down at the beginning of the universe. However, general relativity claims to be only a partial theory, so what the singularity theorems really show is that there must have been a time in the very early universe when the universe was so small that one could no longer ignore the small-scale effects of the other great partial theory of the twentieth century, quantum mechanics. At the start of the 1970s, then, we were forced to turn our search for an understanding of the universe from our theory of the extraordinarily vast to our theory of the extraordinarily tiny.[12]

Hawking continued to surprise and impress the scientific community, moving forward on a new theory of quantum gravity. The study of singularities was the road to the new perspectives: "The singularity theorems discussed earlier indicate that the gravitational field should get very strong in at least two situations, black holes and the big bang. In such strong fields the effects of quantum mechanics should be important. Thus, in a sense, classical general relativity, by predicting points of infinite density, predicts its own downfall.... We do not yet have a complete consistent theory that unifies general relativity and quantum mechanics, but we do know a number of features it should have."[13]

Hawking's Radiation

In 1965, Hawking got a research fellowship at Gonville and Caius College in Cambridge. His ALS had already disabled his writing. He married Jane in

July; their first child, Robert, was born in 1967, and their second, Lucy, in 1970. His illness worsened, and it appeared he had limited time to live. The latter half of the 1960s saw him on crutches, and then in a wheelchair. By 1972 his speech had deteriorated.

Nevertheless, he continued his research, publishing at least one scientific article every year, and growing in reputation as a cosmologist. In 1965 he was invited to give a talk at a relativity meeting in Miami. Other invitations followed, even though his speech limitations now required that friends read the talks for him. In 1966 he won the United Kingdom's prestigious mathematics award, the Adams Prize, for his essay "Singularities and the Geometry of Spacetime." In 1968 he was invited to join the Institute of Theoretical Astronomy in Cambridge.

In those years astrophysics and cosmology were full of new and intriguing discoveries. No clear evidence for black holes had appeared, but theoretical work on them continued, much of it by Hawking and Penrose. In the 1970s they showed that black holes can emit some radiation, even though their enormous gravitation traps everything around them.

Hawking presented his ideas on black hole radiation at the Rutherford-Appleton Laboratory near Oxford in 1974. Although he reports being greeted with general incredulity, the radiation he described is now accepted and generally known as "Hawking radiation." Nothing was supposed to escape from a black hole, but by taking quantum effects into account, Hawking showed that black holes could create pairs of particles in their vicinity, one being absorbed by the black hole and the other being radiated into space.

Hawking radiation had important consequences. Explaining the radiation as a quantum effect was a step toward unifying gravity and quantum mechanics, partially bonding the estranged theories. The radiation was also a thermodynamic effect, establishing a new link between black hole theory and yet another part of physics. Hawking wrote: "My work in the 1970s focused on the black holes that can result from such stellar collapse and the intense gravitational fields around them. It was this that led to the first hints of how the theories of quantum mechanics and general relativity might affect each other—a glimpse of the shape of a quantum theory of gravity yet to come."[14]

In the January 1977 *Scientific American*, Hawking published "The Quantum Mechanics of Black Holes." The article summary reads: "Black holes are often defined as areas from which nothing, not even light, can escape. There is good reason to believe, however, that particles can get out of them by *tunneling*." Hawking highlighted the connection between gravity and quantum physics:

One of the problems facing physicists who sought to apply general relativity to these newly discovered or hypothetical objects [quasars, pulsars, neutron stars, black holes] was to make it compatible with quantum mechanics. Within the past few years there have been developments that give rise to hope that before too long we shall have a fully consistent quantum theory of gravity, one that will agree with general relativity for macroscopic objects and will, one hopes, be free of the mathematical infinities that have long bedeviled other quantum field theories. These developments have to do with certain recently discovered quantum effects associated with black holes, which provide a remarkable connection between black holes and the laws of thermodynamics.[15]

The quantum effects relate to Heisenberg's uncertainty principle and the way it allows for the temporary creation of particle-antiparticle pairs. These virtual particles usually annihilate each other immediately, in a flash of energy. But one of them could get pulled into a nearby black hole, leaving the other free to escape. This exotic process is an application of quantum physics to very strong gravitational fields.

Hawking published his ideas in *Nature* in 1974:

> It seems that any black hole will create and emit particles such as neutrinos or photons at just the rate that one would expect if the black hole was a body with a temperature of [a mathematical formula]. As a black hole emits this thermal radiation one would expect it to lose mass. This in turn would increase the surface gravity and so increase the rate of emission. The black hole would therefore have a finite life of the order of [a very big magnitude is indicated]. For a black hole of solar mass this is much longer than the age of the Universe. There might, however, be much smaller black holes which were formed by fluctuations in the early Universe. Any such black hole of mass less than [a huge quantity] would have evaporated by now.[16]

Although Hawking's physical body was increasingly confined to a wheelchair, his mind remained strangely free to wander the entire space and time of the universe.

In March of this same year, when he was just thirty-two years old, Hawking was inducted into the Royal Society. His biographer, Kitty Ferguson, tells the story:

> During the rite of investiture, a ceremony dating from the seventeenth century, new Fellows walk to the podium to write their names

in the book, the earliest pages of which contain the signature of Isaac Newton. Those present when Hawking was inducted remember that the president of the society, Sir Alan Hodgkin, Nobel laureate in biology, broke tradition and carried the book down to Hawking in the front row. Hawking could still write his name with great effort, but it took him a long time. The gathering of eminent scientists waited respectfully. When Hawking finished and looked up with a broad grin, they gave him an ovation.[17]

This was Hawking's greatest honor, but many others followed. Hawking concluded from his work that

> The most likely outcome seems to be that the black hole just disappears. . . . This was the first indication that quantum mechanics might remove the singularities that were predicted by general relativity. However, the methods that I and other people were using in 1974 were not able to answer questions such as whether singularities would occur in quantum gravity. From 1975 onward I therefore started to develop a more powerful approach to quantum gravity based on Richard Feynman's idea of a sum over histories.[18]

Hawking claimed to have shown in 1970 that the universe has a definite age, a beginning in time, and that the big bang contains a singularity where the laws of physics break down. Now, applying quantum physics to black holes for the first time, he saw a way to remove the initial singularity.

Hawking Meets the Pope

Hawking gave an invited presentation at a meeting of the Pontifical Academy of Sciences at the Vatican in the fall of 1981. The Academy, which had evolved from an earlier organization founded in 1603, numbered Galileo among its many famous members. In 1936 Pope Pius XI opened membership to leading scientists without discrimination on the basis of either race or religion, enabling Hawking the unbeliever to join Galileo the Christian in the august body, which he did in 1986.

The focus of the 1981 meeting of the Academy was "Cosmology and Fundamental Physics" and included the main topics of those branches of science: large-scale structure of the universe; evolution of galaxies, quasars, and radio galaxies; primordial nucleosynthesis; and the very early universe. It was an esoteric scientific meeting for specialists. The published volume from the

meeting includes contributions on the very early universe by Steven Weinberg, Nobel laureate in physics and well-known foe of religion; Dennis Sciama,
Hawking's doctoral adviser; Yakov Zeldovich, leading Russian cosmologist;
and Hawking himself. Martin Rees, the British Royal Astronomer, wrote a
long introduction.

Although Academy meetings have a strictly scientific character, the Academy belongs to the Vatican, and the Pope usually receives the participants in a
special audience. The Pope addresses them in a speech, and they greet the Pope
personally. At this meeting, the audience took place the day after the meeting
ended, at the Pope's summer residence at Castelgandolfo. The Pope's speech
appeared at the beginning of the published volume, with three paragraphs
devoted to the meeting with Hawking.[19]

The first paragraph contains customary greetings. The second highlights
that science and religion address the origin of the universe from different
perspectives:

> Cosmogony and cosmology have always aroused great interest among
> peoples and religions. The Bible itself speaks to us of the origin of the
> universe and its make-up, not in order to provide us with a scientific
> treatise, but in order to state the correct relationships of man with
> God and with the universe. Sacred Scripture wishes simply to declare
> that the world was created by God, and in order to teach this truth it
> expresses itself in the terms of the cosmology in use at the time of the
> writer. The Sacred Book likewise wishes to tell men that the world
> was not created as the seat of the gods, as was taught by other cos-
> mogonies and cosmologies, but was rather created for the service of
> man and the glory of God. Any other teaching about the origin and
> make-up of the universe is alien to the intentions of the Bible, which
> does not wish to teach how heaven was made but how one goes to
> heaven.[20]

The Pope continues: "Any scientific hypothesis on the origin of the world,
such as the hypothesis of a primitive atom from which derived the whole of
the physical universe, leaves open the problem concerning the universe's beginning. Science cannot of itself solve this question: there is needed that
human knowledge that rises above physics and astrophysics and which is
called metaphysics; there is needed above all the knowledge that comes from
God's revelation."[21] This passage may have disturbed Hawking, laboring as
he was to explain the beginning of the universe. Probably the Pope wished to
highlight only that physics cannot of itself prove or disprove the creation of the
universe. But he used the word "beginning." Any philosopher or theologian,

including the Pope, would distinguish "creation"—existence of creatures de-
pending on the action of God—from "beginning"—origins in time. In Hawking's mind, however, the subtle but theologically critical distinction between
"creation" and "beginning" probably got lost, creating further problems.

Afterward, John Paul II quoted Pope Pius XII from thirty years earlier:

> In vain would one expect a reply from the sciences of nature, which
> on the contrary frankly declare that they find themselves faced by an
> insoluble enigma. It is equally certain that the human mind versed
> in philosophical meditation penetrates the problem more deeply.
> One cannot deny that a mind which is enlightened and enriched by
> modern scientific knowledge and which calmly considers this prob-
> lem is led to break the circle of matter which is totally indepen-
> dent and autonomous—as being either uncreated or having created
> itself—and to rise to a creating Mind. With the same clear and crit-
> ical gaze with which it examines and judges the facts, it discerns
> and recognizes there the work of creative Omnipotence, whose
> strength raised up by the powerful *fiat* uttered billions of years ago
> by the creating Mind, has spread through the universe, calling
> into existence, in a gesture of generous love, matter teeming with
> energy.[22]

John Paul II and Pius XII both argue that the material universe must be
created; it cannot be self-sufficient. But the casual reference to "billions of
years ago" may have suggested to Hawking that they were using the big bang
as a proof of the Creation.

After the speech, the participants greeted the Pope one by one. Gribbin
and White provide a report that is not, unfortunately, completely accurate. The
papal address to the conference was not delivered while the conference was
taking place, as they suggest; it occurred after the conference, during the papal
audience at Castelgandolfo. They described Hawking's meeting with the Pope
as follows:

> When it was Hawking's turn, he wheeled on to the stage and up to
> the Pope. The other guests watched as the man who, only days ear-
> lier, had talked of the 'no-boundary' concept and the fact that there
> could be no need for a Creator came face to face with the leader of the
> Catholic Church and, for millions, God's representative on Earth.
> Everyone, believer and cynic alike, was curious to know what would
> be said. However, no one in the room could have been more sur-
> prised by what happened next. As Hawking's wheelchair came to a

halt in front of the Pope, John Paul left his seat and knelt down to bring his face to Hawking's level. The two men talked for longer than any of the other guests. Finally the Pope stood up, dusted down his cassock and gave Hawking a parting smile, and the wheelchair whirred off to the far side of the stage. There were a number of offended Catholics in the hall that afternoon, misinterpreting the Pope's gesture as undue respect. Many of the nonscientists present were unfamiliar with Hawking's latest proposals, but his reputation as a scientist with irreligious views was well known. They simply could not understand why the Pope should kneel before him; to them Hawking's opinions were at the opposite end of the spectrum from orthodox Catholic doctrine. Why had John Paul not taken more interest in them, the faithful?[23]

Gribbin and White miss that John Paul's affectionate treatment of Hawking was typical of his personality, and it is very unlikely that there were Catholics in the audience offended by the pope's very normal and familiar action. Certainly no evidence has appeared to suggest this was the case.

Hawking, however, did not like what the Pope said, or at least what he thought he said. But Hawking's response missed the boat, as we will see now.

The Pope and the Big Bang

Hawking recalls his meeting with the pope in *A Brief History of Time*:

Throughout the 1970s I had been mainly studying black holes, but in 1981 my interest in questions about the origin and fate of the universe was reawakened when I attended a conference on cosmology organized by the Jesuits in the Vatican. The Catholic Church had made a bad mistake with Galileo when it tried to lay down the law on a question of science, declaring that the sun went round the earth. Now, centuries later, it had decided to invite a number of experts to advise it on cosmology. At the end of the conference the participants were granted an audience with the Pope. He told us that it was all right to study the evolution of the universe after the big bang, but we should not inquire into the big bang itself because that was the moment of Creation and therefore the work of God. I was glad then that he did not know the subject of the talk I had just given at the conference—the possibility that space-time was finite but had no boundary, which means that it had no beginning, no moment of

Creation. I had no desire to share the fate of Galileo, with whom I felt a strong sense of identity, partly because of the coincidence of having been born exactly 300 years after his death![24]

Hawking's version of the celebrated encounter with the pope has intrigued millions of his readers and has been illustrated in a popular introduction to Hawking.[25]

Setting aside that the conference was organized by the Academy and not by the Jesuits, Hawking did not understand the Pope's comments. The Pope did *not* say that the big bang was the moment of Creation. He said only that the scientific approach leaves open the metaphysical and religious questions about the creation of the universe, something virtually all scientists admit. Moreover, Hawking said nothing in the meeting about God, or Creation, or there being no need for a Creator, despite what Gribbin and White say and Hawking himself implies to his readers.

Hawking also wrote, "Many people do not like the idea that time has a beginning, probably because it smacks of divine intervention. (The Catholic Church, on the other hand, seized on the big bang model and in 1951 officially pronounced it to be in accordance with the Bible.)"[26] The Catholic Church, however, never made this official pronouncement, and Hawking's widely disseminated misunderstanding of these events demands a response to set the record straight.

Rewriting History

On November 22, 1951, Pope Pius XII delivered a lengthy address to the Pontifical Academy of Sciences, quoted by John Paul II in 1981. Cardinals, diplomats, and other luminaries were present. In the volume published by the Academy that we quoted above, the title of the address is "The Proofs for the Existence of God in the Light of Modern Natural Science." The Pope stated his thesis up front: "Contrary to rash statements in the past, the more true science advances, the more it discovers God, almost as though He were standing, vigilant and waiting, behind every door which science opens."[27] It was an optimistic message. The Pope did not say that the sciences by themselves could prove the existence of God. He explicitly highlighted that such proofs, although based on empirical realities, are philosophical in character. His aim was "to re-examine the classical proofs of St. Thomas on the basis of the new scientific discoveries...to consider, that is, if and to what extent the more profound knowledge of the structure of the macrocosm and the microcosm contributes to

the reinforcement of philosophic arguments."[28] He concentrated on two features of the natural world: the mutability of things, and the teleological order
of the cosmos.

At the end of the speech, Pius XII stated: "Indeed, it seems that the science
of today, by going back in one leap millions of centuries, has succeeded in being
a witness to that primordial *Fiat Lux*, when, out of nothing, there burst forth
with matter a sea of light and radiation, while the particles of chemical elements
split and reunited in millions of galaxies."[29] This is the closest that Pius XII
came to an endorsement of the big bang. Nevertheless, the Pope immediately
added:

> It is true that the facts verified up to now are not arguments of
> absolute proof of creation in time as are those which are drawn from
> metaphysics and revelation, in so far as they concern creation in
> its widest sense, and from revelation alone in so far as they con-
> cern creation in time. The facts pertinent to natural sciences, to which
> we have referred, still wait for further investigation and confirma-
> tion, and theories founded upon them have need of new develop-
> ments and proofs, in order to offer a secure basis to a line of reasoning
> which is, of itself, outside the sphere of the natural sciences.[30]

We then read in the conclusion that modern science has indicated the

> beginning in time at a period about five billion years ago, confirming
> with the concreteness of physical proofs the contingency of the uni-
> verse and the well-founded deduction that about that time the cosmos
> issued from the hands of the Creator. Creation, therefore, in time,
> and therefore, a Creator; and consequently, God! This is the state-
> ment, even though not explicit or complete, that we demand of sci-
> ence, and that the present generation of man expects from it. It is a
> statement which rises from the mature and calm consideration of a
> single aspect of the universe, that is, of its mutability.[31]

Pius XII had said nothing particularly new. He recalled that only metaphysics and revelation can establish that the world is created, in the sense that
its being depends completely on God's action; that revelation says the world
was created in time; and that the natural sciences by themselves cannot
prove the creation of the world, but they can provide knowledge useful for
metaphysics and theology. The only novelty was his optimistic outlook regarding modern cosmology's contribution to arguments for the existence of
God. He took note that science had established that the universe had a finite
age and, therefore, it must have been created by God. But he also warned that

science did not have a definitive word on this topic and that proofs of God's existence lie outside science. He referenced the famous scientist and historian of science Sir Edmund Whittaker (1873–1956), fellow of the Royal Society, Irish Royal Astronomer, and member of the Pontifical Academy of Sciences, an important scientist who had converted to Catholicism.

Monsignor Georges Lemaître, the father of the big bang, was in the audience attending that papal speech in 1951. He would later become president of the Pontifical Academy of Sciences. Lemaître always insisted that the big bang had no consequences for religion: "We may speak of this event as of a beginning. I do not say a creation. . . . The question if it was really a beginning or rather a creation: something starting from nothing, is a philosophical question which cannot be settled by physical or astronomical considerations."[32] Lemaître also spoke with influential prelates in the Vatican to warn the Pope on this issue. In the Pope's next address to a scientific audience, the International Astronomical Union on September 7, 1952, he used a more moderate tone when relating physics and theology.[33]

We also note that no Catholic theologian would consider statements of the sort we have been analyzing above, made in these circumstances, to be official statements of Catholic doctrine.

Hawking on God and Creation

In examining Hawking's views on God and religion we face two difficulties. The first is the complexity and subtlety of the relationship between the *creation* of the universe and the *beginning* of the universe. We have already examined this in detail above, in anticipation of looking more closely at Hawking's specific ideas.

The second is that Hawking's illness, tragically, severely limits his communications. He has not produced books, or even essays, on religion. We have but brief references in his writings, and cryptic comments in his interviews— nothing to examine in depth. We must content ourselves with plausible interpretations of a few published statements, making no claim to certainty about his ideas on God and religion. Nevertheless, since his few remarks have been widely quoted and have appeared in best-selling books, it is important that they be examined carefully.

In a 1989 interview, Hawking said: "It is difficult to discuss the beginning of the universe without mentioning the concept of God. My work on the origin of the universe is on the borderline between science and religion, but I try to stay on the scientific side of the border. It is quite possible that God acts in ways that cannot be described by scientific laws. But in that case one would just have to go by personal belief."[34] Hawking acknowledges here that scientific and religious arenas are different. One can accept that laws established by God ruled the natural world, while also accepting that God acts in other ways not describable by science.

Hawking tries to stay on the scientific side, which most scientists do. Some of these scientists believe in God; some don't. Some think science supports belief in God; some don't. But Hawking poses his questions about God on purely scientific grounds. In a 1986 interview with Renée Weber titled "If there's an edge to the universe, there must be a God," we find the following dialogue:

> WEBER   Why is it so important whether there is or is not an edge to space-time?
>
> HAWKING   It obviously matters because if there is an edge, somebody has to decide what should happen at the edge. You would really have to invoke God.
>
> WEBER   Why does that follow?
>
> HAWKING   If you like, it would be a tautology. You could define God as the edge of the universe, as the agent who was responsible for setting all this into motion.
>
> WEBER   You are invoking God because we need an explanatory principle for the edge.
>
> HAWKING   Yes, if you want a complete theory, then we would have to know what happens at the edge. Otherwise, we cannot solve the equations.[35]

Hawking's responses border on the bizarre. What can it mean to define God as the edge of the universe? This seems like little more than the long-discredited "god of the gaps." Hawking apparently thinks God is ruled out until we get to the boundary of our explanation and discover that there are some things we can't explain, like the initial conditions. So we posit God as the explanation for those things. Hawking sets God and scientific explanation in opposition—we can use one or the other to explain things, but not both. And since we want science to explain everything, we should avoid invoking God. This agrees with another of Hawking's statements in the same interview: "I think the universe is completely self-contained. It doesn't have any beginning or end, it doesn't have any creation or destruction."[36] But this claim is not science. This is a philosophical idea misrepresented as deriving from science. Hawking apparently thinks that science can show that the universe is self-contained, self-sufficient, existing by itself. He comments provocatively: "So long as the universe had a beginning, we could suppose it had a creator. But if the universe is really completely self-contained, having no boundary or edge, it would have neither beginning nor end: it would simply be. What place, then, for a creator?"[37]

Hawking conflates two different issues: a universe with no edges in space and time; and a self-contained universe. He links them by suggesting that if the universe has no edges in space and time, then it is self-contained and not created.

However, to say that something—or everything—is "created by God" is not the same as saying that something "has a temporal origin," a common misunderstanding that occurs when the popular notion of the term—as in "Apple Computer 'created' the iPod"—is used in place of the theological term—as in "God 'created' the world." "Creation" in the religious sense, as articulated in creeds and other authoritative writings of the Judeo-Christian tradition, refers to *dependence in being*. God continually "gives being" to all creatures, sustaining them from moment to moment. God's role is not confined to creaturely "beginnings" or "space-time edges," to use Hawking's terminology. God is the only "self-contained" Being, not dependent on any other being, and is the source of all created beings. These important distinctions clarify that the problem of universal space-time edges has no relation whatsoever to God. Claiming that the universe is self-sufficient because it has no boundaries in space and time makes no sense.

We also note, in preparation for our discussion below, that St. Thomas Aquinas addressed the philosophical problem of God's relation to space-time boundaries in the thirteenth century. Hawking neither created nor solved this problem. This kind of historical consideration is critically important in science and religion because of the perception that science is constantly forcing religion to retreat in the face of new knowledge, making adjustments to theology while retreating. Scientists unfamiliar with theology often believe that science has posed a brand-new problem for theology when, in fact, science has simply stumbled upon an ancient philosophical problem that has already been considered.

On the Eternity of the World

Aquinas saw no contradiction in a universe both created and having always existed, an insight he derived from the Arab philosopher Avicenna. One of his last writings, *On the Eternity of the World*, was a sophisticated treatise defending the claim that "to say that something has been made by God and that it has always existed is not a contradiction."[38] This, of course, is exactly the problem that Hawking thinks his work has created. Aquinas did believe, however, that we know from divine revelation that the world created by God had a temporal beginning.

Let us look at Aquinas's rather careful argument, unfortunately cast in the convoluted scholastic prose that eager secularists would later ridicule. He begins like this:

> Although we accept according to the Catholic faith that the world had a beginning of its duration, nevertheless the problem has arisen of whether it could have always existed. In order that the truth of this problem be explained, first we must distinguish that about which we agree with our adversaries from that about which we differ from them. If, on the one hand, it is thought that something other than God could have always existed in the sense that something could exist but not [be] made by God, this is an abominable error, not only according to the faith but also according to the philosophers, who admit and prove that absolutely nothing would be able to exist unless it were caused by Him who has being in the highest degree and most truly. If, on the other hand, it is thought that something has always existed and still had been caused completely by God, an investigation should be made whether this can be the case.[39]

Aquinas concludes first that, "considering God's infinite power, everyone agrees that God could have made something which always existed." The remaining problem is to see "whether it is possible for something to be made which always existed."[40] He notes the *possibility* of a contradiction in claiming that something is both created and has always existed. Aquinas challenges the apparent inconsistency. "If they should be inconsistent, this could only be because of one of two reasons or both: (1) either because the efficient cause must precede [its effect] in duration, (2) or because the fact that the creature is said to be made out of nothing requires that nonbeing precede in duration."[41] On the first point, Aquinas argues that God produces effects instantaneously, not through motion, and therefore it is not necessary that He precede His effect in duration. On the second point, he argues that we can say something has been made out of nothing if there is not something from which it has been made. Therefore there is no need that the thing first be nothing and later be something.

Aquinas would reject Hawking's confident assertion that a proof that the universe has no boundaries would have "profound implications for the role of God as Creator."[42]

A Universe without Boundaries

A landmark in Hawking's career was his 1970 proof that a universe expanding from the big bang must have a singularity at the beginning and a definite duration in time. This proof rested on certain assumptions he would later challenge:

> The final result was a joint paper by Penrose and myself in 1970, which at last proved that there must have been a big bang singularity provided only that general relativity is correct and the universe contains as much matter as we observe.... in the end our work became generally accepted and nowadays nearly everyone assumes that the universe started with a big bang singularity. It is perhaps ironic that, having changed my mind, I am now trying to convince other physicists that there was in fact no singularity at the beginning of the universe—as we shall see later, it can disappear once quantum effects are taken into account.[43]

Hawking introduced his rather technical ideas at the Vatican in 1981. The paper was titled "The Boundary Conditions of the Universe," and it begins like this:

> This paper considers the question of what are the boundary conditions of the universe and where should they be imposed. It is difficult to define boundary conditions at the initial singularity and, even if one could, they would be insufficient to determine the evolution of the universe. In order to overcome this problem it is suggested that one should adopt the Euclidean approach and evaluate the path integral for quantum gravity over positive definite metrics. If one took these metrics to be compact, one would avoid the need to specify any boundary conditions for the universe. This approach might explain why the apparent cosmological constant is zero, why the universe is spatially flat, and why it was in thermal equilibrium at early times.[44]

The paper, as the reader can readily discern, was deeply mathematical rather than philosophical or theological, and completely unintelligible to the layperson.

Hawking's paper makes no mention of creation, or God, although another paper from the same meeting and printed in the same volume did offer some challenges to Catholic doctrine.[45] Hawking acknowledges that, at the time of the Vatican meeting, he had not fully elaborated his no-boundary proposal, nor had he fully realized what he thought were its implications. He says:

> It was at the conference in the Vatican mentioned earlier that I first put forward the suggestion that maybe time and space together formed a surface that was finite in size but did not have any boundary or edge. My paper was rather mathematical, however, so its implications for the role of God in the creation of the universe were not generally recognized at the time (just as well for me). At the time of the Vatican conference, I did not know how to use the "no boundary" idea to make predictions about the universe. However, I spent the following summer at the University of California, Santa Barbara. There a friend and colleague of mine, Jim Hartle, worked out with me what conditions the universe must satisfy if space-time had no boundary.[46]

Two years later, Hartle and Hawking published their results in the *Physical Review*, the world's leading physics journal. In one of the few sentences in this paper a layperson might understand, they write: "This means that the Universe does not have any boundaries in space or time. . . . There is thus no problem of boundary conditions."[47] They conclude that their work "sheds light on one of the fundamental problems of cosmology: the singularity. In the classical theory, the singularity is a place where the field equations, and hence predictability, break down. This situation is improved in the quantum theory. . . . in the quantum theory there is no singularity or breakdown."[48] The final words in the paper became famous because Hawking repeated them many times: "If this were the case, one would have solved the problem of the initial boundary conditions of the Universe: the boundary conditions are that it has no boundary."[49] We note, however, the all-important-but-easily-overlooked conditional, "If this were the case."

Interesting results in mathematical physics almost always contain assumptions and simplifications. As remarkable as the fit between the natural world and mathematics might be, there are virtually no cases where the fit is so perfect that no simplifying assumptions are required. This is acceptable in physics because such abstract mathematical results often contain predictions that can be tested against new observations. With theories like the no-boundary proposal, however, there are no empirical tests that can be made now, and there probably will be no such tests for decades. This does not mean, however, that the proposal should be dismissed. The mathematical model that eventually became the basis for the big bang theory, for example, was once an untestable abstraction. Many ideas in science originate in this way.

The no-boundary proposal is similar to the idea of relativity theory that the universe is finite but boundless in space. The typical image used to explain this was the surface of a sphere where all points are the same and none of them represents a "starting point." In a similar vein, Hawking says in the glossary of *A Brief History of Time* that the no-boundary condition is "the idea that the universe is finite but has no boundary (in imaginary time)."[50]

Hawking highlights that his proposal works "in imaginary time," something that seems like science fiction to laypersons. But, in fact, it is a fairly mainstream idea in physics. Imaginary numbers are used, for example, to represent the time coordinate in relativity theory. In the case of the Hartle-Hawking proposal, however, imaginary time plays a more substantial role, introduced to eliminate the singularity at the beginning of time. But when we return to our world of real time, the banished singularity returns.

In the Hartle-Hawking proposal, we don't have to assume that at the beginning of the universe a singularity exists where the laws of physics break down. Hawking uses the familiar comparison with the North Pole and the surface of the earth. The North Pole is a point like any other on earth. Asking what happened before the big bang is like asking what is north of the North Pole. It is a meaningless question: There is no mystery at the North Pole; we can walk across the North Pole without noticing anything odd whatsoever.

Does the no-boundary proposal contradict Hawking's earlier ideas? This is his answer: "It might seem therefore that my more recent work has completely undone the results of my earlier work on singularities. But, as indicated above, the real importance of the singularity theorems was that they showed that the gravitational field must become so strong that quantum gravitational effects could not be ignored. This in turn led to the idea that the universe could be finite in imaginary time but without boundaries or singularities. When one goes back to the real time in which we live, however, there will still appear to be singularities."[51]

Not everyone agrees with Hawking's ideas, of course. His collaborator Penrose finds the Hartle-Hawking "no-boundary" proposal interesting, but notes that he has "considerable difficulties" with it.[52] Hawking notes that the empirical confirmation of his proposal is very difficult and insists that his idea is only a proposal: "I'd like to emphasize that this idea that time and space should be finite 'without boundary' is just a *proposal*: it cannot be deduced from some other principle. Like any other scientific theory, it may initially be put forward for aesthetic or metaphysical reasons, but the real test is whether it makes predictions that agree with observation. This, however, is difficult to determine in the case of quantum gravity."[53]

In the foreword to the tenth anniversary edition of *A Brief History of Time*, Hawking writes:

> On the observational side, by far the most important development has been the measurement of fluctuations in the cosmic microwave background radiation by COBE (the Cosmic Background Explorer satellite) and other collaborations. . . . Their form agrees with the predictions of the proposal that the universe has no boundaries or edges in the imaginary time direction; but further observations will be necessary to distinguish this proposal from other possible explanations for the fluctuations in the background. However, within a few years we should know whether we can believe that we live in a universe that is completely self-contained and without beginning or end.[54]

Once again we find Hawking mistakenly conflating the scientifically admissible no-boundaries proposal with the philosophically contradictory self-contained universe. Overlooking this, however, he remains too optimistic regarding his proposal. It is but one of several proposals for a theory of quantum gravity, and prospects for empirically testing any of them are quite slim at the moment. In a 2002 book devoted to predicting the progress of science in the next fifty years, leading cosmologist Lee Smolin explains that there are several theories on the origin of the universe and that the Hartle-Hawking "wave-function of the universe" is one candidate. He notes, though:

> It is possible, but by no means assured, that we will have evidence constraining these theories to the point that we will know whether there was something before the Big Bang or not. This evidence will have to come from using gravitational waves to probe the universe in the earliest period of the expansion. Nothing else can do this, because the universe at early times is opaque to all forms of radiation except gravitational waves. Gravitational wave astronomy is currently under development, but no gravitational waves have yet been observed. There are on the table proposals for space-based gravitational wave detectors. . . . It is possible but by no means certain that this technology will be in place by mid-century.[55]

A Brief History of Time

The no-boundary proposal and its "connection" with God exploded onto the scene in 1988, when Hawking published *A Brief History of Time*, which surprised everyone by becoming a best-seller, despite its challenging content. The success of Hawking's book became a story in its own right as everyone tried to figure out how it had happened, from colleagues convinced that maybe popularization was respectable after all, to publishers who wanted to get in on the action. Hawking himself has provided "A Brief History of *A Brief History*."[56] Gribbin and White explain the book's genesis at length, and Ferguson explains it briefly. Their accounts, however, differ in some respects. As we look at the phenomenon of Hawking's book, we will pick up the details that seem more reliable.

Both biographies agree that Hawking wrote the book for financial reasons. Hawking had managed his illness with great courage, but as his physical challenges grew, so did the expenses associated with increased personal and medical assistance. He was famous, but his income was still modest. Ferguson describes the succession of new medical difficulties:

> Until 1974 Hawking could still feed himself and get into and out of bed. But as such actions became increasingly difficult, the Hawkings finally decided they couldn't go on managing alone. They began a custom of asking one of his research students to live with them. In return for free accommodation and extra attention from Hawking, the student helped him get ready for bed and get up.... By the late 1970s and early 1980s, his speech was so slurred that only his family and closest friends could understand him.... Since 1980, community and private nurses had been coming for an hour or two each morning and evening to supplement the care given by Jane Hawking and the resident research student.[57]

Hawking also had to pay for the education of his children.

To this point Hawking had ignored suggestions that he write a popular book on cosmology. "But by late 1982 he had come to recognize that such a project might provide the answer to his looming financial difficulties, and he decided to revive the idea," Gribbin and White report, adding: "He wanted a lot of money for this book.... At their first organized meeting [with Simon Mitton, from Cambridge University Press] to discuss the book, Hawking opened the conversation by explaining his financial situation, making it clear that he wanted to earn enough money to continue financing Lucy's education and to offset the costs of nursing. He was obviously unable to provide any form of life insurance to protect the family in the event of his death or complete incapacitation."[58]

Mitton criticized Hawking's initial efforts, which had equations on every page, as too technical. But Cambridge University Press ended up offering a contract specifying a 10,000-pound advance and high-percentage royalties. In the meantime, in early 1983, a senior editor at Bantam Books at New York read an article on Hawking in the *New York Times*. He immediately realized that the combination of Hawking's scientific fame and his physical condition was a great story. Just as Hawking was preparing to sign the contract with Cambridge University Press, Bantam offered him a $250,000 advance and a very favorable deal on royalties. This contract was signed.[59]

The result surpassed expectations and surprised even the publishers. In the tenth anniversary edition, published in 1998, we read that it has sold more than 9 million copies worldwide.

Knowing the Mind of God

Hawking's work is inspired by the search for a set of rational, comprehensible laws that describe the universe—a "complete theory," he calls it in the last paragraph of *A Brief History of Time*. With great optimism, he speaks of a time when everyone would understand such a wonderful theory, at least in general terms. Then we could all "take part in the discussion of the question of why it is that we and the universe exist. If we find the answer to that, it would be the ultimate triumph of human reason—for then we would know the mind of God."[60]

This oft-quoted oracular pronouncement by Hawking is very strange. What can it possibly mean? Hawking says he does not believe in God, so what exactly is the "mind of God"? We would hope that the statement is more than just an editorial insertion to make Hawking's book provocative. The conclusion of *A Brief History of Time* seems designed to provoke reaction: "If the universe is completely self-contained, with no singularities or boundaries, and completely described by a unified theory, that has profound implications for the role of God as Creator." He explains:

> Einstein once asked the question: "How much choice did God have in constructing the universe?" If the no boundary proposal is correct, he had no freedom at all to choose initial conditions. He would, of course, still have had the freedom to choose the laws that the universe obeyed. This, however, may not really have been all that much of a choice; there may well be only one, or a small number, of complete unified theories . . . that are self-consistent and allow the existence of structures as complicated as human beings who can

investigate the laws of the universe and ask about the nature of God.[61]

Ferguson's interpretation of this is: "Hawking has not said that the no-boundary proposal rules out the existence of God, only that God wouldn't have had any choice in how the universe began. Other scientists disagree. They don't think the no-boundary proposal limits God very much."[62]

Ferguson goes a step further, noting, "In *A Brief History of Time* Hawking himself suggests that there may still be a role for a Creator," and she refers to a concluding remark: "Even if there is only one possible unified theory, it is just a set of rules and equations. What is it that breathes fire into the equations and makes a universe for them to describe?"[63] This question inspired Ferguson's subsequent book, *The Fire in the Equations.*[64]

This point may be more than just a clever metaphor. Hawking certainly understands that theoretical models are constructions that must be checked against the real world. And even when we find equations with an uncanny match to the real world, as we often do, we still cannot equate these equations with the physical reality they describe so well. The equation of a planetary orbit, for example, is not the same thing as the orbit itself. Hawking's reference to "the fire in the equations" hints at a transcendence that points beyond the basic mathematical description of the world.

In a 1992 Christmas Day interview, Sue Lawly summarized Hawking's ideas and then engaged him in the following conversation:

SUE   You believe that there was no beginning and there is no end, that the universe is self-contained. Does that mean that there was no act of creation and therefore that there's no place for God?

STEPHEN   Yes, you have oversimplified. I still believe the universe has a beginning in real time, at a big bang. But there's another kind of time, imaginary time, at right angles to real time, in which the universe has no beginning or end. This would mean that the way the universe began would be determined by the laws of physics. One wouldn't have to say that God chose to set the universe going in some arbitrary way that we couldn't understand. It says nothing about whether or not God exists—just that He is not arbitrary.

SUE   But I think that many people do feel you have effectively dispensed with God. Are you denying that, then?

STEPHEN   All that my work has shown is that you don't have to say that the way the universe began was the personal whim of God. But you still have the question: Why does the universe bother to exist? If you like, you can define God to be the answer to that question.[65]

A Review in *Nature*

Donald Page, a cosmologist and professor at the University of Alberta, disagrees with Hawking on God. Gribbin and White describe him as "another physicist who was to play a significant role in collaborations and become one of Hawking's lifelong friends."[66]

The Hawkings' plan to invite research students to live with them and help with Stephen's physical care created some interesting relationships. One of the earliest students to do this was the distinguished cosmologist Bernard Carr. Another was Donald Page, a Cal Tech Ph.D. with whom Hawking had written a black hole paper in 1974, while he was himself on leave to Cal Tech and Page was a graduate student. When Page finished his Ph.D. at Cal Tech he had Hawking write him some reference letters, but then Hawking hired Page himself, and Page came to live with the Hawkings.

White and Gribbin recount that "Hawking managed to help Page secure funding for a year and then organized a grant for a further two years of research. Page joined the Hawking household in 1976 and reestablished the close friendship they had enjoyed in California, a friendship that has survived to the present day."[67]

Both Page and Hawking's wife, Jane, were Christians with strong religious views. White and Gribbin report, "Jane once told a reporter that she had been saddened when, soon after he had taken up residence in their home, Page tried to engage Hawking in a religious discussion but was forced to give up. Despite their vastly differing outlooks, the two men have remained friends, simply agreeing not to discuss any form of personal God."[68]

In April 1988, Page reviewed *A Brief History of Time* for *Nature*. Page writes, "Most of the first three quarters of the book covers ideas that are fairly well accepted, but the final quarter concentrates upon more speculative proposals."[69] The final quarter discusses the "no-boundary" proposal on a popular level. Page comments that the proposal is scientifically controversial for four reasons that he lists, adding: "Although many of these caveats are noted in the book, there is the danger that Hawking's enthusiasm for his proposal may lead the less-cautious reader to become more convinced of its correctness than there is yet evidence to warrant. Nevertheless, because of the significance of the proposal if it is correct, its exposition in this timely book is valuable for enabling the public to ponder some of its implications."[70]

Page's own pondering of these implications is quite interesting. He writes:

> After discussing what he considers to be the most common view of God's activity—that God started off the Universe and then let it evolve without intervention—Hawking objects that if the Universe actually has no boundary, and hence no beginning, "What place, then, for a creator?" However, this objection does not apply to the Judeo-Christian view, that God creates and sustains the entire Universe rather than just the beginning. Whether or not the Universe has a beginning has no relevance to the question of its creation, just as whether an artist's line has a beginning and an end, or instead forms a circle with no end, has no relevance to the question of its being drawn.[71]

Page is right. For traditional theists, Hawking's proposal requires no revision of the belief that all created things depend on God—the core of the religious concept of Creation.

Page adds:

> Hawking draws the conclusion that God "had no freedom at all to choose initial conditions," but this is debatable. When I was defending Hawking's proposal to a small group of gravitational theorists in 1982, Bryce DeWitt expressed this view by saying, "You do not want to give God any freedom at all." However, Karel Kuchar quickly rejoined, "But that's His choice." In other words, even if we correctly hypothesize which state God chose for the Universe, that would in no way eliminate the freedom He may have had in making that choice. Choosing the no-boundary state and then actually carrying out the immense task of the creation of the Universe in this state is a far cry from Carl Sagan's claim in his introduction to the book of "nothing for a Creator to do."[72]

The introduction in the original version of the book contained some of Sagan's most aggressively atheistic rhetoric. In the expanded tenth anniversary edition of *A Brief History of Time*, Sagan's introduction was removed.

Cosmology has developed impressively in the past few decades. In 2001 Hawking himself published a new popular book, *The Universe in a Nutshell*, whose chapters, as he writes in the foreword, "correspond to areas I have worked on or thought about since the publication of *A Brief History of Time*. Thus they present a picture of some of the most active fields of current research."[73]

That such comments were written by a man who had contracted ALS decades earlier is nothing short of miraculous.

Hawking the Positivist

Chapter 2 of *The Universe in a Nutshell*, "The Shape of Time," explores many of the ideas we have discussed above. Hawking also, however, introduces ideas about the nature of science and the value of scientific knowledge, claiming, in a few scattered comments, to accept a positivist philosophy of science. We are going to consider these ideas in succession.

Here is Hawking's explanation of his positivism:

> Any sound scientific theory, whether of time or of any other concept, should in my opinion be based on the most workable philosophy of science: the positivist approach put forward by Karl Popper and others. According to this way of thinking, a scientific theory is a mathematical model that describes and codifies the observations we make. A good theory will describe a large number of phenomena on the basis of a few simple postulates and will make definite predictions that can be tested. If the predictions agree with the observations, the theory survives the test, though it can never be proved to be correct. On the other hand, if the observations disagree with the predictions, one has to discard or modify the theory.... If one takes the positivist position, as I do, one cannot say what time actually is. All one can do is describe what has been found to be a very good mathematical model for time and say what predictions it makes.[74]

Popper has surely rolled in his grave over this comment, having spent considerable energy dispelling the myth of his positivism. The positivism embraced by Hawking places his ideas in a new light. He draws his own conclusions, saying simply: "One cannot say what time actually is." Hawking claims we have only models that work, or models that do not work and must be replaced. We can make no claims about reality. In fact, the possibility of even knowing reality has vanished; all we have are models. In the same chapter, speaking of theories of space-time with ten or eleven dimensions, Hawking writes: "I must say that personally, I have been reluctant to believe in extra dimensions. But as I am a positivist, the question 'Do extra dimensions really exist?' has no meaning."[75] When he introduces his central idea of imaginary time, he says of imaginary numbers that "they are a mathematical construct, they don't need a physical realization," and he adds: "One might think this means that imaginary numbers are just a mathematical game having nothing to do with the real world. From the point of view of positivist philosophy, however, one cannot determine what is real. All one can do is find which mathematical models describe the universe we live in."[76] Elsewhere in the book, Hawking applies his positivism to vacuum fluctuations, to p-branes (membrane-like structures that appear in superstring theory), to large extra dimensions, and to deciding whether it is true that "maybe we think we live in a four-dimensional world because we are shadows cast on the brane by what is happening in the interior of the bubble."[77]

These ideas are not new. Hawking used them in 1988 in *A Brief History of Time* and reproduced them in the illustrated edition of 1996. This latter volume has a summary of his philosophy of science:

> I shall take the simpleminded view that a theory is just a model of the universe, or a restricted part of it, and a set of rules that relate quantities in the model to observations that we make. It exists only in our minds and does not have any other reality (whatever that might mean). A theory is a good theory if it satisfies two requirements. It must accurately describe a large class of observations on the basis of a model that contains only a few arbitrary elements, and it must make definite predictions about the results of future observations.... Any physical theory is always provisional, in the sense that it is only a hypothesis: you can never prove it. No matter how many times the results of experiments agree with some theory, you can never be sure that the next time the result will not contradict the theory. On the other hand, you can disprove a theory by finding even a single observation that disagrees with the predictions of the theory. As philosopher of science Karl Popper has emphasized, a good theory is characterized by the fact that it makes a number of predictions that could in principle be disproved or falsified by observation. Each time new experiments are observed to agree with the predictions the theory survives, and our confidence in it is increased; but if ever a new observation is found to disagree, we have to abandon or modify the theory.[78]

Hawking has used these same ideas in more specialized settings. He used them in a serious discussion with Penrose, published as a book introduced as follows: "The debate between Roger Penrose and Stephen Hawking recorded in this book was the high point of a six-month program held in 1994 at the Isaac Newton Institute for Mathematical Sciences at the University of Cambridge. It represents a serious discussion of some of the most fundamental ideas about the nature of the universe."[79] At the final debate Hawking said: "These lectures have shown very clearly the difference between Roger and me. He's a Platonist and I'm a positivist.... I don't demand that a theory correspond to reality because I don't know what it is. Reality is not a quality you can test with litmus paper. All I'm concerned with is that the theory should predict the results of measurements."[80]

Many mathematical physicists would agree with Hawking's positivism. They study aspects of the world that can be approached only with incredibly abstract and sophisticated mathematical tools. They build models and try to derive predictions from them—a challenging task. They accept the models to the degree their predictions are successful; otherwise they replace the models by new ones they hope will work better. This is normal theoretical physics. The trouble begins if we take this as a complete description of the aims of science and of the value of its results. Science makes most sense as a search for true knowledge of a real world. Without this inspiration, modern science would not exist. Galileo wouldn't have had any problems at all; he could have just shrugged away his Copernicanism as a helpful model. Hawking's statements about God, and the beginning of the universe for that matter, all become meaningless in the shadow of the gray light cast by positivism.

Hawking, though, contradicts himself. In speaking of the reach of science, he assures us that science consists only of models, and we don't know a "reality" independent of these models. However, when he speaks of scientific results, he argues with inappropriate confidence for a self-contained universe. He even uses his theory to discuss the existence of God, a remarkable achievement for a tentative model.

Time Travel

Hawking's work in general relativity has led him at times to discuss time travel, an enduring science fiction idea that actually connects to real science. Time travel enters serious scientific consideration through the topic of wormholes that, in principle, connect different space-time coordinates of the universe. These connections offer a tantalizing suggestion that one could travel from one time to another, or from a local spot to one very distant.[81] Hawking defines a wormhole as "a thin tube of space-time connecting distant regions of the Universe. Wormholes might also link to parallel or baby universes and could provide the possibility of time travel."[82] If time travel through a wormhole were possible, that would surely be the most astonishing result in all of science.

This particular story of time travel begins in 1948. The great mathematician Kurt Gödel discovered a solution to Einstein's relativity equations, Hawking tells us, that allowed for a new space-time where travel to the past would be possible. Gödel's result, like most of the other solutions that have been found to the relativity equations, does not correspond to the universe we live in. There are other space-time configurations, though, that do permit travel into the past. One is in the interior of a rotating black hole, a location that crushes everything. Another possible time machine derives from a special combination of cosmic strings. But this possibility, like Gödel's, does not correspond to our universe.

Wormholes have seemed, for some time, like a way to get around the various problems with the other possible time machines. Albert Einstein and Nathan Rosen actually suggested the idea in 1935, although with a different name. But the real possibility seemed unlikely, plagued as it was by so many difficulties. Now, however, it has been given new life: "What one needs, in order to warp space-time in a way that will allow travel into the past, is matter with negative energy density."[83] Hawking notes that if the uncertainty principle were combined with the creation of negative energy densities as shown in the Casimir effect (a peculiar force that arises between two surfaces in a vacuum), time travel would be possible, in principle. He suggests that no time travel has yet occurred because the past has not had the warping of space needed, but this does not rule out the possibility in the future. Hawking examines ways of avoiding the paradoxes involved in time travel, where reality and fiction seem to merge. The traditional logical challenge to time travel is that one could, in principle, go back in time and encounter and maybe even kill's one's younger self. How do we explain this? One response to this paradox is the "alternative histories hypothesis," which suggests that when you go back in time, you enter an alternative history that differs from the history that is your actual past.

Hawking discusses the behavior of virtual particles in the proximity of black holes, concluding, "The radiation by black holes shows that quantum theory allows travel back in time on a microscopic scale and that such time travel can produce observable effects. One can therefore ask: does quantum theory allow time travel on a macroscopic scale, which people could use? At first sight, it seems it should."[84] Hawking's good sense eventually comes to our rescue, as he introduces a plausible but unproven conjecture: "One would avoid these problems if what I call the chronology protection conjecture holds. This says that the laws of physics conspire to prevent *macroscopic* bodies from carrying information into the past."[85]

Hawking has a fine sense of humor to go with his brilliant mind, and one must always suspect that some of his more interesting speculations may have been shaped by his humor. He concludes his time travel chapter in *The Universe in a Nutshell* by saying: "You might wonder if this chapter is part of a government cover-up on time travel. You might be right."[86] Whatever Hawking's physical limitations, they certainly don't prevent him from putting his tongue in his cheek, something that probably should be noted when evaluating any of his extravagant claims.

Hawking in Perspective

University of Nottingham professor of astrophysics Peter Coles has published scientific articles and books, both technical and popular, on cosmology, including one on Hawking to which we now turn.

Coles puts Hawking in perspective, dispelling some of the mythology:

> The first point to be made, and I make it meaning no disrespect whatsoever to Hawking and what he has achieved, is that it is absurd to compare him with Einstein and Newton. These characters ignited true revolutions in science and, in their different ways, the philosophical changes they brought about had great cultural impact. Stephen Hawking has not, by any stretch of the imagination, revolutionized his subject. His work has been often brilliant.... He is rightly regarded as one of the most able theoreticians of his day. But beyond that, the public image is out of all proportion to his place in the history of physical science.[87]

Coles notes a 1999 poll of the world's leading physicists asking for the five physicists who made the most important contributions to their field: Only one of the 130 respondents put Hawking on the list. His extraordinary personal condition, says Coles, plays an important role in his public image as an Oracle of science: "Hawking's whole persona reinforces the 'other-worldliness' of his science. Even the strange artificial voice with which he speaks casts him in the role of a kind of oracle, speaking the secrets of the universe."[88]

Of Hawking's forays onto religious territory, Coles writes: "Hawking's phrase 'to know the Mind of God' is just one example of a border infringement. But by playing the God card, Hawking has cleverly fanned the flames of his own publicity, appealing directly to the popular allure of the scientist-as-priest. I am not by nature a religious man, but I know enough about Christianity to understand that 'knowing the mind of God' is at best meaningless and at worst blasphemous when seen in the context of that particular religion."[89] Coles also notes that while mathematics is interesting and useful, it plays far too large a role in Hawking's philosophical thinking: "[Hawking] thinks it possible to replace religion and metaphysics with a mathematical theory that encodes all the laws of nature. But the philosophical questions to be asked about the universe will inevitably involve some that cannot be answered in the framework of mathematics."[90]

Coles's last statement may be too strong. Hawking sometimes undervalues metaphysics and religion, but in the last paragraph of *A Brief History of Time*, Hawking does not say that a complete scientific theory of the universe means we already know the mind of God. What he says is that such a theory would let us ask why we and the universe exist and that in answering this question we would know the mind of God.

In *The End of Science*, science writer John Horgan discusses Hawking's work. Horgan attended a 1990 symposium in northern Sweden on the birth and early evolution of our universe. Hawking was there, and while Horgan found him in some ways heroic, he had a different impression of his ideas:

> What he was saying struck me as being utterly preposterous. Wormholes? Baby universes? Infinite dimensional superspace of string theory? This seemed more science fiction than science. I had more or less the same reaction to the entire conference.... Over the course of the meeting, I struggled to quell that instinctive feeling of preposterousness, with some success. I reminded myself that these were terribly smart people, "the greatest geniuses of the world," as a local Swedish newspaper had put it.... [But] My initial reaction to Hawking and others at the conference was, to some extent, appropriate.[91]

Horgan, who for years was a senior writer at *Scientific American*, believes much of modern cosmology is preposterous. Empirical support for these various cosmological theories will take decades to get here, if it ever arrives. What are we to make of an entire field of science that has floated so completely free of observation, into a stratosphere of speculation? It is ironic that Hawking calls himself a positivist: The hallmark of the original positivism was to avoid speculation, to admit only facts and "positive" empirical data. Theories were to be no more than explanatory schemes connecting observations. This did not work, of course, which is why positivism all but died as a philosophy of science. It was too much of a straitjacket for science, which needs creative and audacious hypotheses and imaginative techniques to test them against observation. In claiming to be a positivist, Hawking should be critiquing his own theories, perhaps even laughing at them, located as they are at the extreme end of scientific speculation.

Horgan makes an interesting final comment:

> I suspect that Hawking—who may be less a truth seeker than an artist, an illusionist, a cosmic joker—knew all along that finding and empirically validating a unified theory would be extremely difficult, even impossible. His declaration that physics was on the verge of finding *The Answer* may well have been an ironic statement, less an assertion than a provocation. In 1994, he admitted as much when he told an interviewer that physics might never achieve a final theory after all. Hawking is a master practitioner of ironic physics and cosmology.[92]

4

A Light in the Darkness

Carl Sagan

Carl Sagan was one of the most popular scientists of the twentieth century. Half a billion people around the globe watched his TV series *Cosmos*, originally airing in 1980 and rereleased in an enhanced version in 2000. The lavishly illustrated companion book, reprinted many times in different languages, still sells briskly more than two decades after its original publication. The Web site carlsagan.com provides ongoing access to his projects, and new ones are under way, such as educational science programs for kids. Sagan communicated great enthusiasm for the adventure of science and mastered the art of explaining difficult concepts to large audiences. In the first decades of the space era, he collaborated with NASA and enhanced public interest in space exploration. More than any scientist before or since, he brought science to literally millions of people who might not have otherwise paid any attention.

A passionate and productive scientist himself, Sagan was deeply committed to the beneficial application of science. He opposed nuclear weapons, campaigned to protect the environment, and worried about widespread superstition and what he saw as harmful beliefs in everything from astrology to miracle cures. He educated the public about "Nuclear Winter," the idea that a nuclear war could precipitate an unprecedented ice age that might render the earth largely uninhabitable. But his central core was always science and its power to liberate and advance humanity.

Sagan became notorious in certain circles for his forays into religion, which he treated skeptically. But his approach was not overly hostile and was seemingly motivated by his conviction that religious beliefs lack adequate evidentiary support. He did not appear to be on an antireligious crusade of the sort that animates Richard Dawkins and Peter Atkins. His notoriety in the religious community stemmed more from his great influence than the aggressiveness of his critiques.

Bringing the esoteric achievements of science to the general public with integrity and excitement requires a special talent, possessed by few. Good science popularization requires talented scientists who know both the subject and how to explain it. Sagan was unmatched at this.

He died in 1996.

Scientist and Showman

Carl Sagan was born in Brooklyn, New York, on November 9, 1934. His sister Carol, nicknamed Cari, was Carl's only sibling. Their father, Samuel Sagan (1905–79), left Ukraine in 1910, when he was five years old, accompanied by his uncle George. In the United States they joined Samuel's father, who had emigrated earlier from Ukraine. George eventually became wealthy working in the garment industry. Samuel studied at Columbia University in New York, but then his father died, forcing him to abandon his studies and go to work in the industry of his uncle George.

Carl's mother, Rachel Molly Gruber (1907–82), was born in New York, the daughter of Leub Gruber, an immigrant from the area that is now Ukraine. Rachel's mother died when she was young, and Rachel was sent to Europe, but her father remarried, and after a few years she returned to New York. Rachel played a special role in the personality of Carl Sagan. Keay Davidson, one of Sagan's biographers, writes: "Rachel was madly in love with her little boy. She told him he was brilliant. He believed her. . . . 'There is no way of understanding him without understanding her very well,' says Sagan's first wife, scientist-author Lynn Margulis. 'His mother had made him so dependent in this one relationship—on *her*. He was worthy of every attention, all the time, every need [was] always filled.' "[1]

Rachel was right. Her son was brilliant and would eventually become that most rare of public figures—an intellectual celebrity. Sagan initially proved himself a competent astrophysicist, participating in NASA projects. He taught at Harvard University, and then for many years was a professor at Cornell University. He published so many professional articles that there could be no doubt about his competence as a scientist. His fame, however, derived from his appearances on television, first as a guest of Johnny Carson on *The Tonight Show*, and then with his popular series *Cosmos*.

Sagan attended elementary and high school in New York and New Jersey. He entered the University of Chicago in 1951, obtaining bachelor's degrees in liberal arts (1954) and physics (1955) and a master's degree in physics (1956). In 1957, he married Lynn Alexander (later Lynn Margulis) with whom he had two sons, Dorion and Jeremy. Lynn left Carl in 1962, apparently tired of his inattention to household affairs, and went on to become famous on her own terms as a biologist. Margulis is well known for her theory of the origin of eucharyotic cells, one of the main events in the evolutionary history of life on earth. (Eucharyotic cells have nuclei containing hereditary material, and different organelles outside the nucleus.)

His fellow scientists gave Sagan mixed reviews. Harvard denied him tenure in 1968, initiating his move to Cornell, which probably advanced his career as a science popularizer. Years later, in 1992, the National Academy of Sciences denied him admission to that elite body, a decision Margulis attributed to jealousy on the part of his colleagues. Sagan was nominated to the Academy by his old friend Stanley Miller; Academy membership was the highest award for American scientists apart from the Nobel Prize. (Miller was quite famous for his early 1950s experiment imitating the conditions of the primitive earth and producing chemicals essential for life. Countless biology texts present his work in their discussions of the origin of life.)

Margulis, already a member of the Academy, was present for the debate on Sagan's nomination on April 28, 1992. The vote was evenly divided, but a majority of two-thirds was required. Margulis wrote to Sagan explaining the details of that "miserable half hour." "They are jealous of your communications skills, charm, good looks and outspoken attitude especially on nuclear winter," she wrote.[2] Two years later, in 1994, the Academy did award Sagan its Public Welfare Medal in recognition of his popularization of science.

After Sagan's death, a new edition of his book *The Cosmic Connection* included an essay by his third wife, Ann Druyan, titled "Carl Sagan: A New Sense of the Sacred." Druyan complained of "the frequent belittling of his scientific standing, an injustice that even after his death continues as a plodding backbeat to the first two attempts at full length biography." The reason, Druyan noted, was Sagan's engagement with popularizing science. Besides publishing hundreds of papers in scientific journals, working for NASA, editing an international scientific journal, and being a pioneer in more than one area of scientific investigation, Sagan's "transgression was to also write, co-write or edit thirty-one books and 1380 articles, and to give countless public talks, radio and television presentations, including the world's most successful science television series, as well as co-founding the largest public space-interest organization on Earth. All of the above was aimed at engaging public awareness of and respect for the scientific enterprise."[3]

Sagan liked to present his view of science by way of two episodes from when he was five years old. The preface, "My Teachers," from the last book published before his death tells the story. His teachers were his dad and mom. Dad Sam was responsible for the enthusiasm to embark on the scientific adventure. He explained to little Carl, for example, that adding one to any number was an endless process, inspiring his son to begin writing in sequence the integers from 1 to 1,000. When he arrived at the low hundreds, his mother announced that it was time for his bath. Carl was disconsolate, but his father offered to continue writing the numbers. When the bath ended, his father was approaching 900 and, writes Carl, "I was able to reach 1,000.... The magnitude of large numbers has never ceased to impress me." The same year, Carl waited with his mother for Sam's arrival, and she told Carl that there were people out there fighting, across the Atlantic. "I can see them," replied Carl. "No, you can't," replied his mother, "they're too far away." Carl recalls wondering how his mother could know this, and concluded that she was probably right and he was just imagining. But this raised for him the question of how we distinguish what we know from what we imagine. Sagan comments: "My parents were not scientists. They knew almost nothing about science. But in introducing me simultaneously to skepticism and to wonder, they taught me the two uneasy cohabiting modes of thought that are central to the scientific method."[4]

Sagan liked to present his entire life as a synergistic combination of elements derived from these two childhood experiences: skepticism and wonder. He presented himself as a searcher for truth and a promoter of science, defending it against proliferating pseudosciences and delusions. At the same time, he felt obliged to spread the good news of a cosmos whose magnitude and rationality could provide a wonderful sense of awe, an almost religious feeling that could substitute for traditional religion.

Extraterrestrial Worlds

Sagan's career centered on extraterrestrial life. Biographer William Poundstone writes,

> According to one childhood friend, Carl Sagan's defining attribute
> was *clarity of purpose*: from an early age he was seized with the

fabulous mission of searching for life on other worlds. . . . Extrater-
Extraterrestrial life was the maguffin of Sagan's life and career. He
staked out *exobiology*—the would-be study of alien life—as his own
turf. The subject lay in the foreground or background of most of Sagan's
300 scientific articles. It is no exaggeration to say that Sagan's ability to capitalize on the topic's broad appeal made him rich and famous.[5]

Why the broad appeal of the topic? Poundstone writes, "Of all the scientific questions of the busily inquisitive twentieth century, nothing fired the public imagination so much as life on other planets. . . . As anyone who watches
TV or movies knows, extraterrestrial life is our society's primary myth. This is
not to trivialize its standing as a scientific conjecture but to recognize that
certain scientific ideas can have broad and unpredictable cultural influence."[6]
Sagan thought discovery of extraterrestrial life would be a major breakthrough
in science, broadening our consideration of how life works beyond planet
Earth. Perhaps there are other forms of life, speculated Sagan, based on different biochemistry; perhaps these life-forms possess knowledge that would
open unforeseen vistas in science. Moreover, contacting extraterrestrial life
would be particularly impressive if the "aliens" were different from us, promising dramatic consequences for humanity's understanding of its place in the
grand scheme of things.

When Sagan was a boy, science fiction stories about extraterrestrials—
usually Martians—abounded. But the reality of traveling to other worlds began with the launching of the Soviet *Sputnik* in 1957, just as Sagan began his
work as a space scientist.

Sagan's considerable interest in the stars began at an early age. He recalls
asking his parents about the stars, what they were, but to no avail.

> As soon as I was old enough, my parents gave me my first library
> card. . . . I asked the librarian for something on stars. She returned with
> a picture book displaying portraits of men and women with names
> like Clark Gable and Jean Harlow. I complained. . . . She smiled and
> found another book—the right kind of book. I opened it breath-
> lessly and read until I found it. The book said something astonishing, a
> very big thought. It said that the stars were suns, only very far away. . . .
> Later I read another astonishing fact. The Earth . . . is a planet, and
> it goes around the Sun. There are other planets. . . . Well, then, I
> thought, it stood to reason that the other stars must have planets
> too, ones we have not yet detected, and some of those other planets
> should have life (why not?). . . . So I decided I would be an astronomer,
> learn about the stars and planets and, if I could, go and visit them.[7]

Worlds outside the Earth became Sagan's lifelong passion, always present throughout his entire career—first as an astronomy student, then a research scientist, and finally a science popularizer.

The reality of the *Sputnik* orbiting about the Earth pulled everyone's imagination into space. Sagan became intrigued by the possibility of finding life in the solar system, even on the moon. At that time, it was not clear that life on the moon was very improbable.

In 1959 Hermann Joseph Muller, Nobel Prize winner in medicine, invited Sagan to present a paper at a meeting of the National Academy of Sciences hosted by him at Bloomington, Indiana. Sagan gave two talks on his research about life on the moon, and an abstract was published in *Science*. In 1960 he published a paper, coauthored with Stanley Miller, in the *Astronomical Journal* on organic molecules in Jupiter, which found an echo in the *New York Times*.

Sagan presented his doctoral dissertation to the University of Chicago in June 1960. A work of eighty-five pages, titled "Physical Studies of Planets," the dissertation considered the possibility of life and organic molecules on the moon and Jupiter, a speculative subject at the time.

His Ph.D. in hand, Sagan received a two-year fellowship from the University of California at Berkeley. He lived in the Berkeley Hills with his wife Lynn, enrolled in the graduate program at Berkeley. Busy with space projects and writing, Sagan believed he was witnessing the beginning of the space age, a unique transition in history. The Soviets were the first into space, and the United States was fearful and eager to catch up.

In 1961 Sagan published his first major article in *Science*, the journal of the American Association for the Advancement of Science. The article proposed a greenhouse model for the atmosphere of Venus, together with a proposal for how to make Venus habitable. Sagan's greenhouse model for Venus caught the attention of the scientific community and made its way into the popular media. Sagan became involved in the space program, working in Pasadena, in the Jet Propulsion Laboratory of the California Institute of Technology. He tried unsuccessfully to persuade that laboratory that the *Mariner 2*, to be launched to Venus, should carry a camera.

While in California, Sagan began working as a consultant on planetary atmospheres for RAND (Research And Development). In 1961 he published a report on the atmospheres of Mars and Venus. In 1962 he became associate editor of *Icarus*, a new space science journal, and six years later became its editor in chief.

Sagan's scientific star was clearly rising, and in 1962 he was appointed assistant professor at Harvard University. This was also the year that Lynn divorced him and the *Mariner 2* reached Venus and made measurements confirming Sagan's greenhouse model for the atmosphere of the planet.

Interlude on Earth

Sagan arrived at Harvard in 1963 and within two years obtained a major NASA grant to investigate "biochemical activities of terrestrial microorganisms in simulated planetary environments." He also got a NASA grant to study exobiology. He was a consultant to several corporations, served on various committees, and advised NASA, the National Academy of Sciences, the RAND Corporation, the Air Force, and other agencies. He was becoming very influential.

In collaboration with the Russian scientist I. S. Shklovskii, Sagan published *Intelligent Life in the Universe* in 1966. This was but one of the meaningful relationships he maintained over many years with Russian scientists, hoping to promote cooperation between the world's two superpowers. He published, with Jonathan Norton Leonard, *The Planets*, part of a *Time-Life* series of popular science books. He also served as an adviser on the film *2001: A Space Odyssey*. His biographer Davidson comments:

> At Harvard, Sagan would become a nationally known scientific figure—not famous, exactly, but getting there.... Also in the mid-1960s, the mass media would begin exploiting Sagan. He was not a complete unknown to journalists.... In those days, few U.S. newspapers had full-time science reporters.... Hence Sagan would be a revelation.... By the time Sagan left Harvard, science reporters knew him on sight. They gravitated toward him at NASA press conferences, while his neglected colleagues were left staring at their microphones.[8]

Sagan was involved in many different projects, which suited him just fine, in contrast to his colleagues, most of whom focused exclusively on narrow research topics that generated little public attention. He was becoming a well-known public personality, sought after for his ability to interpret the latest scientific news in a way that everyone could understand. He had not, however, established good relations with his colleagues. Davidson comments:

> For all this, he would pay a price. His interests were dizzyingly diverse—too diverse. Most professors ... resent young go-getters who stake claim in a dozen different specialties, commenting suavely to media on topics far from their training.... He made few

[connections] at Harvard.... Also during Sagan's Harvard years, he would become more overtly political.... After four years at Harvard, campus officials denied his bid for tenure. A key reason is a furious letter, written by someone out of Sagan's past, someone to whom Sagan had demonstrated inadequate obeisance. Of course, Harvard rarely grants tenure to anyone, even a potential superstar like Carl Sagan. What is telling, though, is this: hardly anyone lifted a finger to keep him.[9]

The negative letter was written by Harold Urey, the Nobel Prize winner who inspired Stanley Miller's experiment, whom Sagan had met while at Chicago. Years afterward, Urey confessed to Sagan and lamented writing the letter.[10]

So Sagan went to Cornell, but not before, in April 1968, marrying Linda Salzman. This second marriage would not last long. Sagan's success as a scientist and a popularizer of science was not matched by his performance in his private life. He came to regret this, and took more care with his third and last marriage.

Becoming a Star

In 1968 Sagan arrived at Cornell, where he held a position until the end of his life, although for long periods he was absent. He soon became famous, participating in the *Mariner 9* mission, codesigning the *Pioneer* plaque, writing the best-seller *The Cosmic Connection*, and appearing on *The Tonight Show*. Davidson notes Sagan's ascendancy during the 1968–78 decade:

At Cornell, Sagan flexed his new-found artistic muscles in his breakthrough best-seller, *The Cosmic Connection*. He became a television star, the upbeat educator of sleepy-eyed millions viewing *The Tonight Show*. During the Viking mission, he was the television networks' favorite talking head, whose playful speculations about an inhabited Mars maddened his colleagues but titillated viewers. And like a performance artist with a NASA-sized budget, he engaged in grand forms of self-expression: he sent "messages" to aliens aboard star-bound space-probes, the *Pioneers 10* and *11* and the *Voyagers 1* and *2* ... (two plaques and two records encoded with the sounds and imagery of Earth).... He retained credibility with his orthodox colleagues partly by attacking their antithesis, the airhead purveyors of pseudoscience and occultism then storming the cultural marketplace.... Meanwhile, within ivory towers, a growing number of

academics began questioning the reliability of science itself. . . .
Science and reason (they warned) were in danger—and with them,
Western civilization. Carl Sagan became their hero. . . . Not content to
be their attack dog, he developed a more complex view of the tension between rationalism and irrationalism, one prefigured by the
structure of the human brain. He expressed this view in his first
truly literary work, the book that climaxed his 1968–1978 decade:
The Dragons of Eden. A crazy salad of ideas about myths, dreams, and
evolution, *Dragons* won the Pulitzer Prize. Thereafter, the intelli-
gentsia realized that Sagan was no longer merely a scientist or a late-
night TV show guest. He was a luminary.[11]

In 1973 Sagan published *The Cosmic Connection*, recounting the story of
how his grandfather asked the twelve-year-old Carl, with his emerging interest
in astronomy, "But how will you make a living?"[12] Davidson notes that the
book itself provided its own answer: "It sold so well that Dell bought the mass
paperback rights from Doubleday for $350,000. As an adult, Sagan had always
preferred a high standard of living—and now he had the money to back it up."[13]

The first part of *The Cosmic Connection* deals with space exploration, a
central topic throughout Sagan's career. The second part deals with the solar
system. The third looks at extraterrestrial life, asking if the Earth has already
received visits from aliens—Sagan says no—and how we might search for
extraterrestrial intelligence. Sagan was closely linked to the SETI (Search for
Extra Terrestrial Intelligence) and subsequent programs.

After Sagan's death, a new edition of *The Cosmic Connection* appeared in
2000, with three new contributions. In the foreword, physicist Freeman Dyson
comments on Sagan's vision and work. Sagan's third wife and collaborator Ann
Druyan writes an essay titled "Carl Sagan: A New Sense of the Sacred." And
David Morrison provided an epilogue discussing the advances since the book
first appeared in 1973 and their relationship to Sagan's predictions.[14]

Dyson writes:

Carl's vision as recorded in this book had two aspects, the long-range
and the short-range. The long-range aspect was the awakening of
mankind to awareness of the majesty of the cosmos and the possibility of extraterrestrial life. The short-range aspect was a program of
human activities in space to be pursued during the last three decades of the twentieth century. The book gives roughly equal emphasis to the two parts of the vision. But the outcomes for the two
parts of the vision have been very different, as events over the twenty-
seven years since the book was published show. The long-range part

of the vision has been magnificently fulfilled, while the short-range part has failed miserably. . . . He expected (see Chapter 23) international manned expeditions to the planets and self-sustaining colonies on the Moon before the end of the century. He expected at least one large telescope to be built and dedicated to a full-time search for extraterrestrial civilizations. The end of the twentieth century has now come and gone. There are no colonies in the Moon and no manned expeditions to planets. The dream of a rapid expansion of human voyages into the cosmos has faded. The International Space Station falls ludicrously short of Carl's expectations for a pioneering space venture.[15]

In spite of those short-range disappointments, Dyson shares Sagan's enthusiasm about the long-range vision:

For three decades, Carl was the preeminent voice of science speaking to the broad public. In television shows and films and books, he used his gifts as a performer to dramatize the excitement of exploring and the joy of discovery. He was a great preacher. He knew how to spice his gospel of cosmic connection with stories and jokes so that he did not seem to be preaching. His audiences came to his performances to be entertained and went away converted. . . . This book is a record of short-range visions that failed and of long-range visions that remain alive. . . . It is a monument to a great man who succeeded, in spite of failures and disappointments, in changing our view of our planet, changing the way we think about the universe.[16]

Sagan's first appearance on *The Tonight Show* was November 30, 1973, and inaugurated his role as a major public intellectual. In the next thirteen years, he was invited an average of twice each year. Davidson comments, "Carl Sagan was a near-magical figure. . . . After *The Tonight Show*, he became America's best-known scientist."[17]

Messages to the Galaxy

As his star rose steadily in the firmament of public acclaim, Sagan worked on many projects, including helping design two messages sending information about humanity to intelligent aliens. Such projects made Sagan appear to be humanity's "ambassador" to the extraterrestrial universe—quite a role.

The messages to extraterrestrials included in *Pioneer 10*, *Pioneer 11*, *Voyager 1*, and *Voyager 2* derive from Sagan's childhood experience of visiting the New York World's Fair of 1939–40. Both Poundstone and Davidson recount the event. The latter writes:

> One of the Fair's most publicized gimmicks was the burial of a time capsule at Flushing Meadows. It contained mementos of the 1930s to be recovered by our descendents millennia hence. The time capsule thrilled Carl.... As an adult, Carl and his colleagues would create his own time capsules—capsules destined to survive not for millennia inside the Earth, but for millions of years in the galaxy. The *Pioneer* plaques and the *Voyager* records—all are long-term spin-offs of Sagan's wide-eyed scamper through the World's Fair.[18]

Pioneer 10 was launched in early 1972, and was the first spacecraft to obtain close-up images of Jupiter. Its historic close encounter to Jupiter in December 1973 opened exploration of the outer solar system. The mission ended in 1997. *Pioneer 10* carried a now-famous plaque with a pictorial message of humankind: drawings of a man and woman, and scientific data that would enable aliens to find our location in the solar system. Sagan, of course, was enthusiastic about this project.

The *Pioneer 11*, launched in April 1973, carried the same plaque, by then rather famous and beginning to receive criticism. Some claimed it was anthropocentric and difficult to understand. Others asked if it might not provide information for malicious extraterrestrials to attack us!

Voyager 1 and *Voyager 2* were launched in 1977 to study Jupiter, Saturn, and their moons. When they finally departed the solar system, they too carried messages to aliens that Sagan had helped develop: photos of the earth, music, and greetings in different languages.

It seems unlikely that the plaques of the *Pioneer* or the records of the *Voyager* will ever be received by aliens. Space is vast, and these tiny space ships move slowly and inconspicuously through its great emptiness. But the messages do illustrate Sagan's enthusiastic approach to communicating with aliens—something his public was only too eager to hear about.

The culmination of Sagan's first decade at Cornell was the 1977 publication of *The Dragons of Eden*. He noted in the introduction that he knew little of the anatomy and physiology of the brain, which made his ideas quite speculative.[19]

In the same introduction, Sagan notes that we have just started using radio telescopes to communicate across interstellar distances, hoping to contact alien civilizations. Knowing more about the evolution of intelligence on earth may help determine the nature of the messages the elusive aliens may send to us. Sagan returns to this topic in the book's final chapter: "Knowledge Is Our Destiny: Terrestrial and Extraterrestrial Intelligence." He argues for using computer technology to scan radio frequencies that could originate from extraterrestrial intelligences. He is optimistic about the number of alien civilizations and thinks they will be different from us but capable of understanding our messages. After all, the laws of nature in their world are the same as in ours.

Sagan was convinced that discovering alien intelligence would be good news for our nuclear age, for it would show that technologically advanced civilizations can overcome the danger of nuclear destruction. These oracular insights and Sagan's work on the plaque aboard the *Pioneer 10* and *11*[20] were cementing his role as not only an ambassador for science, but as a spokesperson for the entire human race in its quest to make contact with aliens.

A Wonderful Cosmos

In October 1976, Sagan received a proposal to make the thirteen-episode television series that would launch him to enduring worldwide fame. It was a difficult time in his personal life. His marriage to Linda was ending, and he would soon ask Ann Druyan to become his third wife (and last wife, as it turned out). And in 1979 Sagan had to take care of his father, who died of cancer that year.

The series, titled *Cosmos* and directed by Adrian Malone, required considerable time and resources. Sagan moved to California in mid-1978, leaving Cornell for two years and living in Los Angeles with Ann Druyan. Other collaborators also moved there. The series cost $8.2 million and was accompanied by a book of the same name; the book had the same thirteen chapters as the film series, the same arguments and ideas, and sometimes even the same words.

The first episode of *Cosmos* aired Sunday night, September 28, 1980. Sagan's fellow scientists reacted favorably, and the show did wonders for the public image of science.

Cosmos was entertaining and well done, with exotic locales and expensive "special effects" typically not found in educational productions. Sagan spoke of pyramids from Egypt, with the real pyramids visible behind him; he discussed Japanese fish standing on the coast of Japan; the library of Alexandria in ancient Egypt was re-created in miniature, for example, and Sagan magically made to appear speaking within it.

Sagan wanted his audiences to share the sense of wonder accompanying scientific knowledge. The extraterrestrial issue, of course, was a key ingredient in generating this excitement. In the last chapter of *Cosmos* Sagan writes: "The cost of major ventures into space—permanent bases on the Moon or human exploration of Mars, say—is so large that they will not, I think, be mustered in the very near future unless we make dramatic progress in nuclear and 'conventional' disarmament. Even then there are probably more pressing needs here on Earth. But I have no doubt that, if we avoid self-destruction, we will sooner or later perform such missions."[21] Sagan's considerable influence generated important public support for NASA's projects.

Extraterrestrial adventures, in Sagan's mind, were linked to our deepest questions. At the end of the seventh episode, "The Backbone of Night," he says:

> As long as there have been humans we have searched for our place in the cosmos. Where are we? Who are we? We find that we live on an insignificant planet of a humdrum star, lost in a galaxy tucked away in some forgotten corner of the universe in which there are far more galaxies than people. We make our world significant by the courage of our questions and by the depth of our answers. We embarked on our journey to the stars with a question first framed in the childhood of our species, and in each generation asked anew with undiminished wonder: "What are the stars?" Exploration is in our nature. We began as wanderers, and we are wanderers still. We have lingered long enough on the shores of the cosmic ocean. We are ready at last to set sail for the stars.[22]

For Sagan, the extraterrestrial path led to a deeper understanding of who we are. This was his religion, the glorious search for meaning through science.

Godless Materialism

Some of Sagan's comments in *Cosmos* had a materialistic, antireligious tone, and it wasn't long until he was under attack as an enemy of religion. "I am a collection of water, calcium and organic molecules called Carl Sagan," he said. "You are a collection of almost identical molecules with a different collective label. But is that all? Is there nothing in here but molecules? Some people find this idea somehow demeaning to human dignity. For myself, I find it elevating that our universe permits the evolution of molecular machines as intricate and subtle as we are."[23] Here we find Sagan denying the existence of a spiritual dimension to reality, using what had become his typical style of argument: presenting his philosophical view indirectly in a scientific context.

Sagan typically did not argue against basic religious ideas; rather, he presented difficulties associated with the ideas. Davidson notes:

> Sagan would always feel ambivalence about certain elements of the skeptics movement. Some of its members were too lacking in "compassion" for those deluded by foolish ideas, he complained. He refused to sign astronomer Bart Bok's anti-astrology petition because, in Sagan's view, its tone was too authoritarian; in an age when the public increasingly distrusted "experts," astrology buffs would not be converted to reason by an elitist-sounding petition signed by a band of astronomers. More subtle means were required to combat pseudoscience. One must not talk to people as if they are children babbling about Santa Claus; rather, they must be educated, patiently and respectfully so. And for that educational mission, Sagan was ideally suited.[24]

When dealing with the origin of the universe, Sagan raised the question of God. In the *Cosmos* book he writes:

> If the general picture of an expanding universe and a Big Bang is correct, we must then confront still more difficult questions. What were conditions like at the time of the Big Bang? What happened before that? Was there a tiny universe, devoid of all matter, and then the matter suddenly created from nothing? How does that happen? In many cultures it is customary to answer that God created the universe out of nothing. But this is mere temporizing. If we wish courageously to pursue the question, we must of course ask next where God comes from. And if we decide this to be unanswerable, why not save a step and decide that the origin of the universe is an unanswerable question. Or, if we say that God has always existed, why not save a step and conclude that the universe has always existed?[25]

Theologians recognize this timeless question, posed many times and with a stock response: asking where God comes from makes no sense as God, at least in the Abrahamic faiths, is the source of all being and has been understood that way since long before the big-bang theory raised so many interesting questions about the origin of the universe. *Cosmos* was addressed to the general public, of course, and Sagan might respond that it would be distracting to develop theological issues in detail. But Sagan advances his arguments as if they are scientific, never distinguishing between a central scientific concept and a philosophical claim coming from outside science. In the opening episode of the television series he says, "We wish to pursue the truth, no matter where it leads. But to find the truth, we need imagination and skepticism both. We will not be afraid to speculate. But we will be careful to distinguish speculation from fact." This commitment, however, didn't even last through the first sentence of the series (and the book): "The Cosmos is all that is or ever was or ever will be."[26] In Sagan's *Cosmos* there is no place for God. No claims are made, of course, that science has proven God does not exist. But this is the obvious conclusion if one takes the arguments seriously, for they are presented as if they naturally follow from science.

The series and the book, however, are devoted almost entirely to scientific issues. References to religion are rare and peripheral, although consistently negative. The only major exception is chapter 7, "The Backbone of Night," which is quite negative about religion.

The Conflict Thesis

Without explicitly acknowledging it, Sagan endorses the view that science and religion are in perpetual conflict, consistent with the "conflict thesis" that has received much scholarly attention over the past few decades.[27] This metaphor for understanding the interaction of science and religion was popularized in the second half of the nineteenth century by the influential books *History of the Conflict between Religion and Science* by John William Draper (1874) and *A History of the Warfare of Science with Theology in Christendom* by Andrew Dickson White (1896).

In the *Cosmos* book, at the beginning of chapter 7, Sagan includes a lengthy monologue on primitive cultures. The origin of religion is described as a reaction to mysterious and unknown aspects of the natural world, with the obvious corollary that scientific progress explains religion away, because its myths are no longer necessary. Primitive religion, says Sagan, centered on myths about capricious gods running the natural world. Humanity was finally rescued a few centuries before Christ by the pre-Socratics of ancient Greece, who developed scientific thinking and provided explanations for natural phenomena without gods.

Sagan is quite enamored with the pre-Socratics. An entire scene of the series, "Ancient Greek Scientists," takes place on the island of Samos. Sagan strolls along the island, surrounded by beautiful landscapes and animated residents. He comments:

Here, twenty-five centuries ago, on the island of Samos and in the other Greek colonies which had grown up in the busy Aegean Sea, there was a glorious awakening. Suddenly, people believed that everything was made of atoms, that human beings and other animals had evolved from simpler forms, that diseases were not caused by demons or the gods, that the Earth was only a planet going around a sun which was very far away. This revolution made cosmos out of chaos. Here, in the sixth century B.C., a new idea developed, one of the great ideas of the human species. It was argued that the universe was knowable. Why? Because it was ordered. Because there are regularities in nature which permitted secrets to be uncovered. Nature was not entirely unpredictable. There were rules which even she had to obey. This ordered and admirable character of the universe was called cosmos. And it was set in stark contradiction to the idea of chaos. This was the first conflict of which we know between science and mysticism, between nature and the gods.[28]

By these lights, science and religion have been at odds since the dawn of Western civilization, often said to have begun with the pre-Socratics. Sagan leaves audiences with the impression that this same science-versus-religion opposition continued indefinitely, an impression reinforced by occasional reiterations. Pre-Socratic Ionia, he says, was an ideal place for science to be born because it was located at a crossroads of different civilizations, stimulating the skepticism Sagan considers a key ingredient of science:

What do you do when you are faced [with different gods].... You might decide that Marduk and Zeus were really the same. You might also decide, since they had quite different attributes, that one of them was merely invented by the priests. But if one, why not both? And so it was that the great idea arose, the realization that there might be a way to know the world without the god hypothesis; that there might be principles, forces, laws of nature, through which the world could be understood without attributing the fall of every sparrow to the direct intervention of Zeus.[29]

The options at play in pre-Socratic Greece remain and are still, says Sagan, the choices available to us—natural forces or divine intervention. This false dichotomy derives from a simplistic theological misunderstanding that God's action and natural forces are opposed. Sagan imputes this same dichotomy to his Greek heroes, Thales and Democritus. They did not achieve important results, he admits, but they did have the right approach. Thales, for example, is thought to have believed that "the world was not made by the gods, but instead was the result of material forces interacting in nature."[30] Sagan celebrates Thales' materialism as a primitive scientific method, wisely replacing religious myths with natural explanations.

This account is biased to the point of being misleading. While *Cosmos* was certainly not the place to take sides in esoteric academic disputes, Sagan's simplifications, communicated to hundreds of millions of viewers, trespass all acceptable limits. He opposes his materialist heroes, Thales and Democritus, about whom we know next to nothing, to Plato and Aristotle, who he says would have stopped scientific progress: Plato and Aristotle, he claims, "were comfortable in a slave society. They offered justifications for oppression. They served tyrants. They taught the alienation of the body from the mind (a natural enough ideal in a slave society).... Plato, who believed that 'all things are full of gods,' actually used the metaphor of slavery to connect his politics with his cosmology."[31] This passage, incidentally, echoes typical Marxist rhetoric of the 1970s.

Sagan apparently did not know that while Plato was indeed happy with the idea that "all things are full of gods," he and other classic authors attributed the idea to Thales! Werner Jaeger, a leading authority on the pre-Socratics, notes that Plato interpreted Thales' comment about the gods as meaning that natural philosophy should not be regarded as a source of atheism, and Jaeger adds: "In attaching this new content to Thales' ancient dictum, Plato is naturally interpreting it in his own way; we can only guess what Thales really had in mind.... Aristotle suggests that he may here have been thinking of magnetic attraction.... The assertion that everything is full of gods would then mean something like this: everything is full of mysterious living forces.... This interpretation is still far from certain."[32] This, and countless other examples we could mention, indicate that the history of science and religion is much more complex and interesting than Sagan's biased account suggests.

Sagan delights in pointing out those ancient thinkers persecuted for their antireligious ideas. His selective reading of history is guided by a search for charges to make against religion. For instance, speaking of Democritus he writes:

> He believed that the prevailing religions of his time were evil and that neither immortal soul nor immortal gods exist: "Nothing exists, but atoms and the void." There is no record of Democritus having been persecuted for his opinions—but then, he came from Abdera. However, in his time the brief tradition of tolerance for unconventional views began to erode and then to shatter. People came to be

punished for having unusual ideas.... his insights were suppressed, his influence on history made minor. The mystics were beginning to win.[33]

Sagan understands history as a simple opposition between religion and science, which gets him trouble when dealing with Plato and the Pythagoreans. On the one hand, he writes, "The Pythagoreans would powerfully influence Plato and, later, Christianity. They did not advocate the free confrontation of conflicting points of view. Instead, like all orthodox religions, they practiced a rigidity that prevented them from correcting their errors."[34] He charges Pythagoras and Plato with having suppressed the scientific method invented by the Ionians.[35] On the other hand, however, he must face the uncomfortable fact that the mathematical approach of Pythagoras and Plato was crucial to the scientific revolution in the seventeenth century. The Copernican theory was even referred to as "Pythagorean" in its day, reflecting the degree to which Copernicus's arguments were reminiscent of those used by Pythagoras two thousand years earlier.

Suppression and Reawakening

Much of chapter 7 of *Cosmos* and the corresponding television episode is devoted to the science-and-religion-in-perpetual-conflict thesis. Sagan's conclusion is aggressive: "The books of the Ionian scientists are entirely lost. Their views were suppressed, ridiculed and forgotten by the Platonists and by the Christians, who adopted much of the philosophy of Plato. Finally, after a long, mystical sleep, in which the tools of scientific inquiry lay moldering, the Ionian approach was rediscovered. The western world reawakened. Experiment and open inquiry slowly became respectable once again. Forgotten books and fragments were read once more. Leonardo and Copernicus and Columbus were inspired by the Ionian tradition."[36]

Enthusiasm for the Ionians is widespread. We find it in scientists like E. O. Wilson, who devoted the first chapter of his book *Consilience* to "The Ionian Enchantment," and in philosophers like Karl Popper, who was able to detect among them a precursor to his philosophy in the rarely quoted Xenophanes. But Sagan goes too far. The Nobel laureate physicist Steven Weinberg sees in the Ionians only a pale qualitative anticipation of some modern ideas, arguing,

> None of the pre-Socratics, neither at Miletus nor at Abdera, had anything like our modern idea of what a successful scientific

explanation would have to accomplish: the *quantitative* understanding of phenomena. How far do we progress toward understanding why nature is the way it is if Thales or Democritus tells us that a stone is made of water or atoms, when we still do not know how to calculate its density or hardness or electrical conductivity? And of course, without the capacity for quantitative prediction, we could never tell whether Thales or Democritus is right.[37]

Sagan gets carried away identifying materialist thinking with science, in comfortable and self-evident opposition to religion. He sees science as an inevitable cultural development, eventually arising in any civilization free from external hindrances, like religion. If science is not flourishing, there must be suppression by religion. He writes in *Cosmos*: "The scientific worldview works so well, explains so much and resonates so harmoniously with the most advanced parts of our brains that in time, I think, virtually every culture on the Earth, left to its own devices, would have discovered science. Some culture had to be first. As it turned out, Ionia was the place where science was born."[38]

Sagan's idiosyncratic interpretation is open to dispute. One has only to note that many careful studies of the Scientific Revolution of the seventeenth century see it as quite original and not at all a reawakening of the Ionian Enchantment. Rather, its roots lie in the medieval period, which Sagan dismisses. As a physicist, for example, Sagan surely knew that mathematical physics, the first branch of science to be developed, is difficult and often deeply counterintuitive; it deals with abstract models that capture some aspects of the natural world to perfection while ignoring others; it is deeply quantitative at all levels and appeared only once—in the seventeenth century in Western Europe. But this science did not just fall from the sky, or appear on some newly discovered Ionian parchment. Centuries of careful preliminary work were needed until modern science was born, midwifed by the generation that gave us Galileo and Kepler. And much of the necessary prerequisite work was done in the medieval period,[39] which Sagan considers a part of the "Dark Ages."

Thomas Kuhn, in a groundbreaking scholarly work on the Copernican revolution, wrote:

During the seventeenth century, just when its full utility was being demonstrated for the first time, scholastic science was bitterly attacked by men trying to weave a radically new fabric of thought. The scholastics proved easy to ridicule, and the image has stuck. Medieval scientists more often found their problems in texts than in nature; many of those problems do not seem problems at all; by modern standards the practice of science during the Middle Ages was incredibly inefficient. But how else could science have been reborn in the West? The centuries of scholasticism are the centuries in which the tradition of ancient science and philosophy was simultaneously reconstituted, assimilated, and tested for adequacy. As weak spots were discovered, they immediately became foci for the first effective research in the modern world. The great new scientific theories of the sixteenth and seventeenth centuries all originate from rents torn by scholastic criticism in the fabric of Aristotelian thought. Most of those theories also embody key concepts created by scholastic science. And more important even than these is the attitude that modern scientists inherited from their medieval predecessors: an unbounded faith in the power of human reason to solve the problems of nature. As the late Professor Whitehead remarked, "Faith in the possibility of science, generated antecedently to the development of modern scientific theory, is an unconscious derivative from medieval theology."[40]

Reviving Ancient Myths

From childhood, Sagan liked ancient myths and built stories around them, a skill put to good use in *Cosmos*. But he also liked to revive old clichés about religion. A case in point is his treatment of the historical figure of the ancient female mathematician Hypatia of Alexandria. Apparently it was Druyan who suggested that Sagan make Hypatia one of the heroes of the series.[41]

The ancient library of Alexandria, with Hypatia as a central figure, occupies much of the last chapter of *Cosmos*. Here is Sagan's account:

The last scientist who worked in the Library was a mathematician, astronomer, physicist and the head of the Neoplatonic school of philosophy—an extraordinary range of accomplishments for any individual in any age. Her name was Hypatia. She was born in Alexandria in 370. At a time when women had few options and were treated as property, Hypatia moved freely and unself-consciously through traditional male domains. By all accounts she was a great beauty. She had many suitors but rejected all offers of marriage. The Alexandria of Hypatia's time—by then long under Roman rule— was a city under grave strain. Slavery had sapped classical civilization of its vitality. The growing Christian Church was consolidating its power and attempting to eradicate pagan influence and culture.

Hypatia stood at the epicenter of these mighty social forces. Cyril, the Archbishop of Alexandria, despised her because of her close friendship with the Roman governor, and because she was a symbol of learning and science, which were largely identified by the early Church with paganism. In great personal danger, she continued to teach and publish, until, in the year 415, on her way to work she was set upon by a fanatical mob of Cyril's parishioners. They dragged her from her chariot, tore off her clothes, and, armed with abalone shells, flayed her flesh from her bones. Her remains were burned, her works obliterated, her name forgotten. Cyril was made a saint. The glory of the Alexandrian Library is a dim memory. Its last remnants were destroyed soon after Hypatia's death. It was as if the entire civilization had undergone some self-inflicted brain surgery, and most of its memories, discoveries, ideas and passions were extinguished irrevocably. The loss was incalculable.[42]

Sagan's story is long on drama, short on facts. There are few historical sources to support the repeated use of the Hypatia affair against Christianity. Contemporary scholars have shown that the episode was quite complex. Analyzing all the available data, including indirect information from people related to Hypatia, Byzantine historian Maria Dzielska concludes that it is difficult to determine whether Hypatia was persecuted because of her paganism. She was not an active pagan. She was, in fact, sympathetic to Christianity and protective of her Christian students. And two of her students were even consecrated Christian bishops! Hypatia's death was not related to science but was the consequence of political quarrels between prefect Orestes and patriarch Cyril, who had no direct involvement. Some of Cyril's supporters apparently were involved in spreading rumors against Hypatia and attacking her, but powerful leaders can hardly be held responsible for the misbehavior of mobs nominally under their rule. The whole affair has little to do with the anti-Christian legend that portrays it as a consequence of the increasing power of the Church acting against ancient philosophy and science. Neither pagan religion nor mathematics nor Greek philosophy disappeared when Hypatia died. The greatest successes of the Alexandria school were reached after Hypatia's death, at the end of the fifth and the beginning of the sixth centuries.[43]

Dzielska analyzes Hypatia's modern legend, following each one of its steps. At the beginning of her work she writes:

Long before the first scholarly attempts to reconstruct an accurate image of Hypatia, her life—marked by the dramatic circumstances of her death—had been imbued with legend. Artistically embellished,

distorted by emotions and ideological biases, the legend has enjoyed wide popularity obstructing scholarly endeavors to present
Hypatia's life impartially, and it persists to this day. Ask who Hypatia
was, and you will probably be told: "She was that beautiful young
pagan philosopher who was torn to pieces by monks (or, more generally, by Christians) in Alexandria in 415." This pat answer would be
based not on ancient sources, but on a mass of belletristic and historical literature, a representative sample of which is surveyed in
this chapter. Most of these works present Hypatia as an innocent
victim of the fanaticism of nascent Christianity, and her murder
as marking the banishment of freedom of inquiry along with the
Greek gods.[44]

Contact

The success of *Cosmos* brought Sagan worldwide fame. Moreover, Davidson
notes that "his fame brought him a fortune. His colleagues' hearts ached when
he received a $2 million advance from Simon & Schuster in early 1981 to write
the novel *Contact*.... The advance was the largest ever made for a book that
had not yet been written. A film version was expected in 1984."[45]

The novel *Contact* was published in 1985,[46] but production of the film
was delayed until after Sagan's death. It was not released until 1997, and then
only after additional work had been done by Sagan, Druyan, and producer
Lynda Obst.

Contact embodied Sagan's lifelong passion for intelligent extraterrestrial life. The protagonist of the novel is Eleanor (Ellie) Arroway, a woman,
a scientist, and an agnostic who successfully contacts aliens. The novel also
explores intellectual topics such as the limits of science and the validity of
religion.

Religion was treated differently in the novel than in the film. Davidson
comments:

> In the novel *Contact*, Sagan had depicted American religion in one of
> its more primitive forms: tent-revival evangelism.... Sagan wasn't
> fighting modern religion.... he was still waging the "warfare of sci-
> ence with theology" that Andrew Dickson White had fought a century
> earlier. And this is why the novel *Contact*'s treatment of religion is
> of far less intellectual interest than its treatment of scientific issues.
> Religiously speaking, he was beating a dead horse. The film treatment

of religion is subtler. . . . thanks to Sagan's new maturity on religious
issues, and thanks partly to the good sense of his two female com-
patriots, the film's main representative of religion is an intelligent
neo-yuppie played by Matthew McConaughey. A religious man himself, McConaughey refused to utter the one sentence that Ann Druyan
had hoped would make the film: "My God was too small." The line
was sacrilegious, McConaughey told her. The more she talked to him
about it, the more she realized the depth of his intelligent and sincere
faith; in time they became good friends.[47]

Why does Davidson speak of "Sagan's new maturity on religious issues"?
He notes that Sagan's attitude toward religion changed in the late 1980s, at
least in public, when he established "political alliances with religious leaders
in an effort to fight nuclearism and environmental recklessness. His vacil-
lating comments about religion during the making of *Contact* show how much
his views had evolved since his youthful quarrels with [his mother] Rachel."[48]
Davidson also suggests that a turning point in Sagan's public attitude toward
religion was his encounter with Pope John Paul II in 1984: "Sagan discovered
that organized religion could be a powerful ally in his effort to save the world
from nuclear and environmental disaster. Exactly how he came to this realization is unclear. It may have stemmed from his meeting in 1984 with the
most majestic religious leader of the Western world, Pope John Paul II." [49]

Based on an interview with Druyan, present on that occasion, Davidson
reports Sagan's encounter with the pope:

A group of about fifteen scientists, including Sagan and Stephen Jay
Gould, the famous paleontologist and essayist, were invited by the
Pontifical Academy to "brief the Pope about what the nuclear winter
scenario was," Druyan recalls. "So we were ushered into his Vatican
apartments." . . . Sagan gave a talk. . . . The talk lasted thirty to forty-
five minutes, explaining the risks of nuclear winter. John Paul asked
Sagan questions, and "it was clear he had been paying attention and
he understood what Carl was saying." Afterward, Druyan asked the
Pope to bless a religious medal that she wished to give her house-
keeper, a native of Peru. Druyan was startled by the skeptical look
of John Paul's face. Surrounded by scientists, "he wanted to make
it very clear to us that he didn't believe in this [superstition]! That
it meant nothing to him! . . . I was shocked!" Nonetheless, he per-
functorily blessed the medal. Atheists aren't the only cynics. . . . The
ultimate result was a papal statement warning of the danger of
nuclear winter, and of nuclear weapons in general. The statement

undoubtedly made the nuclear winter scientists' warning seem more credible to much of the world. After all, if the Pope was worried about nuclear winter, then it must be a serious issue! The Pope had unwittingly done a big favor for Carl Sagan, one of the century's more glamorous atheists. Perhaps for this reason, Sagan began to rethink his attitude toward religion. True, to him it was anathema; but it might also be useful.[50]

(Druyan and Davidson can be forgiven for misconstruing the pope's reaction as cynicism. There is a venerable Catholic tradition, updated during the pontificate of John Paul II, of pronouncing benedictions or blessings on people and symbols of everyday activities, like travels. There is nothing cynical in the Pope's benediction of a medal.)

Years later, in a posthumously published book, Sagan showed an unprecedented attitude, devoting a chapter to meetings with religious leaders: "It has been my good fortune to participate in an extraordinary sequence of gatherings throughout the world: The leaders of the planet's religions have met with scientists and legislators from many nations to try to deal with the rapidly worsening world environmental crisis."[51] Shortly before, in the same chapter, he made it clear that a new epoch of understanding between science and religion had begun: "For centuries, there has been a conflict between the two fields. . . . But times have changed." He quoted approvingly Pope John Paul II: "Science can purify religion from error and superstition; religion can purify science from idolatry and false absolutes. Each can draw the other into a wider world, a world in which both can flourish."[52] Sagan had certainly not become a religious man, but his view of religion was considerably tempered.

Science, Pseudoscience, and Religion

Sagan is typically portrayed as a preeminent skeptic, a poster child for the humanist movement. He was a popular scientist in the United States and an outspoken opponent of obscurantism. His most conspicuous convert to skepticism was Michael Shermer, currently the publisher and editor in chief of *Skeptic* magazine. In 1996 *Skeptic* ran a tribute to Sagan on the occasion of his death. The cover shot was a picture of Sagan with his hands around a candle, symbolizing science, "a candle in the dark." The phrase was the subtitle of Sagan's last book, published that same year while he was still alive. *Skeptic's* tribute consisted of quotes taken from Sagan's works, and three articles, one by Shermer himself.

Shermer eulogizes Sagan. But he also includes a deeply personal account of Sagan's influence on him, first with *The Dragons of Eden*, then with *Cosmos*, and then with another episode that would be decisive for American skeptics:

> Most significantly, in the Fall of 1987, Sagan delivered a lecture I attended in Pasadena, California, entitled "The Burden of Skepticism." It came at a crossroads in my life when I was trying to find my intellectual moorings. After reminding us of the joys and responsibilities of science and skepticism, Sagan concluded: "If we teach school children the habit of being skeptical perhaps they will not restrict their skepticism to aspirin commercials and 35,000 years old channelers. Maybe they will start asking awkward questions about economic or social or political or religious institutions, and then where will we be? Skepticism is dangerous. In fact, it is the business of skepticism to be dangerous. That is exactly its function." ... I wanted to be a part of the business of skepticism and start asking awkward questions of any and all institutions and beliefs. It was a defining moment. I wanted to be a skeptic. Immediately after the lecture I applied to the Claremont Graduate School, earned a Ph.D. in the history of science, and within six months of graduating in 1991 founded the Skeptics Society. In a way, the Society was born at that 1987 lecture.[53]

Doing and popularizing science, for Carl Sagan, was something of a secular religion. He preached of the excellence of science. If we have any hope of really knowing who we are, we should look to science. He considered it a sacred duty to fight pseudoscientific notions that presented unfounded fantasies as real science. At the same time, Sagan considered traditional religions to have been superseded by scientific progress. Last but not least, he realized that future scientific progress depends on ideas that nonscientific people (including politicians and voters) have about science. He considered it his duty to bring to the general public an appreciation of science and its results, not only as a means to advance science, but also as a legitimate end in itself—the simple satisfaction of knowing about our world.

Religious communities, of course, share with Sagan and the skeptics a preference that their religion not be mixed with pseudoscientific fantasies. They also prefer their religion not to be compared with science as if science and religion shared the same concerns. But Sagan often mixed all the ingredients in the same pot. He did not believe in God, of course, and was concerned only with promoting science. Druyan puts it like this: "For Carl Sagan, it was the permanently revolutionary method of science, with its systematic and unblinking questioning of authority and dispassionate testing of all hypotheses, that promised the greatest prize of all—a deeper understanding of who, what, when and where we are in space and time. . . . He was completely free of the spiritual narcissism that demanded a central place in the universe for him and his kind."[54]

Davidson spoke of Sagan in religious terms: "Underneath, he was a scientific messiah. He saw space exploration as an evolutionary leap forward, not merely as the latest feint in the chess game of superpowers. Despite his business-suit demeanor, Sagan was more like an artist or a rabbi or a hippie. His concerns were transcendental. Aliens like gods! Relativistic travel to Andromeda, and beyond! Sagan was one of those rare people who measure time in centuries, millennia, and geological layers, not in fiscal years, obsessing in future possibilities that we surely won't live to see."[55]

Sagan's mother was a religious believer, but his father had little interest in religion. In New Jersey the family attended the temple; the young Carl was enrolled in a Hebrew school and received a religious education. At thirteen he celebrated his bar mitzvah, the Jewish ceremony of maturity. But this was precisely the time he became convinced there were contradictions in the Bible. He noted "two different, contradictory accounts of the origin of the world in Genesis. That propelled me away [from religion]," he said in an interview. Sagan's lifelong rejection of religion emerged at this early age. His doubts

> upset his mother, Rachel. Despite her flinty skepticism about most matters, she trusted in the unseen world. . . . Her only son—her future genius—was rejecting the faith of his fathers? Their religious quarrels, Sagan later admitted, were "traumatic" because for Rachel "there were a lot of emotional, traditional connections" at stake. "There was a time," he recalled, "when my mother and I would have—fights, I guess is the word, on this issue. I think it only lasted about a year." Then Rachel realized that it was "hopeless" for her to try to change Sagan's mind, and they stopped fighting.[56]

Like so many intellectuals who reject their childhood faith, Sagan did not pursue alternative responses to his concerns. That Genesis contains two different creation stories is problematic only for a biblical literalist. Most scholars are quite content to see the accounts as complementary rather than contradictory. On the other hand, Sagan's loss of religious faith coincided with his steadily growing interest in extraterrestrial life. One is tempted to say that Sagan's faith was not so much lost as "relocated." As a youth, he took seriously the extraterrestrial nature of UFOs, then a hot topic. It was an interest he took with him to the University of Chicago, where it became curiously entangled with his interpretation of the Bible.

There is a telling anecdote about this that would be hard to believe were it not from a reliable source, Seymour Abrahamson. Sagan met Abrahamson at Christmas in 1951. Abrahamson was a graduate student in genetics, working at Indiana University under the Nobel laureate Hermann Muller. Abrahamson introduced Sagan to Muller, and Sagan worked with Muller on biology for the next two summers. Muller was passionate about science fiction and engaged Sagan in long discussions on extraterrestrial life and intelligence. Poundstone reports that Sagan later credited these discussions with Muller as being "critical" in directing him toward the serious consideration of aliens: "If not for meeting Muller I might possibly have bowed under the weight of conventional opinion that *all* these subjects were nonsense."[57]

Poundstone recounts, from his interview with Abrahamson, that one Sunday morning Sagan was with Abrahamson and his fiancée, and

> Sagan propounded a new theory: that Moses, Jesus, and all the great religious figures of ages past were really extraterrestrial beings. The miracles of the Bible had all happened as described. Moses parted the Red Sea, Jesus turned water into wine, and so forth. They used advanced technology that was perfectly ordinary on *their* planet—but which we earthlings could take only as proof of divinity.... That afternoon, Abrahamson took his fiancée and Sagan out to dinner.... In the middle of dinner, without any warning, Sagan slammed his fist on the table, sending the dishes rattling. He looked Abrahamson in the eye and bellowed, "I tell you, Jesus Christ *is* extraterrestrial!" The restaurant fell silent. It took a subjective eternity for conversations to resume with something of their former spontaneity. Abrahamson and his fiancée wanted to crawl under the table.[58]

Davidson reports Nina Landau, a friend of the Sagans from Berkeley, saying of Carl: "He was totally consumed with the idea that there was probably life on other planets, in outer space. He was on *fire* with his ideas. He would go on and on."[59] Davidson comments: "Sagan's loss of faith intersected neatly with his growing fascination with extraterrestrial life. He had rejected a supernatural explanation of the origin of life (and everything else); therefore he needed to find a scientific one. A great deal was at stake."[60]

Eventually Sagan would come to critique the extraterrestrial explanation of UFOs as being without scientific foundation.

If one sees religion as myths invented to explain the mysteries of the natural world, it is easy to see science superseding religion on its own terrain.

This false dichotomy—that mysteries are to be explained by either science or religion—is always present in Sagan's view of religion. He could not resist the temptation to view religion as pseudoscience, proffering bogus explanations that look vaguely scientific. This temptation is especially troubling in the United States, where fundamentalist groups continually lobby for a biblically inspired "creation science" or "Intelligent Design" as a scientific alternative to evolutionism, repeating Sagan's mistake in comparing religious and scientific explanation. Sagan criticized pseudoscience and religion in the same context, upsetting many religious people.

In time Sagan came to see that religion and science did not need to be in conflict, a view shared by the great majority of thoughtful Christians.

A Demon-Haunted World

The Demon-Haunted World, published the year he died, was Sagan's assault on pseudoscience, which paralleled his campaign for science. He viewed them as competing vehicles of communication: The more one rises, the more the other declines, like playmates on a seesaw: "Pseudoscience is embraced, it might be argued, in exact proportion as real science is misunderstood.... If you've never heard of science ... you can hardly be aware you're embracing pseudoscience. You're simply thinking in one of the ways that humans always have."[61]

Sagan seemed aware that Christianity per se has no direct connection to pseudoscience. As we showed above, in earlier publications he considered science in constant conflict with religion. Instead, in *The Demon-Haunted World* he advances a different and, we would add, more *mature* view. He writes: "Of course many religions, devoted to reverence, awe, ethics, ritual, community, family, charity, and political and economic justice, are in no way challenged, but rather uplifted, by the findings of science. There is no necessary conflict between science and religion."[62] He adds:

> The religious traditions are often so rich and multivariate that they offer ample opportunity for renewal and revision, again especially when their sacred books can be interpreted metaphorically and allegorically. There is thus a middle ground of confessing past errors, as the Roman Catholic Church did in its 1992 acknowledgement that Galileo was right after all, that the Earth does revolve around the Sun: three centuries late, but courageous and most welcome none the less. Modern Roman Catholicism has no quarrel with the Big

Bang, with a Universe 15 billion or so years old, with the first living things arisen from prebiological molecules, or with humans evolving from ape-like ancestors—although it has special opinions on "ensoulment." Most mainstream Protestant and Jewish faiths take the same sturdy position.[63]

Sagan apparently changed his mind on religion, now claiming no *necessary* conflict between science and religion. He continued to critique religion, though, and elsewhere in *The Demon-Haunted World* he wrote: "But tenets at the heart of religion can be tested scientifically. This in itself makes some religious bureaucrats and believers wary of science. Is the Eucharist, as the Church teaches, in fact and not just as productive metaphor, the flesh of Jesus Christ, or is it, chemically, microscopically and in other ways, just a wafer handed to you by a priest?"[64] He also objects to prayer: "Does prayer work at all? Which ones?... Why is the prayer needed? Didn't God know of the drought? Was he unaware that it threatened the bishop's parishioners? What is implied here about the limitations of a supposedly omnipotent and omniscient deity?... Is God more likely to intervene when many pray for mercy or justice than when only a few do?"[65] So, while Sagan's wholesale assault on religion was tempered, he continued to critique specifics, albeit without doing enough homework to understand how theologians and thoughtful believers view things like the Eucharist or prayer.

Sagan also retained his materialist views. In *The Demon-Haunted World* he wrote:

But why should "psychic" experiences challenge the idea that we are made of matter and nothing but? There is very little doubt that, in the everyday world, matter (and energy) exist. The evidence is all around us. In contrast, as I've mentioned earlier, the evidence for something non-material called "spirit" or "soul" is very much in doubt. Of course each of us has a rich internal life. Considering the stupendous complexity of matter, though, how could we possibly prove that our internal life is not wholly due to matter? Granted, there is much about human consciousness that we do not fully understand and cannot yet explain in terms of neurobiology. Humans have limitations, and no one knows this better than scientists. But a multitude of aspects of the natural world that were considered miraculous only a few generations ago are now thoroughly understood in term of physics and chemistry.... All the mammals—and many other animals as well—experience emotions: fear, lust, hope, pain, love, hate, the need to be led. Humans may brood about the future more, but there is nothing in our emotions unique to us. On the other hand, no other species does science as much or as well as we. How then can science be "dehumanizing"?[66]

No wonder, then, that so many saw Sagan as a staunch foe of religion. There were exceptions, though. After Sagan's death, at a memorial service in Manhattan's St. John the Divine Cathedral, Rev. Joan Campbell reflected: "Carl Sagan was one of religion's most severe critics and best friends. Carl demanded of religion clarity, honesty, and excellence—qualities we would do well to demand of ourselves.... He would say to me with a smile, 'You're so smart. Why do you believe in God?' And I would say to him, 'You're so smart. Why don't you believe in God?' "[67]

The Scientific Way of Thinking

Davidson's biography opens with these words: "All his life, Carl Sagan was troubled by grand dichotomies—between reason and irrationalism, between wonder and skepticism. The dichotomies clashed within him. He yearned to believe in marvelous things—in flying saucers, in Martians, in glistening civilizations across the Milky Way. Yet reason usually brought him back to Earth. Usually; not always."[68] He adds:

> As we shall see, the adult Sagan's insistence on the inevitability of cosmic intelligence is important partly because it undergirded his quasi-religious belief in alien super-beings. He believed that these creatures, perhaps dwelling in other galaxies, were benevolent and might help us to solve our terrestrial problems. Viewed from a psychological perspective, they were secular versions of the gods and angels he had long since abandoned. His secular "faith" stemmed from the choice he made when he reached the two paths diverging in the evolutionary yellow wood—the paths of divergence and convergence. Assuming intelligence to be a universal phenomenon, he chose the latter path, and that would make all the difference.[69]

Sagan *believed* in intelligent extraterrestrials. He believed the aliens' civilization would be more advanced than our relatively recent one. And he believed they would be benevolent. Davidson is quite convinced that Sagan had a bona fide "secular faith":

> Carl Sagan, too, believed in superior beings in space, creatures so intelligent, so powerful to resemble gods. They are superior partly

because their civilizations are millions of years old and have developed technologies unimaginable to us. They have evolved far enough to outgrow their warlike ways. And they are benevolent; they will even share the secrets of the cosmos with us, if we'll simply tune in to their radio transmissions. In short, they are all-powerful, all-knowing, all-loving. Is it any wonder that Sagan's first son, science writer Dorion Sagan, scoffs that "the search for extraterrestrial intelligence is a replacement for religion in a secular age"?[70]

We can hardly exaggerate Sagan's optimism about contact with extraterrestrials. He celebrated the possible content of the first alien message we might get, if only we have the wisdom to listen:

> In particular, it is possible that among the first contents of such a message may be detailed prescriptions for the avoidance of technological disaster, for a passage through adolescence to maturity. Perhaps the transmissions from advanced civilizations will describe which pathways of cultural evolution are likely to lead to the stability and longevity of an intelligent species, and which other paths to stagnation or degeneration or disaster.... Perhaps there are straightforward solutions, still undiscovered on Earth, to problems of food shortages, population growth, energy supplies, dwindling resources, pollution and war.[71]

The anticipated alien message, for Sagan, was essentially a "Bible from the sky," addressing what he saw as the great needs of humanity. Davidson even notes that Sagan fretted that the aliens might not be interested in us, that "the aliens would ignore us, that extremely advanced societies might regard us as indifferently as we regard the ants at our feet."[72]

Sagan's quasi-religious hopes are scientific to the degree they could be fulfilled using scientific tools. But despite his own yearnings for a scientific religion, he could never find much of value in conventional religion, even for other people. Chapter 2 of *The Demon-Haunted World*, for example, is virtually a hymn praising the advantages of science over religion. Sagan describes science as "a way of thinking," as "an attempt, largely successful, to understand the world, to get a grip on things, to get hold of ourselves, to steer a safe course." He acknowledges the limitations of science: "Science is far from a perfect instrument of knowledge. It's just the best we have." And it does not provide certainty: "Except in pure mathematics nothing is known for certain.... But the history of science—by far the most successful claim to knowledge accessible to humans—teaches that the most we can hope for is successive improvement in our understanding, learning from our mistakes, an asymptotic approach to the Universe, but with the proviso that absolute certainty will always elude us."[73]

Sagan longed for science to be at the center of the human quest for meaning and purpose, as both the goal and the proper way to reach that goal: "Science is not only compatible with spirituality," he writes, "it is a profound source of spirituality."[74] We agree. We note that science presupposes a powerful human capacity for abstraction, argument, evidence, self-reflection, distinguishing objective from subjective phenomena, critical evaluation of theories, truth-seeking, and more. Furthermore, science demands a profound appreciation for the *value* of truth. These are qualities usually labeled as "spiritual," and we join Sagan in affirming that science demands them and affirms their importance. On the other hand, our remarkable scientific progress is evidence that we *possess* these qualities, all of which transcend the material in a significant and unique way. The transcendent uniqueness of humans in the natural world is shown clearly by the steady progress of science.

But unfortunately Sagan cannot free himself from the false dichotomy that juxtaposes science and religion as incompatible. He strains to pull spiritual realities into his materialistic worldview, to be understood in the same way that we understand protons and electrons. His concept of religion is so deeply flawed that his arguments seem like little more than potshots at straw men. He says, for example, "Religions are tough. Either they make no contentions which are subject to disproof or they quickly redesign doctrine after disproof. The fact that religions can be so shamelessly dishonest, so contemptuous of the intelligence of their adherents, and still flourish does not speak very well for the tough-mindedness of the believers."[75]

This is a common claim by scientists hostile to religion and has a standard twofold response: First, noting Sagan's bitter charge of dishonesty, we call attention to Sagan's shoddy scholarship in promoting the outmoded conflict thesis of Draper and White, a nineteenth-century cliché that no competent scholar accepts today. Sagan charges religion with dishonesty and then immediately proceeds to praise White's articulation of the conflict thesis, strangely unaware that recent scholarship has thoroughly discredited it:[76] "Andrew Dickson White was the intellectual guiding light, founder and first president of Cornell University. He was also the author of an extraordinary book called *The Warfare of Science with Theology in Christendom*."[77] We can excuse Sagan for praising the founder of his university. But praising White's book as "extraordinary" is like praising Marx for his brilliant insights into economics.

Sagan continues to use White's outdated scholarship, ignoring newer sources on the very topics he is discussing. For example, he follows White in

saying, "The aged Galileo was threatened by the Catholic hierarchy with torture because he proclaimed the Earth to move."[78] White wrote:

> There [before the Inquisition], as was so long concealed, but as is now
> fully revealed, he was menaced with torture again and again by ex-
> press order of Pope Urban, and, as is also thoroughly established
> from the trial documents themselves, forced to abjure under threats,
> and subjected to imprisonment by command of the Pope; the In-
> quisition deferring in this whole matter to the papal authority. All the
> long series of attempts made in the supposed interest of the Church to
> mystify these transactions have at last failed. The world knows now
> that Galileo was subjected certainly to indignity, to imprisonment, and
> to threats equivalent to torture.[79]

But what recent scholarship has determined from the relevant documents
is that Galileo was menaced with torture but once, at the very end of the
proceedings, as an intimidating formality to ensure that he did not lie. Nobody
intended to torture him, and most scholars are convinced that Galileo knew
this very well. Moreover, although he was technically condemned to prison, he
did not spend a single day in prison, not during the trial and not afterward: The
prison sentence was immediately commuted to house arrest, first for six
months in the palace of his friend the bishop of Siena, and then in his villa near
Florence.[80] White's account of the Galileo affair is, to say the least, misleading.

The second, more systematic, objection to Sagan's version of the conflict
thesis is its false assumption that science and religion are comparable enterprises, competing for the same goals and appropriately compared on the same
grounds. Science, says Sagan, makes accurate predictions, is reliable, has an
observable record of success, accepts the facts, and is willing and able to discover its failings and limitations. Science takes account of the magnificence
and intricacy of the universe. Alas, says Sagan, we cannot find these qualities in
religion.[81] But, as he repeatedly observes, science deals with natural patterns
that can be submitted to experiments, providing reliable methods of investigation that are simply not applicable to the investigation of spiritual realities
that transcend the material world. The success of science is largely due to the
self-limitation of its subject; the more limited the scope, the more successful
the science. Outside those limits are deeper dimensions of the human experience. Rational inquiry is also possible and desirable as we try to understand
those dimensions, but we must now take into account that mysterious human
freedom that doesn't lend itself to simple replication in the laboratory.

Scientific thinking is a search for truth. And scientific method entails a
rigorous discipline in collecting data in prescribed ways, and reflecting upon

that data in equally prescribed ways. Scientists seek to explain the natural world by reducing it to a few simple laws of nature, the appropriate application of reductionism. Sagan aptly observes:

> Of course, we may make mistakes in applying a reductionist programme to science. There may be aspects which, for all we know, are not reducible to a few comparatively simple laws. But in the light of the findings of the last few centuries, it seems foolish to complain about reductionism. It is not a deficiency but one of the chief triumphs of science. And, it seems to me, its findings are perfectly consonant with many religions (although it does not *prove* their validity). Why should a few simple laws of Nature explain so much and hold sway throughout this vast Universe? Isn't this just what you might expect from a Creator of the Universe? Why should some religious people oppose the reductionist programme in science, except out of some misplaced love of mysticism?[82]

Such reflections clarify that the dichotomy opposing science and religion, nature and God, is mistaken. If we conceive of God in the most traditional way as the source of all being, we do not see scientific knowledge of nature competing with the Creator of those laws, to see which can provide the best explanation.

We go one step further. Sagan correctly notes that the idea of an ordered cosmos is a necessary presupposition for the entire scientific enterprise. He correctly criticizes ancient religious worldviews where capricious deities governed the world whimsically, notions that hindered the development of science. We add that the Judeo-Christian worldview was completely different, even opposed to those pagan ideas. It has been argued that modern science was born in the Christian West because there existed a pervasive Christian intellectual matrix that, during many centuries, led thinkers to see the world as the rational ordered work of an omniscient and omnipotent Creator who also created humans and endowed them with the faculty of knowing the world. This idea is present in numerous authors and has been developed at length by Stanley L. Jaki, although not without criticism.[83] Surely modern science needed geniuses that could combine theory and experience, mathematics and experimentation. But those pioneers of modern science, like Copernicus, Kepler, Galileo, and Newton—all deeply religious in various ways—testify to the relevance of the Christian cultural matrix for the birth of modern science.

By the time Carl Sagan would put pen to paper in the latter half of the twentieth century the scientific community had changed dramatically. No longer were scientists typically religious and those who were tended to keep their science separate from their religion. The scientific community had secularized, although it certainly was not antireligious. Furthermore, especially in America, millions of fundamentalists were rejecting much of modern science, following pseudo-scientific gurus offering specious creation science or intelligent design alternatives. Many scientists, of course, were still religious, and many Christians were not rejecting science, but Sagan's professional career overlapped the ascendancy of a strong religious coalition opposing science.

Sagan shared with the religious founders of science a deep and abiding respect for truth and objectivity and humility in the face of nature's secrets. He also had a deep faith in the rational order of nature, although he simply took that for granted rather than locating it in the rationality of God, as Kepler and Newton would have done. Near the end of his life he came to appreciate the reverence religious people had for the creation and he partnered with religious groups to help mobilize these sentiments on behalf of the environment.

Sagan remains relevant, and his ideas and books still circulate widely. In 2006, a decade after his death, a collection of interviews with him was published. One of them, reprinted from *U.S. Catholic*, "God and Carl Sagan: Is the Cosmos Big Enough for Both of Them?"[84] reiterates the point we made earlier that the religious hostility to Sagan derives more from his great influence than the stridency of his critiques of religion. This is in contrast to, say, Richard Dawkins, whose assaults on religion are more aggressive. Nevertheless, Sagan was very much a materialist himself and certainly made it clear in his writing that religion offers little of value in the development of a mature worldview. Fortunately, though, he put far more energy into promoting science than demeaning religion.

5

Understanding a
Pointless Universe

Steven Weinberg

Steven Weinberg is one of the most distinguished figures in contemporary physics. In 1979 he won the Nobel Prize in physics for
groundbreaking work in showing how the weak nuclear interaction
related to electromagnetism. This "electroweak" theory, as it is known,
was developed in the early 1960s in collaboration with Sheldon Glashow and Abdus Salam, who shared the Nobel Prize with Weinberg.

Unifying the weak and electromagnetic interactions was a critically important contribution to physics at the most fundamental
level, representing real progress in the search for a theory that would
bring all of physics under a single explanatory paradigm. Shortly
before winning his Nobel Prize, in 1977, Weinberg published the
best-selling and now-classic *The First Three Minutes*, describing the
development of the universe immediately after the big bang. He was
drawn into considerable public controversy over the Superconducting
Super Collider (SSC), conceived as the largest laboratory of subatomic
particles in the world. Containing a 10-foot-wide underground tun-
nel forming an astonishing 83-kilometer-long oval ring, the collider
was approved by the White House in 1987, and construction began
shortly thereafter, only to be halted when the House of Representatives voted in 1993 to terminate the program. Prior to this decision
Weinberg had watched in dismay as sentiment turned against the
$8 billion project that was so close to his heart. His 1992 book
Dreams of a Final Theory, where he discusses the reach of physical
science and also his views on philosophy and God, was an attempt to

restore flagging enthusiasm for the supercollider. A good essayist, he has made contributions to other contemporary cultural and political issues, collecting some of them in a 2001 book titled *Facing Up*.

Weinberg's writing is a model of uncluttered clarity—sober, direct, well-suited to popularizing science, and very sharp in its polemics. He loves the classical works of literature, painting, history, and music, and comes across in print as a Renaissance man. His attitude toward God is negative, even harsh, and he is well-known as a public opponent of religion. In this arena he is equally direct and uncompromising.

A Nobel's Career

Steven Weinberg was born in New York City on May 3, 1933, to a family of Jewish immigrants recently arrived from Europe. Much of his mother's family remained in Germany and died in the Holocaust. His father worked as a stenographer in the tribunals, or courts. He grew up in the Bronx, near Yankee Stadium (where Lou Gehrig was finishing his distinguished career), but was never passionate about sports.

He studied in the Bronx High School of Science. "My early inclination toward science received encouragement from my father, and by the time I was 15 or 16 my interests had focused on theoretical physics," he says.[1] He began to excel in physics, inspired by a popular book written by Sir James Jeans, explaining that nature is based on simple but powerful laws. Theoretical physics would remain Weinberg's lifelong passion.

Weinberg's academic career started at the universities of Cornell and Princeton: "I received my undergraduate degree from Cornell in 1954, and then went for a year of graduate study to the Institute for Theoretical Physics in Copenhagen (now the Niels Bohr Institute). There, with the help of David Frisch and Gunnar Källén, I began to do research in physics. I then returned to the U.S. to complete my graduate studies at Princeton. My Ph.D. thesis, with Sam Treiman as adviser, was on the application of renormalization theory to the effects of strong interactions in weak interaction processes,"[2] an attempt to eliminate the infinities plaguing theories of the nuclear interactions.

Weinberg did postdoctoral work at Columbia, Berkeley, Harvard, and MIT. After receiving his Ph.D. from Princeton in 1957, he worked first at Columbia and then at Berkeley from 1959 to 1966. He met his wife Louise, now a law professor, at Cornell, and they were married in 1954. Their daughter, Elizabeth, was born in Berkeley in 1963.

While at Berkeley, Weinberg investigated a variety of topics, but late in 1965 he began focusing on what physicists call strong interactions—the forces that act within the nuclei of atoms—and symmetry breaking, a powerful way to study strong interactions. From 1966 to 1969 he was Loeb Lecturer at Harvard and then a visiting professor at MIT, where he accepted a professorship in 1969.

While visiting MIT in 1967, his work turned in the direction of the unification of the weak and electromagnetic interactions, the work eventually recognized with a Nobel Prize. In 1973 he became the Higgins Professor of Physics at Harvard. Finally, in 1982 he became the Josey Regental Professor of Science at the University of Texas at Austin.

In addition to his scientific work, Weinberg also has a remarkably rich grasp of military history. His expertise in the subject grew to the point where he was invited to publish a review essay in 2003 in the *New York Review of Books*. The physics Nobel laureate reviewed twenty books on wars from antiquity to World War II, highlighting the insidious danger of *"institutionalized vainglory"* as a motive for war.[3] He has also written on a broad cross section of other political topics.

Weinberg has received many awards in addition to his Nobel Prize. He has honorary doctorates from several universities, including the University of Chicago, the City University of New York, the University of Rochester, Yale University, the University of Barcelona, and Columbia University. In 1968 he was elected to the American Academy of Arts and Sciences, and in 1972 to the National Academy of Sciences. He was elected to the American Philosophical Society and the Royal Society of London as a Foreign Honorary Member. In 1991 he was awarded the National Medal of Science. The list could go on.

The greatest honor for a scientist, of course, is the Nobel Prize. Weinberg's work leading to the Nobel was on electroweak theory, a unification of two of the four interactions in nature—the weak nuclear and electromagnetic interactions. On October 15, 1979, the Royal Swedish Academy of Sciences issued the news. On December 8 he received the award in Stockholm, in the presence of Sweden's Royal Family and a large public audience. Professor Bengt Nagel of the Royal Academy of Sciences began his presentation speech as follows: "This year's Nobel Prize in Physics is shared equally between Sheldon Glashow, Abdus Salam and Steven Weinberg for their contributions to the theory of the unified weak and electromagnetic interaction between elementary particles, including *inter alia* the prediction of the weak neutral current."[4]

The Basic Forces of Nature

Nagel's speech included a long, detailed account of the history and significance of the work of the new Nobel Prize winners: "Important advances in
physics," he said,

> often consist in relating apparently unconnected phenomena to a
> common cause. A classical example is Newton's introduction of the
> gravitational force to explain the fall of the apple and the motion of the
> moon around the earth. In the 19th century it was found that elec-
> tricity and magnetism are really two aspects of one and the same
> force, the electromagnetic interaction between charges. Electromag-
> netism, with the electron playing the leading part and the photon—
> the electromagnetic quantum of light—as the swift messenger,
> dominates technology and our everyday life.[5]

The two examples were carefully chosen, representing the two forces known and
studied scientifically prior to the twentieth century: gravity and electromagnetism. The most important theories in the physical sciences during that era were
Newtonian mechanics, explaining the motion of bodies, including gravity, and
Maxwell's theory of electromagnetism, explaining and unifying electrical and
magnetic phenomena. These theories, and the study of heat and energy in
nineteenth-century thermodynamics, are often called "classical physics."

The first decades of the twentieth century have been called "Thirty Years
That Shook Physics."[6] Entirely new and puzzling visions of nature opened up
to physicists, from Einstein's relativity to quantum theory. Radioactivity was
discovered, and the atom was probed to reveal a complex internal structure,
with electrons buzzing about an unimaginably dense nucleus. Two entirely
new forces—or *interactions*, as they came to be called—were discovered operating within the nucleus: the weak interaction to explain radioactivity and
the strong interaction to explain how the positively charged—and thus mutually repulsive—protons could be packed so tightly in the nucleus.

Gravitation and electromagnetism, the forces of classical physics, are both
long-range. But the two newly discovered nuclear interactions act only at the
astonishingly small distances encountered inside the nucleus of the atom,
typically a trillionth of a millimeter. The strong force, for example, has been
compared to "glue," binding things tightly if they are in contact, but having no
power to "pull" across any distances.

Physicists thus know four fundamental forces or interactions in the natural world: gravitation, electromagnetism, and the strong and weak nuclear

forces. While the first three seem obviously important in terms of what they "do," the fourth could seem quite irrelevant. This is not the case, however, and the press release from the Academy of Sciences highlighted several of the significant roles played by the weak force, some of which are even relevant for the very existence of human beings on earth. The energy of the sun, for example, on which life depends, is produced when hydrogen fuses into helium in nuclear reactions occurring in the interior of the sun. The critically important transformation of hydrogen into deuterium is caused by the weak interaction. Without the weak interaction, the sun would not shine. The *intensity* of the weak interaction also has important consequences. A much stronger interaction would make the life span of the sun too short for life to evolve. There are also practical applications. Radioactive elements used in medicine and technology, for example, get their radioactivity from the weak interaction. And carbon-14 dating, used commonly to ascertain the age of organic archaeological remains, is based on the weak interaction.

Scientists constantly seek new theories to explain new phenomena, and the weak interaction was no exception. The great Italian physicist Enrico Fermi, who received the Nobel Prize in 1938, developed the first theory of the weak interaction in 1933. And, although Fermi's theory was improved in 1957, it remained unsatisfactory until the 1960s.

A Brilliant Idea

Weinberg explains the inspiration for his Nobel Prize–winning theory of the weak interaction. It was 1967. "I was feeling strung out. I had taken a leave of absence from my regular professorship at Berkeley a year earlier so that my wife could study at Harvard Law School. We had just gone through the trauma of moving from one rented house in Cambridge to another, and I had taken over the responsibility of getting our daughter to nursery school, playgrounds, and all that. More to the point, I was also stuck in my work as a theoretical physicist."[7]

He was then a visiting professor at MIT and had his big idea driving to work one day. Perplexed by the strong interaction, he suddenly realized that the theory he was using could be applied, instead, to the weak interaction:

> For the previous two years, I had made progress in understanding what physicists call the strong interactions—the forces that hold particles together inside atomic nuclei. Some of my calculations had even been confirmed by experiments. But now these ideas seemed to be leading to nonsense . . . suddenly on my way to MIT (on October 2,

1967, as near as I can remember), I realized that there was nothing wrong with the sort of theory on which I had been working. I had
the right answer, but I had been working on the wrong problem. The
mathematics I had been playing with had nothing to do with the
strong interactions, but it gave a beautiful description of a different
kind of force, known as the weak interaction. This is the force that
is responsible, among other things, for the first step in the chain of
nuclear reactions that produces the heat of the sun. . . . I got safely to
my office and started to work out the details of the theory. Where
before I had been going around in circles, now everything was easy.
Two weeks later, I mailed a short article on the electroweak theory to
Physical Review Letters, a journal widely read by physicists. The theory was proved to be consistent in 1971. Some new effects predicted
by the theory were detected experimentally in 1973. By 1978, it was
clear that measurements of those effects agreed precisely with the
theory. And in 1979, I received the Nobel Prize in physics, along with
Sheldon Glashow and Abdus Salam, who had done independent
work on the electroweak theory. I have since learned that the paper I
wrote in October 1967 has become the most cited article in the history of elementary particle physics.[8]

Weinberg's work was in *elementary particle physics*, an area plagued by
unmanageable infinite quantities. Sometimes these infinities can be avoided
by a process called "renormalization." Weinberg's new theory had infinities.
Fortunately, a Dutch physicist proved in 1971 that the Glashow-Weinberg-
Salam electroweak theory could be renormalized. This is what Weinberg
means when he says that "the theory was proved to be consistent in 1971." He
tells us the story:

In 1971 I received a preprint from a young graduate student at
the University of Utrecht named Gerard 't Hooft, in which he claimed
to show that this theory actually had solved the problem of the
infinities. . . . At first I was not convinced by 't Hooft's paper. I had
never heard of him, and the paper used a mathematical method developed by Feynman that I had previously distrusted. A little later
I heard that the theorist Ben Lee had taken up 't Hooft's ideas and was
trying to get the same results using more conventional mathematical methods. I knew Ben Lee and had great respect for him—if he took
't Hooft's work seriously, then so would I. . . . After that I took a more
careful look at what 't Hooft had done and saw that he had indeed
found the key to showing that the infinities would cancel.[9]

As it turned out, Weinberg's theory of the weak interaction also applied to the electromagnetic interaction. The theory unifies both interactions, as if they were two aspects of what came to be called the "electroweak" theory. This was a major breakthrough, showing how two of the four known interactions relate to each other. Physicists are eager to find a theory to unify all four of the interactions, an explanation that would provide a better, more comprehensive, understanding of the natural world.

A unified theory would also shed light on the origin and evolution of the universe. If we trace our expanding universe back to the "beginning," we arrive at a point where all the matter and energy of the universe is concentrated in a state of enormous density and temperature. At those extremely high energies, physicists believe that the four interactions were indistinguishable, merged into some kind of "superforce." When the big bang initiated the expansion of the universe, each of the four interactions broke off from the superforce. First, gravity appeared, then the strong interaction. Finally, the weak and electromagnetic interactions separated. All this took very little time, considerably less than a trillionth of a second. If physicists could reconstruct these early stages of the universe, they would understand much more about the fundamental nature of the physical world.

The electroweak theory predicted the existence of *weak neutral currents*, discovered in 1973 and providing dramatic empirical confirmation of the theory. Solid theories in physics must have measurable consequences, and Weinberg's theory passed the test with flying colors.

Will You Return the Nobel Prize?

The Nobel Prize in physics is rarely awarded for theoretical work unless such work is supported by completed experiments. For the electroweak theory, some physicists reportedly joked to the Nobel Prize winners: And what if your theory is refuted by experiments? Will you return your Nobel Prize?

The electroweak theory in 1979 did have some experimental support, which probably played a role in the prize deliberations. Nagel explained in his speech that the theory predicts "there should exist a new kind of weak interaction. It was formerly assumed that weak processes could occur only in connection with a change of identity of the electron to neutrino (or vice versa); such a process is said to proceed by a charged current, since the particle changes its charge. The theory implies that there should also be processes connected with a neutral current in which the neutrino—or else the electron—acts without changing identity. Experiments in the 70's have fully confirmed these predictions of the theory."[10]

This new interaction was named "weak neutral current," and its experimental observation was a landmark in the development of contemporary physics. In 1974, Weinberg published an article on theories of unification in *Scientific American*, reporting that weak neutral currents were within the range of available experiments, although he was cautious:

> For some years these neutral current processes, as they are called, remained at the edge of detectability, and many physicists doubted their existence. Within the past year, however, evidence for neutral-current processes has at last begun to appear. A pan-European collaboration involving some 55 investigators from seven different institutions, working at the European Organization for Nuclear Research (CERN) in Geneva, has found two events in which muon-type antineutrinos are scattered by electrons and several hundred events in which they are scattered by protons or neutrons. Such scattering events can apparently be explained only by the exchange of a neutral intermediate vector boson, or Z particle, and are therefore direct evidence for a new kind of weak interaction. Moreover, the inferred collision rates agree well with rates predicted by the new theory. An American consortium working at the National Accelerator Laboratory in Batavia, Ill., and another group working at the Argonne National Laboratory have apparently also found neutral-current events.... The existence of neutral-current processes is not yet definitely established.[11]

Shortly thereafter, the team from the Fermi National Accelerator Laboratory in Batavia, Illinois, published an article in *Scientific American* describing the experimental detection of weak neutral currents. They highlighted the relevance of unification theories: "Progress in the understanding of nature has often come through the recognition that seemingly diverse phenomena have a common origin. The classic example of such a unification was provided in the 19th century when electricity, magnetism, light and radio waves were all found to be linked by the equations of electromagnetism formulated by James Clerk Maxwell. We may now be on the verge of a comparable unification in the domain of elementary-particles physics."[12] Another result of interest was published in the summer of 1978, reporting an experiment at Stanford's SLAC electron accelerator, where an effect from a direct interplay between the electromagnetic and weak parts of the unified interaction was observed.[13]

The electroweak theory impressed the physics community with its remarkably successful predictions, the hallmark of the most robust and reliable theories. In addition to predicting the weak neutral currents mentioned above, it predicted three new particles necessary to carry the electroweak interaction.

These particles—the "weak vector bosons"—were called W^+, W^-, and Z^0 and acted as carriers of the weak interaction, just as the photon "carries" or communicates the electromagnetic interaction between charged particles. While the photon has no mass, the electroweak theory predicted a large mass for the W and Z particles. (The predicted mass was about one hundred proton masses. Large masses for carrier particles are correlated with short ranges for the interactions they carry.)

In 1979 no particle accelerator had enough power to produce these particles. But a team of more than one hundred physicists at CERN, directed by the Italian physicist Carlo Rubbia, was searching for them. (Physicists "search" for particles by trying to design an experiment in which they "appear.") Their work was challenging and systematic and was performed on the world's best equipment, the 27-kilometer-long CERN accelerator, 100 meters beneath the border between France and Switzerland. In a 1982 *Scientific American* article, Rubbia's group described their work:

> The unified electroweak theory is about to be put to a decisive experimental test. A crucial prediction of the theory is the existence of three massive particles called intermediate vector bosons (also known as weakons). The world's first particle accelerator with enough energy to create such particles has recently been completed at the European Organization for Nuclear Research (CERN) in Geneva.... The colliding-beam machine has just completed its preliminary runs and is scheduled to resume operating next month.... If the intermediate vector bosons exist and if they have the properties attributed to them by the electroweak theory, they should be detected soon. They are currently the most prized trophies in all physics, and their discovery would culminate a search that began more than 40 years ago.[14]

This was an extremely risky prediction, characteristic of the highest-quality science. Physicists knew exactly the results that should be obtained before they started looking. The experiment would have the last word.

CERN and the Vatican

CERN is known for remarkable results in both science and technology. In 1989, for example, CERN scientist Tim Berners-Lee invented the World Wide Web, originally developed to enable information sharing between scientists working all over the world. But CERN's primary research agenda is high-energy physics, the search for the most basic components of the material world. The experiments are often very similar: Two beams of subatomic particles are accelerated to extremely high energies in opposite directions, and then redirected to collide. Sophisticated instruments detect the various and complex results of the collision, including the creation of particles that simply don't appear at lower energies. Physicists carefully design the experiments to test important theories.

CERN is a magical place. Its remarkable experiments create exotic materials such as new particles and the mysterious antimatter so popular in science fiction. Perhaps it is not surprising that most people have encountered CERN in a work of fiction, rather than a scientific journal.

In June 2005, an illustration of a spaceplane appeared on CERN's main Web page. The caption read: "Does CERN own an X-33 spaceplane? Find out what's fact and what's fiction in Dan Brown's *Angels and Demons*." Brown's signature mix of entangled fact and fiction motivated CERN to post a questionnaire whose first question was: "Does CERN exist?"

Brown's best-seller tells the story of a secret society out to destroy the Vatican with a bomb made from antimatter stolen from CERN. Brown's scenario sounded plausible enough that CERN felt obliged to clarify the issue of antimatter—as well as their own existence!—and what they were doing with it. They noted, not surprisingly, that the *Angels and Demons* scenario is pure fiction. Antimatter cannot be used as an energy source. Unlike solar energy, coal, or oil, antimatter does not occur in nature, and every particle, such as those Rubbia's group were making for the electroweak experiment, required far more energy for its creation that it could give back during annihilation.

Prior to Brown's imaginative work, the only known link between CERN and the Vatican was the far less ominous visit of Pope John Paul II on June 15, 1982.

CERN does indeed exist. It is a scientific facility employing thousands of people; it is an international collaboration of European countries that, at the beginning of the twenty-first century, leads the world in high-energy physics. CERN was developed to achieve European preeminence in "big" science; this was secured in 1984, when Rubbia and Simon Van der Meer shared the physics Nobel Prize for their contributions to the project that led to the discovery of the particles that carry the weak interaction.

Weinberg had no need to return his Nobel Prize.

The First Three Minutes

Weinberg's first popular science book, *The First Three Minutes*, published in 1977, became a best-seller and a classic. It originated in a talk at Harvard in

1973 that Erwin Glikes, the president of Basic Books, suggested be turned into a book. Weinberg recalls: "At first I was not enthusiastic about the idea. . . . My work has been much more concerned with the physics of the very small. . . . However, I found that I could not stop thinking about the idea of a book on the early universe. What could be more interesting than the problem of Genesis?"[15]

The book is a passionate account of the discoveries leading to the modern big-bang picture of the universe's origin: "The present book is concerned with the early universe, and in particular with the new understanding of the early universe that has grown out of the discovery of the cosmic microwave radiation background in 1965."[16] This discovery transformed cosmology. In 1965 two theories, the *steady state*, implying an uncreated and basically unchanging universe, and the *big bang*, which looks to a point of origin for a steadily evolving universe, had been in competition. Background radiation was a specific prediction of the big-bang theory, and its discovery in 1965 by Arno Penzias and Robert Wilson confirmed the big bang, laid the steady-state theory to rest, and won them a Nobel Prize.

The idea of the big bang emerged in the 1920s, when Edwin Hubble determined that the galaxies are moving away from each other. If the universe is presently expanding, this means that, going back in time, the universe is converging and we should find an epoch where all the matter and energy of the universe were concentrated in a state of enormous density and temperature. After the big-bang event, radiation was emitted and then, much later, discovered by Penzias and Wilson—a kind of fossil of the early universe, spread everywhere and observable also from any place. Weinberg shows, as in a kind of movie, the sequence of the events in the first three minutes of the universe.

The First Three Minutes is a masterpiece of popular science praised by academics and the general public. Its most famous and oft-quoted statement appears on the last page:

> It is almost irresistible for humans to believe that we have some special relation to the universe, that human life is not just a more-or-less farcical outcome of a chain of accidents reaching back to the first three minutes, but we are somehow built from the beginning. . . . It is very hard to realize that this all is just a tiny part of an overwhelmingly hostile universe. It is even harder to realize that this present universe has evolved from an unspeakably unfamiliar early condition, and faces a future extinction of endless cold or intolerable heat. The more the universe seems comprehensible, the more it also seems pointless.[17]

After this infamous sentence, the book ends by suggesting we can still create meaning for our lives:

> But if there is no solace in the fruits of our research, there is at least some consolation in the research itself. Men and women are not content to comfort themselves with tales of gods and giants, or to confine their thoughts to the daily affairs of life; they also build telescopes and satellites and accelerators, and sit at their desks for endless hours working out the meaning of the data they gather. The effort to understand the universe is one of the very few things that lifts human life a little above the level of farce, and gives it some of the grace of tragedy.[18]

Weinberg's famous statement is mysterious. What does he mean by "The more the universe seems comprehensible, the more it also seems pointless"? He certainly means that the progress of science has not revealed a Creator with a cosmic plan for our lives. But would this have been a reasonable expectation? Why should we expect to uncover a meaning or a plan for our lives in the laws of science? Is one located there?

Modern Cosmologists

In 1990, Alan Lightman and Roberta Brawer published interviews with twenty-seven cosmologists, including Weinberg, who commented on his famous statement: "I don't think I expressed myself exactly the way I should have, but I think I'm going to leave a more detailed explanation for something else I write.... If you say things are pointless, you have to ask, 'Well, what point were you looking for?' And that's what's needed, I think, to be explained. What kind of point would have been there that might have made it *not* pointless. That's what I really would have to explain."[19]

At the end of most of the interviews, Lightman and Brawer asked the distinguished cosmologists about Weinberg's statement. The answers varied greatly. Sir Fred Hoyle says we should know much more if we want to face that issue. Allan Sandage says Weinberg's statement is silly, and he prefers to believe in purpose because otherwise you become a Nietzschean nihilist, which is even more pointless. Gérard de Vaucouleurs agrees with Weinberg but is keeping an open mind. Maarten Schmidt sees the issue in reverse, finding the universe ever more incomprehensible. Wallace Sargent says he has zero religious impulses and sees no reason why he should expect the universe to have a point. Dennis Sciama finds the question inscrutable. Sir Martin Rees likes to think that life may spread from earth to other parts of the universe, and if life exists elsewhere, there is even less reason to believe the universe is pointless. Charles Misner is impressed with the beauty and intelligibility of the universe and says that in religion there are serious ideas like the existence of God and the brotherhood of man.[20]

Weinberg's statement is perceived as a pronouncement about the existence of God and a divine plan. To the question "Have you ever thought about whether the universe has a point or not?" Marc Davis answers: "I try not to think about the question too much, because all too often I agree with Steven Weinberg, and it's rather depressing. Philosophically, I see no arguments against his attitude, that we certainly don't see a point. To answer in the alternative sense really requires you to invoke the principle of God, I think."[21] Not everyone agrees, however. Stephen Hawking disagrees with Weinberg because he feels proud of our achievement in understanding better and better the order of the universe, but he does not mention God in this context.[22] Not surprisingly, Don Page, a colleague of Hawking and a practicing Christian, responds differently:

> Yes, I would say that there's definitely a purpose. I don't know what *all* of the purposes are, but I think one of them was for God to create man to have fellowship with God. . . . I do believe the Bible is God's revealed word to us, so I think that's one purpose that has been revealed to us. . . . In some sense, the physical laws seem to be analogous to the grammar and the language that God chose to use. . . . It's a bit like if you tried to analyze the grammatical structure of some of Shakespeare's writing, but you didn't look at all at what the plays meant, or what the story was there. There can be these different descriptions on different levels.[23]

A well-known statement with such varied and complex interpretations is truly an oracular pronouncement. We can at least know what Weinberg meant, however, if we take into account explanations he has provided of his personal philosophy.

Weinberg's Personal Agenda

In 1990, Weinberg contributed a personal statement to an edited volume titled *Living Philosophies*. He addressed the question, How should we decide what we ought to believe? He expressed doubts about how much control we can exercise on our beliefs, adding that we ought to follow something like the methods of science. Of his beliefs, he noted that his experience as a physicist led him to believe that there is order in the universe. Finally, he explained what he did not believe: "It would be wonderful if, in uncovering the principles underlying the universe, we had discovered ourselves; if we had found that a grand cosmic drama was going on, in which human beings play a starring role. We haven't. Nothing that scientists have discovered suggests to me that human beings have any personal place in the laws of physics or in the initial conditions of the universe."[24] Weinberg comments that the "anthropic principle" *might* be an exception, but he rules it out, saying that even if the laws or constants of nature are so specific that they enable our existence, we are still only a part of a mega-universe, and there can be an infinitely large number of other universes hostile to life.

He also took this occasion to clarify the ending of *The First Three Minutes*:

> At the end of my book *The First Three Minutes*, I allowed myself to remark that "the more the universe seems comprehensible, the more it also seems pointless." This one sentence got me into more trouble with readers than anything else I've ever written, but all I meant was that if we search in the discoveries of science for some points to our lives, we will not find it. This does not mean that we can't find things that give point to our lives. If science can't provide us with values, neither can it invalidate them.[25]

But if that's all, why so much fuss? That we will not find the meaning of our lives in the laws of physics or chemistry or astrophysics or cosmology is a platitude. Why would a Nobel laureate write this at the end of a popular book? Why would other people bother to discuss and interpret such a statement? We wonder whether Weinberg's question is really meaningful. How could we find a cosmic drama, with us in starring roles, in the discoveries of physics? The search for this kind of meaning is outside science. Many people do actually believe that a divine plan exists, but they do not expect science to discover it.

Weinberg included his contribution to *Living Philosophies* in his 2001 book *Facing Up*. In the introduction Weinberg says plainly:

> Toward the close of the essay I had a little to say about what I do believe, or really, as I see in rereading it, about what I do not believe. I do not believe in a cosmic plan in which human beings have any especial place, or in any system of values other than the ones we make up for ourselves. I ended with a description of our world as a stage, onto which we have stumbled with no script to follow.... But the tragedy is not in the script; the tragedy is that there is no script.[26]

We note Weinberg's clarity. But we also wonder what all this has to do with science.

Weinberg apparently admits two different, even contradictory, positions. On the one hand, he says science neither provides nor invalidates values. On the other, he says he does not believe in a preordained plan and adds that scientific discoveries offer no hint that such a plan exists. He appears to be implicating science in problems that, as he himself acknowledges, have nothing to do with it. But the turmoil provoked by the last paragraphs of *The First Three Minutes* arises from the impression that he is mixing his scientific prestige with his personal unbelief and thus trespassing the legitimate borders of authentic science.

Big Science and Wider Issues

Weinberg's second popular book, *Dreams of a Final Theory*, published in 1992, defended the Superconductor Super Collider (SSC), a huge subatomic particles facility containing an 83-kilometer-long oval accelerator. Named Texatron for its Texas location, the SSC's estimated cost was $8 billion, and the facility would have made the United States the world leader in high-energy physics.

Formal research and development on the SSC started in 1983. In 1986, *Scientific American* published an article on the SSC, fictitiously set in 1995:

> The year is 1995. A pastoral landscape or farmland or prairie gives almost no hint that a tunnel, large enough to walk through and curved into a ring some 52 miles around, lies buried below the surface. Inside the tunnel there is a small tramway for maintaining two cryogenic pipelines, each about two feet in diameter. Within each pipeline is a much smaller, evacuated tube that carries a beam of protons, which are kept in course by powerful superconducting magnets surrounding the tube. With every circuit of the ring the energy of the protons in the two beam pipes is boosted by a pulse of radio waves; in 15 minutes the protons are accelerated around the ring in opposite directions more than three million times. Suddenly electromagnetic gates are opened and the beam paths are made to cross. Pairs of protons collide, and some of the energy of the collision can be transferred at a rate that far exceeds the instantaneous output of all the power plants in the earth into a region whose diameter is 100,000 times smaller than the diameter of a proton. There, for a time so brief that it is to the second what the second is to

100,000 times the age of the universe, we shall have a glimpse of the universe at the moment of creation. . . . It is remarkable that such a vision is well within the reach of twentieth-century technology.[27]

A presidential decision to build the SSC was made in January 1987, and a site selection process was initiated. A total of forty-three proposals were received, and seven were selected for further review. The Ellis County, Texas, site was announced as the preferred site in November 1988, leading to the creation of the SSC laboratory in January 1989.

Many scientists and engineers relocated to Texas to construct the SSC. A staff of more than two thousand people, including more than 250 foreign scientists and engineers from thirty-eight countries, was assembled.

But in 1993 the U.S. House of Representatives halted the project after 14 miles of tunneling and $2 billion. In 1994 John Horgan noted in *Scientific American* that future high-energy physics experiments now relied mainly on the upgrading of the CERN facility.[28]

Debates about the SSC emerged, with Weinberg in their midst. His 1992 *Dreams of a Final Theory* appeared at an opportune moment: Funding for the SSC had been cut off by a June vote but restored in August. Nobody knew what was going to happen to the SSC. In the prologue Weinberg wrote: "This is not a book about the Super Collider. But the debate over the project has forced me in public talks and in testimony before Congress to try to explain what we are trying to accomplish in our studies of elementary particles."[29] The last chapter dealt with the SSC, and the edition we quote also contains an afterword, "The Super Collider, One Year Later," written after the project was halted. The rest of the book deals with the search for a *final theory*, a complete explanation of the constitution of matter. This lofty goal was the rationale for the expense of the SSC.

Dreams of a Final Theory pulled Weinberg into a broad range of issues. Later on he wrote, "Then in the 1980s I started to speak and write in defense of spending on research in science, and in particular on the Superconducting Super Collider, a large and controversial facility for research in elementary particle physics. I found that I had a taste for controversy, and I began to accept invitations to write and speak on wider issues—on the follies that I found in the attitudes toward science of many sociologists, philosophers, and cultural critics, and on the ancient tension between science and religion."[30]

No longer would Weinberg's oracular pronouncements be confined to an enigmatic paragraph closing a book. Inviting controversy, the particle physicist from New York proved himself a talented polemicist. *Dreams of a Final Theory* contains full chapters on philosophy and, surprisingly, the existence of God.

What about God?

Weinberg calls himself "an unreligious American Jew."[31] In the *Dreams* chapter on God, he begins by quoting a psalm of David: "The heavens declare the glory of God; and the firmament showeth his handiwork." Since that time, however, Weinberg continues, the stars have lost their wonder and are now explained by science. He concludes quite dramatically: "The stars tell us nothing more or less about the glory of God than do the stones on the ground around us."[32] His argument has a familiar theme: Scientific progress has superseded ancient theological explanations; the world has been "demystified" and "disenchanted." Scientific progress has erased all evidence of the hand of God acting in nature, and God is not even to be found in the beauty and depth of science itself.[33]

Weinberg concedes a novel role to the "final theory":

> If there were anything we could discover in nature that *would* give us some special insight into the handiwork of God, it would have to be the final laws of nature. Knowing these laws, we would have in our possession the book of rules that governs stars and stones and everything else. So it is natural that Stephen Hawking should refer to the laws of nature as "the mind of God." . . . Whatever one's religion or lack of it, it is an irresistible metaphor to speak of the final laws of nature in terms of the mind of God.[34]

But can the laws of nature bear this weight? Technically, they are not even laws; they are our statement of the regularities we have discovered in nature. "The mind of God" is a seductive, even irresistible metaphor for mathematical physicists, but we must keep in mind, before we ask too much of it, that it is a metaphor. There are very few mathematical physicists in the world, and it is unlikely that God chose a revelatory scheme that only they could understand. In contrast, many people have no difficulty finding God through the contemplation of nature. Others see God in the power of self-organization revealed by contemporary science, or in the marvels of the biological world.

Weinberg says the final laws of nature are the best place to discover the hand of God. But then he argues that even here we do not find a personal God: "Will we find an interested God in the final laws of nature? There seems something almost absurd in asking this question."[35] He is right: He has posed an absurd question. He has fabricated a straw man and proceeded to demolish it.

At this point, Weinberg brings out his heavy artillery to show that, contrary to what religious people may think, scientific progress demonstrates the steady marginalization of God. The world is being demystified, first in physics, then in biology:

> All our experience throughout the history of science has tended . . . toward a chilling impersonality in the laws of nature. The first great step along this path was the demystification of the heavens [he refers to Copernicus, Bruno, Kepler, Newton, Hubble]. . . . Life, too, has been demystified. . . . Most important of all were Charles Darwin and Alfred Russel Wallace, who showed how the wonderful capabilities of living things could evolve through natural selection with no outside plan or guidance. The process of demystification has accelerated in this century, in the continued success of biochemistry and molecular biology in explaining the workings of living things.[36]

What has all this to do with the final laws of nature? Weinberg's rather simple argument goes like this: The best chance of finding God is in the final (and as yet undiscovered) laws of nature; the more science progresses, the less relevant God becomes; therefore we will not find God anywhere.

This argument is troubled. First, as Weinberg points out, we do not know the final laws of nature. So even if we do not anticipate "finding God" in these laws, we should not be making claims about what will or will not be found there. Furthermore, most people would find God more easily by looking somewhere else in nature. And finally, claiming that scientific progress rules out God is nonsense. Such progress reveals how the natural world works. How does this challenge the existence of God? Does detailed knowledge of computers let us deny the existence of computer engineers, or software designers? How does this argument work, exactly? Do not many believers, including some mathematical physicists, find that the rationality of the world speaks to them of God? Science plays a complex role in religion, and various people react to it in dramatically different ways. The safest position is to simply note that science, on balance, is neutral to religion.

Not surprisingly, Weinberg considers evolution to pose especially strong challenges to religion. After extensive discussion, he concludes: "Judging from this historical experience, I would guess that, though we shall find beauty in the final laws of nature, we will find no special status for life or intelligence. A fortiori, we will find no standards of value or morality. And so we will find no hint of any God who cares about such things. We may find these things elsewhere, but not in the laws of nature."[37]

We are disappointed to find such weak arguments in the writing of an otherwise illustrious scholar. To be fair, we note that Weinberg recognizes in a footnote that "it should be apparent that in discussing these things

I am speaking only for myself and that in this chapter I leave behind me any claim to special expertise."[38] Nevertheless, he proceeds with an emaciated rigor in such contrast to his work in physics. He concludes things we knew in advance—like the inability of science to find God. He insists, "As we have discovered more and more fundamental physical principles they seem to have less and less to do with us.... no one has ever discovered any correlation between the importance of anything to us and its importance in the laws of nature."[39] But he also comments: "Of course it is not from the discoveries of science that most people would have expected to learn about God anyway."[40] So why does he claim otherwise?

Weinberg also deals briefly with the problem of evil, one of most enduring arguments against the existence of God. His articulation is concise, but sharp and personal, perhaps offering insight into his general hostility toward God:

> Religious people have grappled for millennia with the theodicy, the problem posed by the existence of suffering in a world that is supposed to be ruled by a good God. They have found ingenious solutions in terms of various supposed divine plans. I will not try to argue with these solutions, much less to add one more of my own. Remembrance of the Holocaust leaves me unsympathetic to attempts to justify the ways of God to man. If there is a God that has special plans for humans, then He has taken very great pains to hide His concern for us. To me it would seem impolite if not impious to bother such a God with our prayers.[41]

Weinberg's reaction to the Holocaust is shared by a great many thoughtful people and must be deeply respected. His worldview has been shaped by the knowledge that many of his relatives were brutally murdered in one of the most terrible experiences in history. His reflections on this are thoughtful and worth reading, and they allude to theological formulations that attempt to deal with it. But he is writing as a distinguished physicist, and we must note that this has nothing to do with science.

Refining Our Understanding of God?

In the *Dreams* chapter on God, Weinberg suggests that religiosity is just wishful thinking. He refers to the interviews by Lightman and Brawer, that among the comments of cosmologists on his "pointless universe" statement, "my favorite response was that of my colleague at the University of Texas, the astronomer Gerard de Vaucouleurs. He said that he thought my remark was 'nostalgic.' Indeed it was—nostalgic for a world in which the heavens declared the glory of God." He adds: "It would be wonderful to find in the laws of nature a plan prepared by a concerned creator in which human beings played some special role. I find sadness in doubting that we will." He concludes: "The more we refine our understanding of God to make the concept plausible, the more it seems pointless."[42]

Weinberg makes little effort, however, to refine "our understanding of God" and poses the question of God rather naively. This claim, in referring directly to the existence of God, is more serious than the one about the "pointless universe." Weinberg also casts himself as a victim, searching in vain for an ultimately pointless God and forever disappointed. But Weinberg's expectation that God should show up in the laws of physics, or the steady advance of scientific explanation, or even the miraculous interruptions of evils like the Holocaust, were doomed from the start. Poorly conceived searches rarely find what they are looking for.

At the end of the *Dreams* chapter Weinberg returns to the wishful thinking idea with an example from George Orwell's *1984*. Under terrible pressure from inquisitor O'Brien, poor Winston Smith cannot bear the pain of the torture and convinces himself that two plus two *is* five. Likewise, we must adjust our beliefs to bear our pain. But growing up, Weinberg adds, our species has had to learn "that we are not playing a starring role in any sort of grand cosmic drama."[43]

Weinberg concludes on a stoic note. We want to believe there is more than meets the eye: "The honor of resisting this temptation is only a thin substitute for the consolations of religion, but it is not entirely without satisfactions of its own."[44] Weinberg has joined the small scientific army waging war on religion. His book, written to rally support for the supercollider, contains a powerful assault on God and religion. We wonder about the connection.

In *The End of Science*, John Horgan describes two meetings with Weinberg. He reports, "Weinberg hoped that a final theory would eliminate the wishful thinking, mysticism, and superstition that pervades much of human thought, even among physicists." The deeper layers of physics grow steadily colder and more impersonal; the world becomes demystified. Weinberg calls us to grow up: "If that's the way the world is, it's better we find out. I see it as a part of the growing up of our species, just like the child finding out there is no tooth fairy. It's better to find out there is no tooth fairy, even though a world with tooth fairies in it is somehow more delightful."[45] Oddly enough, he embraces the coldly rational and demystified world he finds in science: "I sort of enjoy my tragic view. After all, which would you rather see, a tragedy or . . . Well, some people would prefer to see a comedy. But . . . I think the tragic view adds a certain dimension to life. Anyway, it's the best we have."[46]

Again we find ourselves asking what this has to do with science.

Science and Its Cultural Adversaries

Weinberg's 2001 book *Facing Up* was subtitled *Science and Its Cultural Adversaries*. The adversaries are sociologists, philosophers, and cultural critics with negative attitudes toward science. Religious people are also considered adversaries.

Weinberg's title illustrates the opposition he finds between science and religion. His symbol is Tycho Brahe, the great sixteenth-century astronomer who built the city-observatory Uraniborg on the island of Hven in Denmark. Weinberg visited the island and discovered that the only remembrance of Brahe is a statue, appropriately looking at the sky, *facing up.* "The researches of Brahe, Kepler, Newton, and their successors," he tells us, "have presented us with a cold view of the world. As far as we have been able to discover the laws of nature, they are impersonal, with no hint of a divine plan or any special status for human beings. In one way or another, each of the essays in this collection struggles with the necessity of facing up to these discoveries. They express a viewpoint that is rationalist, reductionist, realist, and devoutly secular. Facing up is, after all, the posture opposite to that of prayer."[47]

Having established that physics could not find God, Weinberg now goes after religion, choosing a deliberately antireligious title for his book and embracing the old-fashioned view that science naturally opposes religion.

Everyone agrees that scientists search for natural patterns, not for miracles. In this sense science is not religious. But "not religious" does not mean "antireligious," and it seems oddly inappropriate that a Nobel Prize winner needs to have this pointed out. But Weinberg assumes that scientific and religious explanations are incompatible, subtly but clearly linking science and secularism: "The values of science and secularism that are disliked by some liberal intellectuals in the West are the same ones that I have tried to defend throughout this collection [of essays in *Facing Up*]."[48]

Weinberg dislikes Stephen Jay Gould's separation of science and religion into "non-overlapping magisteria":

> One often hears that there is no conflict between science and religion. For instance, in a review of Johnson's book, Stephen Gould remarks that science and religion do not come into conflict, because

"science treats factual reality, while religion treats human morality."
On most things I tend to agree with Gould, but here I think he
goes too far.... But Gould's view is widespread today among scientists and religious liberals. This seems to me to represent an important retreat of religion from positions it once occupied.[49]

Weinberg is right that most religions include claims about factual reality. But
scholars who work in this area consider the view that the progress of science
entails a simple and steady retreat by religion as far too simplistic.[50] Christianity, for example, has never pretended to provide a scientific explanation of everything. To be sure, people did think the world was only a few thousand years
old, as suggested by the Bible, when no contrary scientific evidence was available. And some retreats from common opinions, such as the Darwinian revolution, have not been easy. But these are theologically peripheral topics. The
central doctrines of Christianity have not been displaced by scientific progress.

A case in point is evolution. This is not Weinberg's specialty, but he
identifies it as a major conflict between science and religion. He rejects Phillip
Johnson's idea that evolution requires a divine plan, but adds:

In another respect I think that Johnson is right. He argues that there
is an incompatibility between the naturalistic theory of evolution
and religion as generally understood.... The inconsistency between
the modern theory of evolution and belief in an interested God
does not seem to me one of logic—one can imagine that God established the laws of nature and set the mechanism of evolution in
motion with the intention that through natural selection you and
I would someday appear—but there is a real inconsistency in temperament. After all, religion did not arise in the minds of men and
women who speculated about infinitely prescient first causes but
in the hearts of those who longed for the continual intervention of an
interested God.[51]

We defer at this point to Francisco Ayala, a leading contemporary evolutionist and well-known exponent of orthodox neo-Darwinism. In an article
criticizing Intelligent Design, he makes a point about the limits of science:
"Science is a wondrously successful way of knowing," he says.

What I want to add is something that seems rather obvious to me:
science is a way of knowing, but it is not the only way. Knowledge
also derives from other sources, such as common sense, artistic and
religious experience, and philosophical reflection.... There are matters of value, meaning, and purpose that are outside science's scope.

Even when we have a satisfying scientific understanding of a natural object or process, we are still missing matters that may well be thought by many to be of equal or greater import. Scientific knowledge may enrich esthetic and moral perceptions, and illuminate the significance of life and the world, but these are matters outside science's realm.[52]

Likewise, God's action in the world may be outside science's realm, but also be compatible with it.

There are no compelling reasons to consider religion a cultural adversary of science. Many scientists, in fact, are religious, including some of Weinberg's stature. Abdus Salam, for example, shared Weinberg's Nobel Prize and was deeply religious. A native of Pakistan, Salam promoted science in developing countries, founding in 1964 a prestigious International Center for Theoretical Physics in Trieste, Italy, with a mission to foster advanced studies and research, especially in developing countries. In his speech at the Nobel awards banquet, Salam quoted the Holy Book of Islam about the perfection of God's creation, adding:

> This in effect is the faith of all physicists; the deeper we seek, the more is our wonder excited, the more is the dazzlement for our gaze. I am saying this, not only to remind those here tonight of this, but also for those in the Third World, who feel they have lost out in the pursuit of scientific knowledge, for lack of opportunity and resource. Alfred Nobel stipulated that no distinction of race or colour will determine who received of his generosity. On this occasion, let me say this to those, whom God has given His Bounty. Let us strive to provide equal opportunities to *all* so that they can engage in the creation of physics and science for the benefit of all mankind. This would exactly be in the spirit of Alfred Nobel and the ideas which permeated his life. Bless You![53]

Is There a Benevolent God?

"A Designer Universe?" in *Facing Up* is the transcript of a 1999 talk Weinberg delivered in Washington as part of the Program of Dialogue between Science and Religion promoted by the American Association for the Advancement of Science. The program asked whether the universe shows signs of Intelligent Design. Weinberg shared the stage with his old friend Sir John Polkinghorne, another mathematical physicist; in 1975 Polkinghorne had announced to

Weinberg and his wife, who were sitting in Polkinghorne's kitchen, that he was giving up his professorship at the University of Cambridge and take holy orders in the Church of England. "I almost fell off my chair," Weinberg recalls.[54]

The *New York Review of Books* published Weinberg's talk. He notes: "It has given rise to more comment—some quite hostile—than any other article I have written."[55]

There were numerous letters to the editor, many generated by an inflammatory broadside Weinberg launched against religion: "With or without religion, good people can behave well and bad people can do evil; but for good people to do evil—that takes religion."[56] Weinberg argued, "The prestige of religion seems today to derive from what people take to be its moral influence. . . . On balance the moral influence of religion has been awful."[57] He looked at some controversial issues as examples. Regarding slavery in particular he concluded that "where religion made a difference, it was more in support of slavery than in opposition to it."[58]

The charge that "for good people to do evil—that takes religion" would play badly in almost any context and demanded clarification: "In saying that it takes religion for good men to do evil I had in mind someone like Louis IX," explained Weinberg. "By all accounts he was modest, generous, and concerned to an unusual degree with the welfare of the common people of France, but he was led by his religion to launch the war of aggression against Egypt that we know as the Sixth Crusade."[59] Weinberg may have had Louis IX in mind when he made the original comment, but he said absolutely nothing about him; instead he made an astonishingly defamatory charge against religion in general. And, of course, there are concerns that Weinberg has decontextualized Louis IX, but this is not our point. We simply note that a Nobel laureate in physics has used the platform provided by that recognition to launch a most vicious attack on religion.

Weinberg finds it

> hard to see why anyone would think that religion is a cure for the world's problems. People have been at each other's throats over differences in religion throughout history, a sad story that continues today in Northern Ireland, the Balkans, the Middle East, Sudan, and India. . . . Of all the elites that can oppress us, the most dangerous are those bearing the banner of religion. . . . Religious leaders may object that the harm in all these cases is done by perversions of religion, not by religion itself. But religious wars and persecutions have been at the center of religious life throughout history.[60]

We acknowledge Weinberg's point but are compelled to respond that religious wars and persecutions are almost never purely religious affairs. More typically, religion has been mixed with secular power and interests who have exploited it as a device to gather support for a cause, like Hitler's claim to be a good Christian. Almost everyone, past and present, has been religious in some way, and it is hard to generalize that their religion motivates their occasionally dreadful behavior. Furthermore, we remind the reader that Weinberg is something of an expert on the history of war and has even written about the motivations of those who wage war.[61] He most certainly knows that his charges are caricatures.

In the *Designer* chapter, Weinberg goes after the idea of a benevolent God. Scientific laws, he notes once again, replace God as an explanation: "Today we understand most of these things in terms of physical forces acting under impersonal laws."[62] He examines various anthropic arguments based on the fine-tuning of the laws and constants of nature; such arguments conclude that our planet is very well adapted to produce intelligent life, but they ask, How could it be otherwise if intelligent life exists? But Weinberg concludes that there may be other universes where things are different. He looks to Linde and Vilenkin for support: "According to the 'chaotic inflation' and 'eternal inflation' theories of André Linde, Alex Vilenkin, and others, the expanding clouds of billions of galaxies that we call the Big Bang may be just one fragment of a much larger universe in which big bangs go off all the time, each one with different values for the fundamental constants."[63] In making these arguments, Weinberg seems to forget that just about everyone, including religious believers, agrees on the value of scientific explanations of the world, even the possibility of other worlds, which may or may not demystify the fine-tuning of this one. Furthermore, these explanations leave untouched the universal human sense of wonder at the world, and the metaphysical urge that leads us to search for explanations beyond the material.

Weinberg acknowledges that he is not especially well suited to the task of looking for a benevolent designer, "Being a physicist is no help with questions like this," he admits, "so I have to speak from my own experience." Abandoning science, he turns to the problem of evil: "My life has been remarkably happy, perhaps in the upper 99.99 percentile of human happiness, but even so, I have seen a mother die painfully of cancer, a father's personality destroyed by Alzheimer's disease, and scores of second and third cousins murdered in the Holocaust. Signs of a benevolent designer are pretty well hidden. The prevalence of evil and misery has always bothered those who believe in a benevolent and omnipotent God. Sometimes God is excused by pointing to the need for free will."[64] Weinberg comments, however, that it seems unfair to his relatives to be murdered in order to preserve free will for Germans. This is a bit oversimplified, however, and unfortunately Weinberg does not engage the serious literature on this topic. The issue is not that free will must be preserved for some persons, but for all persons. A benevolent Creator can certainly endow us with free will without assuming the obligation to prevent all free acts that are not good. This is, briefly, a part of the response to evil perpetrated by humans. Moving to natural evil, in which nonhuman agencies, like earthquakes and bacteria, cause human suffering, Weinberg asks, "How does free will account for cancer?"[65] Again, we note, briefly, that a benevolent Creator could create a world built on natural laws that were not set aside or suspended every time they led to something evil.

Whether or not these all-too-brief responses to the problem of evil are adequate, the point is that Weinberg is simply pontificating from his platform of prestige, without seriously engaging these difficult issues.

Weinberg concludes, "One of the great achievements of science has been, if not to make it impossible for intelligent people to be religious, then at least to make it possible for them not to be religious. We should not retreat from this accomplishment."[66] He wages his secularist war with enthusiasm, but this war is being lost across a broad front, as Oxford theologian Alister McGrath argues in *The Twilight of Atheism*.[67] Consider, for example, the preeminent place of Christianity in the West, where modern science has grown up. Official teachings in many Christian denominations have changed very little as a consequence of the progress of science, so much so that some people complain about this fact. Science is not secularizing the world, and intelligent people are not fleeing religion, en masse, to worship at the temple of scientific progress.

Science Wars

In the preface to *Facing Up*, Weinberg tells the reader that the essays in that book reflect that he is secularist, rationalist, reductionist, and realist. The entries on "rationalism" and "realism" in the index indicate that they are closely related for Weinberg, appearing mainly in connection with Thomas Kuhn and the "Science Wars," the subject of five of the book's essays. Weinberg, in agreement with most scientists, rejects claims that knowledge in the exact sciences (physics, chemistry, molecular biology) is a "social construction," a bizarre claim advanced by some humanities scholars, including the so-called "strong programs" in the sociology of scientific knowledge at the Universities of Edinburgh and Bath. Weinberg is very interested in the philosophy and sociology of science, holding a realist position much in agreement with the actual practice of the sciences.

Commenting on philosopher and historian of science Thomas Kuhn, Weinberg writes:

> I would say that physics in [the twentieth] century offers a remarkable example of stability. Each new theory has preserved and even explained its predecessors as valid approximations in appropriate contexts. Kuhn's description of revolutionary scientific change as a "paradigm shift" akin to a religious conversion does not apply to anything in our century's physics, but it does apply to the shift from Aristotelian to Newtonian physics at the birth of modern physical science. It was *this* shift that I think inspired Kuhn's view of scientific revolutions.[68]

Kuhn's "Aristotelian" experience took place in the summer of 1947,[69] and Weinberg heard it recounted the last time he met Kuhn, at a ceremony in Padua in 1992. Weinberg even got Kuhn to clarify some of his ideas.[70] In *The End of Science*, Horgan also comments on Kuhn's experience. Kuhn was at Harvard University puzzling over how Aristotle, so brilliant in many respects, could be so utterly mistaken in his understanding of the heavens. Staring out his dormitory window, Kuhn had a revelation. Aristotle made sense; it was simply that his use of terminology differed from that of modern physicists. Understood on its own terms, Aristotelian physics made sense and was not inferior to modern physics. It was simply different. This provided Kuhn with what became the central insight of his philosophy of science: Theories are *incommensurable*—they cannot be compared. Horgan comments: "Kuhn has tried, throughout his career, to remain true to that original epiphany he experienced in his dormitory at Harvard. During that moment Kuhn saw—he knew!—that reality is ultimately unknowable; any attempt to describe it obscures as much as it illuminates. But Kuhn's insight forced him to take the untenable position that because all scientific theories fall short of absolute, mystical truth, they are all equally untrue; because we cannot discover *The Answer*, we cannot find any answers."[71]

Weinberg writes: "What does bother me on rereading *Structure* [Kuhn's book *The Structure of Scientific Revolutions*] and some of Kuhn's later writings is his radically skeptical conclusions about what is accomplished in the work of science. And it is just these conclusions that have made Kuhn a hero to the philosophers, historians, sociologists, and cultural critics who question the objective character of scientific knowledge, and who prefer to describe scientific theories as social constructions, not so different in this respect from democracy or baseball."[72] Kuhn later regretted, and Weinberg mentions this, the extreme conclusions of the so-called "strong program" in the sociology of science.

Weinberg is a realist and is disturbed by claims that science is a social construction and that scientific theories are not, even in principle, "true." He writes: "Even more radical than Kuhn's notion of the incommensurability of different paradigms is his conclusion that in the revolutionary shifts from one paradigm to another we do not move closer to the truth."[73] He represents the position of virtually all scientists when he says: "What drives us onward in the work of science is precisely the sense that there are truths out there to be discovered, truths that once discovered will form a permanent part of human knowledge."[74]

Many contemporary philosophers, like the American philosophy and comparative literature professor Richard Rorty, reject Weinberg's robust realism. Weinberg wrote:

> I remarked in a recent article in *The New York Review of Books* that for me as a physicist the laws of nature are real in the same sense (whatever that is) as the rocks on the ground. A few months after the publication of my article I was attacked for this remark by Richard Rorty. He accused me of thinking that as a physicist I can easily clear up questions about reality and truth that have engaged philosophers for millennia. But that is not my position. I know that it is terribly hard to say precisely what we mean when we use words like "real" and "true." That is why, when I said that the laws of nature and the rocks on the ground are real in the same sense, I added in parentheses "whatever that is." I respect the efforts of philosophers to clarify these concepts, but I'm sure that even Kuhn and Rorty have used words like "truth" and "reality" in everyday life, and had no trouble with them. I don't see any reason why we cannot also use them in talking about the history of science.[75]

Weinberg's specialty in physics, remarkably, is the one that presents the most difficulties for realism. He studies the physics of particles so small and inaccessible that we have no possibility of direct access to them or their properties. Experiments deal only with consequences of the theories, and sometimes even the consequences are quite far removed the actual phenomena. Furthermore, the theories are themselves very abstract mathematical constructions containing terms that often do not have a direct referent in the "real world." Physicists working in this area often consider their theories mathematical "models" and claim no correspondence to the real world in the sense of a photograph. They make extensive use of quantum physics, whose realism has been controversial ever since its inception, with no agreement even among its founders. Since its formulation in the 1920s, quantum physics has provoked different interpretations. Books on realism in quantum physics would fill many shelves.[76] Rom Harré, a philosopher of science at Oxford University, devoted an entire book to analyzing scientific realism with a special emphasis in the problems posed by quantum physics, and he did not solve the problem.[77]

Weinberg is one of the architects of the so-called Standard Model of particles and interactions, established in the 1970s. In this model (note the official name "model"), elementary particles, the basic components of matter, are conceived of as "bundles" or "quanta" of energy. In Weinberg's own words: "The Standard Model is a quantum field theory. Its basic ingredients are fields, including the electric and magnetic fields of 19th-century electrodynamics. Little ripples in these fields carry energy and momentum from place to place, and quantum mechanics tells us that these ripples come in bundles, or quanta, that are recognized in the laboratory as elementary particles."[78] Nobody knows how to represent these particles in a "realistic" way. Are they really particles, or waves, or particles with associated waves? Or are they something else, like the vibrations of "strings"? The name "wavicles" was once proposed to label them. We can be certain that the images of tiny marbles or miniature solar systems pictured by many people and in popular texts are certainly far from the truth. Today physicists say that they are the quanta of the fields studied by the Standard Model.

Physicists attempt to go beyond the Standard Model. Weinberg and others are working toward a unified theory of all the four fundamental interactions, "but the discovery of this theory will probably not be possible without radically new ideas," he says, adding, "Some promising ones are already in circulation. There are five different theories of tiny one-dimensional entities known as strings, which in their different modes of vibration appear at low energy as various kinds of particles and apparently furnish perfectly finite theories of gravitation and other forces in ten space-time dimensions."[79] Such an unusual theory will pose a variety of interesting problems, conceptual and otherwise. Will we still be able to speak of truth and reality, for example, in the same way as in ordinary life if we embrace a model of reality with ten dimensions? That we can create such abstract theories that fit empirical data so well is truly amazing, but we must always be cautious when the theories are so abstract. Weinberg's strongly realist intuitions are the instinctive to physicists, but the use of the notion of *truth* in this field requires philosophical elaboration.

Not surprisingly, Weinberg fought for science in the so-called Science Wars. The origin of this sobering but highly entertaining intellectual adventure was an article by physicist Alan Sokal, who wanted to discredit the shoddy scholarship in some of the postmodern assaults on the objectivity of science. Sokal wrote a scholarly-sounding article, full of highbrow nonsense and preposterous quotes from the more pompous of the postmodern critics of science. The article was articulate and succeeded in masquerading as a serious postmodern analysis of quantum gravity. The title was "Transgressing the Boundaries: Toward a Transformative Hermeneutics of Quantum Gravity."[80] He sent it to *Social Text*, a leading journal in the field of cultural studies and popular outlet for postmodern critiques of science. They published it, thinking it credible and pleased to have an article taking this position from a respected physicist. Almost immediately afterward Sokal published in *Lingua Franca* another article exposing the hoax and thoroughly humiliating the editors of *Social Text*.[81] The affair exploded into books and articles.

Weinberg contributed an article on the side of science, warning the social constructivists, "Those who seek extrascientific messages in what they think they understand about modern physics are digging dry wells." But he admitted "two large exceptions": "The discoveries of physics may become relevant to philosophy and culture when we learn the origin of the universe or the final laws of nature, but not for the present." But why these exceptions? Regarding the origin of the universe, Weinberg explains, "Discoveries in science sometimes reveal that topics like matter, space, and time, which had been thought to be the proper subjects for philosophical argument, actually belong in the province of ordinary science." This claim is uncontroversial, as philosophers learned long ago to consider the discoveries of science when dealing with those topics. Weinberg adds, "The other, more important, exception to my statement is the profound cultural effect of the discovery, going back to the work of Newton, that nature is strictly governed by impersonal mathematical laws."[82] Again we find Weinberg taking advantage of another opportunity to claim that scientific discoveries are at odds with the existence of a God who cares about the universe. Oddly enough, Newton himself did not hold this position.

Beyond Reductionism

Weinberg's contributions to the *New York Review of Books* began in 1995. The *Review* had published an article by the great physicist Freeman Dyson criticizing reductionism in physics. Weinberg wrote to Robert Silvers, the editor of the *Review*, offering to write a response defending reductionism. Silvers suggested that instead Weinberg could write an essay review of the book *Nature's Imagination*, where Dyson's article had originally appeared. The book, an edited volume of contributions from leading scholars on reductionism, was based on a 1992 meeting at Jesus College, Cambridge.

Reductionism is actually not an especially popular idea and is usually associated with extreme views held by the members of the Vienna Circle in the 1930s. The central idea of the Vienna Circle was the "principle of empirical verification," which asserts that only the statements of empirical science are meaningful, because they can be "reduced" to sensory experiences. Metaphysics and theology are thus meaningless because the principle cannot be applied to their statements. The bad news was that the critically important principle of empirical verification could not be effectively applied to the empirical sciences. Sir Karl Popper, a friend of some members of the Vienna Circle, in his 1934 book *The Logic of Scientific Discovery*, wrote: "Positivists, in their anxiety to annihilate metaphysics, annihilate natural science along with it."[83] It turns out that none of the most basic concepts of empirical science can be reduced to sensory experiences.

The reduction of one science to another (of biology to chemistry, and chemistry to physics) is extremely difficult. At each level we find entities and properties that don't reduce to a simple aggregation of their component parts. Each of the different levels we find in the natural world seems to have its own unique features that cannot be deduced from the lower levels.

Reductionism is usually associated with materialism. But the difficulties with materialism are so great that today materialists sometimes define their position as "nonreductive physicalism." Everything is ultimately physical, they affirm, but the "emergent" properties of higher levels cannot be "reduced" to lower levels.

The symposium at Jesus College included Oxford chemist Peter Atkins, a champion of reductionism who presented a paper titled "The Limitless Power of Science," and Mary Midgely, who answered energetically with her paper "Reductive Megalomania." In the introduction, Dyson launched an attack against reductionism: "I have already made it clear that I have a low opinion of reductionism, which seems to me to be at best irrelevant and at worst misleading as a description of what science is about. . . . If we try to squeeze science into a single philosophical viewpoint such as reductionism, we are like Procustes chopping off the feet of his guests when they do not fit on to his bed."[84]

Weinberg presents himself as a reductionist and sees the progress of science since Newton as a triumph of reductionism: "From Newton's time to our own we have seen a steady expansion of the range of phenomena that we know how to explain, and a steady improvement in the simplicity and universality of the theories used in these explanations. Science in this style is properly called reductionist."[85]

Unfortunately, not everyone defines reductionism in the same way. Weinberg introduces a distinction:

> We ought first of all distinguish between what . . . I like to call grand and petty reductionism. Grand reductionism is . . . the view that all of nature is the way it is (with certain qualifications about initial conditions and historical accidents) because of simple universal laws, to which all other scientific laws may in some sense be reduced. Petty reductionism is the much less interesting doctrine that things behave the way they do because of the properties of their constituents. . . . Petty reductionism is not worth a fierce defense. Sometimes things can be explained by studying their constituents—sometimes not.[86]

Weinberg describes his image of reductionism:

> One can illustrate the reductionist worldview by imagining all the principles of science as being dots on a huge chart, with arrows flowing into each principle from all the other principles by which it is explained. The lesson of history is that these arrows do not form separate disconnected clumps, representing sciences that are logically independent, and they do not wander aimlessly. Rather, they are connected, and if followed backward they all seem to branch outward from a common source, an ultimate law of nature that Dyson calls "a finite set of fundamental equations."[87]

In 1992, Weinberg was invited to contribute to a book on twentieth-century physics. He decided to accept the invitation because one of the other contributors was Philip Anderson:

> Anderson is a brilliant theorist, one of the leading figures of the past century in the theory of condensed matter physics. . . . More to the point, and to my regret, he has also been a leading detractor of the reductionist tendencies of elementary particle physics, as shown for instance in his celebrated essay "More Is Different." And he has been an important opponent of new accelerator construction. I felt that I could not let Anderson have the last word on the past hundred years of physics.[88]

Anderson won the 1977 Nobel Prize for physics. His 1972 essay "More Is Different" appeared in the leading journal *Science*, where we read: "The more the elementary particle physicists tell us about the nature of the fundamental laws, the less relevance they seem to have to the very real problems of the rest of science."[89] He warns readers not to think that just because the elementary entities of science X—like the molecules of chemistry—obey the laws of science Y—like atomic physics—this implies that science X—chemistry—is just an application of science Y—physics: "At each stage entirely new laws, concepts, and generalizations are necessary, requiring inspiration and creativity to just as great a degree as in the previous one. Psychology is not applied biology, nor is biology applied chemistry."[90] He concludes: "The arrogance of the particle physicist and his intensive research may be behind us . . . but we have yet to recover from that of some molecular biologists, who seem determined to try to reduce everything about the human organism to 'only' chemistry, from the common cold and all mental disease to the religious instinct."[91]

This controversy is both scientific and practical: Weinberg's reductionism encourages investment in projects like the SSC, while Anderson, in fact, opposed the project.

As a scientific matter, no one, Weinberg included, thinks we will ever be able to derive the entire content of all the sciences one from another in a chain leading to physics. Nor will be able to predict, using the laws of physics, the entire content of the other sciences. So what is the compelling attraction of reductionism, if it is doomed to failure from the start, at least in its purest version? Weinberg explains: "There is another reason for some of the opposition to reductionism, and specifically to the perspective provided by grand reductionism. It is that this perspective removes much of the traditional motivation for belief in God."[92]

This concern is real, only if we interpret reductionism as materialism. But "materialism" is not in Weinberg's vocabulary. Nor does it appear in the index of any of his books. This may be due to the fact that "reductionism" sounds scientific, while "materialism" sounds philosophical. Probably Weinberg wishes to avoid direct engagement with philosophical issues, which for him would be much like quicksand.

Weinberg leaves us with his dream of a final theory, underscoring that "a final theory will be final in only one sense—it will bring to an end a certain sort of science, the ancient search for those principles that cannot be explained in terms of deeper principles."[93] He adds, "Our best hope is to identify the final theory as one that is so rigid that it cannot be warped into some slightly different theory without introducing logical absurdities like infinite energies."[94] The dream of a final theory is a great inspiration, if we ask no more from it than that. But as a literal blueprint for scientific progress it seems more like wishful thinking.

6

A Pulitzer for the Ants

Edward O. Wilson

If we were to single out a contemporary scientist whose mind and heart could be identified with the scientific enterprise, it would be Edward Osborne Wilson. He has devoted his entire life to the natural sciences, making numerous breakthroughs and founding the new science of sociobiology. *Time* magazine ranked him one of the most influential people of the twentieth century. He has also worked tirelessly to promote what he considers the worldview stemming from science. Science, for E. O. Wilson, is a kind of religion, destined to succeed traditional religions, and endowed with the task of satisfying the human needs that religion used to fulfill, only in a better way.

E. O. Wilson was born in Birmingham, Alabama, on June 10, 1929. He received his B.S. (1949) and M.S. (1950) in biology from the University of Alabama, after which he went to Harvard University, receiving his Ph.D. in biology in 1955. He remained at Harvard as a professor of zoology and curator in the Museum of Comparative Zoology. In 1997 he became professor emeritus and has held the title of research professor since that date.

Wilson is a world authority on ants. He published in 1990, in collaboration with the German biologist Bert Hölldobler, the Pulitzer Prize–winning *The Ants*, a massive work of 732 beautifully illustrated pages.[1] His studies on the social behavior of ants, published in 1971 in *The Insect Societies*,[2] formed the basis for the scientific study of other social animals, launching the new science of *sociobiology*, also the title of one of his most influential and polemical books, published in 1975.[3] Controversy arose from the last chapter of *Sociobiology*, where Wilson proposed to extend the sociobiological perspective to the study of human beings. Undaunted by the critics, he published the Pulitzer Prize–winning *On Human Nature*[4] in 1978, applying the insights of sociobiology to human behavior. In 1998, at age sixty-nine, he published the best-seller *Consilience*,[5] further developing his ideas and proposing a unification of the different branches of knowledge under the guidance of the natural sciences. In the last few years he has been a tireless promoter of ecology and biodiversity.[6]

The Little Boy of Paradise Beach

In his autobiography, *Naturalist*, Wilson described himself as a shy boy who, at the tender age of seven, would devote entire days to observing the natural world. One of his strongest recollections is the following: "I stand in the shallows off Paradise Beach, staring down at a huge jellyfish in water so still and clear that its every detail is revealed as though it were trapped in glass. The creature is astonishing. . . . I study it from every angle I can manage from above the water surface."[7] As Wilson unfolds his story, we realize that the curious little boy, captivated for hours observing animals in his local habitat, became the curious great scientist who devoted countless hours observing animals in varied and exotic habitats around the world.

Wilson's boyhood haunts, mainly South Alabama and North Florida, around Pensacola, were nurturing environments for a developing naturalist. When Wilson had the chance to go to university, there could be no doubt he would study biology.

Two unusual accidents conspired to direct the emerging naturalist to entomology, the study of insects. The first was loss of vision in his right eye when he was a boy fishing at Paradise Beach. A pinfish with ten needlelike spines flew out of the water and into the young fisherman's face, depriving him of his stereoscopic vision. The second was an adolescent loss of most of his hearing in the uppermost registers, making it hard to hear and locate birds. After describing these limitations, he writes:

> I was destined to become an entomologist, committed to minute
> crawling and flying insects, not by any touch of idiosyncratic genius,
> not by foresight, but by a fortuitous constriction of physiological
> ability. I had to have one kind of animal if not another, because the

fire had been lit and I took what I could get. The attention of my surviving eye turned to the ground. I would thereafter celebrate the little things of the world, the animals that can be picked up between thumb and forefinger and brought close for inspection.[8]

Wilson's passion for animals has not diminished over the course of a long and distinguished career. His childhood passion for explanations has also stayed alive. Incessantly seeking new horizons for himself and others, at Harvard he consistently counseled his students to follow his footprints off the beaten paths of science into unexplored panoramas. With a boy's enthusiasm and a scholar's ingenuity he repeatedly proposed new vistas, forever seeking evolutionary explanations for just about everything, from our preferences for hilltop mansions[9] to our aversion for incest.

A Southern Baptist Discovers Evolution

Wilson's lifelong scientific passion, shared by others, is evolution. But Wilson is unusual in his enthusiasm to expand evolution into an all-encompassing scientific explanation, with nothing outside its explanatory purview. The scope of current evolutionary theory is not so broad, of course, and Wilson knows this. But, starting with sociobiology's illumination of the evolution of social behaviors, Wilson has been steadily crusading to enlarge the relevance of evolutionary explanations so that they may finally include those ambits that currently seem impervious to them.

In the first chapter of his best-selling *Consilience*, titled "The Ionian Enchantment,"[10] Wilson recounts "the time I was captured by the dream of unified learning. It was in the early fall of 1947, when at eighteen I came up from Mobile to Tuscaloosa to enter my sophomore year at the University of Alabama." His mentor, assistant professor Ralph Chermock, handed him a copy of Ernst Mayr's *Systematics and the Origin of Species* (1942), one of the main articulations of the so-called modern synthesis of Darwinism and genetics. Wilson comments, "Then I discovered evolution. Suddenly—that is not too strong a word—I saw the world in a wholly new way.... A new enthusiasm surged through me. The animals and plants I loved so dearly reentered the stage as lead players in a grand drama. Natural history was validated as a real science."

"I had experienced the Ionian Enchantment," Wilson says. "That recently coined expression I borrow from the physicist and historian Gerald Holton.[11]

It means a belief in the unity of the sciences—a conviction, far deeper than a mere working proposition, that the world is orderly and can be explained by a small number of natural laws." The Greeks of old, living around the Ionian Islands in the Mediterranean, were the first recorded thinkers to try to explain the world using a few basic principles. Wilson had discovered evolution—a single foundation on which to develop the grand narrative of the origins and nature of the entire world, including human beings.

In Wilson's perspective, the new explanatory principle would replace religion. On the one hand, he felt liberated from traditional religion and launched on a life full of new adventures: "I found it a wonderful feeling not just to taste the unification metaphysics but also to be released from the confinement of fundamentalist religion. I had been raised a Southern Baptist. . . . More pious than the average teenager, I read the Bible cover to cover, twice. But now at college, steroid-driven into moods of adolescent rebellion, I chose to doubt. . . . Most of all, Baptist theology made no provision for *evolution*. The biblical authors had missed the most important revelation of all!" But he would not abandon the deep aspirations at the heart of religion. He would simply replace traditional religion with evolutionary science: "Still, I had no desire to purge religious feelings. . . . Could Holy Writ be just the first literate attempt to explain the universe and make ourselves significant within it? Perhaps science is a continuation on new and better-tested ground to attain the same end. If so, then in that sense science is religion liberated and writ large. Such, I believe, is the source of the Ionian Enchantment: Preferring a search for objective reality over revelation is another way of satisfying religious hunger."

By these lights, science and religion are not independent pathways. They serve the same purpose, but in such a way that science supersedes and even replaces religion. In the future, having unified knowledge under the umbrella of evolutionary science, we will have solved the riddle of our existence: "When we have unified enough certain knowledge, we will understand who we are and why we are here." Science is the key.

All this sounds very much like a grand and far-reaching intellectual adventure. After decades of productive scientific work, Wilson is still the intrepid adolescent fisherman from Alabama, eager for big new adventures. While not sure we will attain the goal, he thinks the adventure is worth the effort. The first chapter of *Consilience* ends with the mythological flight of Icarus, who flew toward the sun until his wings, fashioned of feathers and wax, came apart and he fell into the sea. Wilson quotes the famous Royal Astronomer Sir Arthur Eddington, saying: "Let us see how high we can fly before the sun melts the wax in our wings."

A Gracious but Stubborn Materialist

Wilson's writing style is gracious, and those who have met him find him a real "southern gentleman" in the best sense of both of those terms. In his quest to make evolution a new religion, he is careful not to present himself as a foe of the old religion, which he treats with respect and even nostalgia.[12] But he treats religion and its traditions as poetry and sentiment, not capable of providing any sort of objective framework for our lives, a capacity Wilson assigns exclusively to empirical science.

Wilson presents ethics and religion in the form of a dialogue between two partners, a transcendentalist who believes in God and uses religious arguments and an empiricist who uses exclusively scientific arguments. The empiricist says:

> So I may surprise you by granting this much: It would be a sorry day if we abandoned our venerated sacral traditions. It would be a tragic misreading of history to expunge *under God* from the American Pledge of Allegiance. Whether atheists or true believers, let oaths be taken with hand on the Bible, and may we continue to hear *So help me God.* Call upon priests and ministers and rabbis to bless civil ceremony with prayer, and by all means let us bow our heads in communal respect. Recognize that when introits and invocations prickle the skin we are in the presence of poetry, and the soul of the tribe, something that will outlive the particularities of sectarian belief, and perhaps belief in God itself. But to share reverence is not to surrender the precious self and obscure the true nature of the human race. We should not forget who we are. . . . [Empiricism] has destroyed the giddying theory that we are special beings placed by a deity in the center of the universe as the summit of Creation for the glory of the gods. We can be proud as a species because, having discovered that we are alone, we owe the gods very little.[13]

Lest the reader get lost in the rhetoric of the arguments, as a part of the same discussion, Wilson clarifies that "the argument of the empiricist, to repeat my earlier confession, is my own."[14] Good manners characterize Wilson's writings, which have been recognized with two Pulitzer Prizes. Behind them, however, a stubborn materialist labors tirelessly to explain everything by means of science. The label "empiricist" that Wilson uses to represent his position sounds softer than "materialism," but there is little doubt that we are dealing with a materialist in the strongest sense of the word—those who try to reduce everything to physics. Of the scientific method he writes: "Behind the mere smashing of aggregates into smaller pieces lies a deeper agenda that also takes the name of reductionism: to fold the laws and principles of each level of organization into those at more general, hence more fundamental levels. Its strong form is total consilience, which holds that nature is organized by simple universal laws of physics to which all other laws and principles can eventually be reduced. This transcendental world view is the light and way for many scientific materialists. (I admit to being among them.)"[15]

Curiously, Wilson immediately clarifies of his worldview that "it could be wrong. At the least, it is surely an oversimplification. At each level of organization, especially the living cell and above, phenomena exist that require new laws and principles. . . . Perhaps some of them will remain forever beyond our grasp. . . . That would not be all bad. I will confess with pleasure: The challenge and the crackling of thin ice are what give science its metaphysical excitement."

So what are we to make of this? On the one hand, Wilson consistently argues in favor of an objective approach, represented by empirical science, with its monopoly on truth. He even argues for physicalism—the reduction of all sciences to physics and the strongest form of materialism. At the same time, however, he is aware that physicalism, and reductionism and scientific materialism in general, had suffered serious defeats in previous times. Wilson aptly notes that the natural world is composed of many levels that possess their own properties and laws, and there appears to be no way to reduce these levels to more basic levels. So Wilson admits at the outset that his proposal faces substantial barriers, but he is not deterred and adopts an intriguing position. Rather than proposing a solution, he embraces the challenge as a grand adventure. Of course, he likes the challenge and considers it exciting. But advancing a grand challenge is not the same as articulating a grand conclusion. Any number of implausible goals may be advanced as grand, even noble, adventures, but one must distinguish between the adventure and rigorously defensible conclusions discovered in the course of the adventure. So when Wilson suggests that his great adventure might "explain away" the humanities and religion by reducing them to physics, we must not be seduced into thinking that this has already occurred, or is even in progress.

An Ambitious Scientist

That Wilson likes the "metaphysical excitement" of expanding science to its outer limits and beyond is closely related to Wilson's character, described appropriately as "ambitious." In his autobiography we meet a shy boy, seriously engaged from an early age with the nature surrounding him. Soon, upon his arrival at the University of Alabama, he morphs into an ambitious myrmecologist, intent on classifying all the ants in the entire state of Alabama. He changed his mind very soon when he discovered evolution, but his goals remained far-reaching. At a very young age he was researching at Harvard University, continually engaged in the ambitious projects in his field, and even creating an entirely new field of science.

While at Harvard, Wilson ran afoul of James Watson, who jointly with Francis Crick discovered the double-helix structure of DNA in 1953. Unraveling the secret of DNA was one of those rare scientific achievements that influence the future course of science, redirecting research agendas for decades and turning the responsible scientists into household names. Wilson devotes an entire chapter of his autobiography to his relationship with Watson under the title "The Molecular Wars," making no secret of his view that Watson was an enemy:

> When he [Watson] was a young man, in the 1950s and 1960s, I found him the most unpleasant human being I had ever met. He came to Harvard as an assistant professor in 1956, also my first year at the same rank. . . . He arrived with a conviction that biology must be transformed into a science directed at molecules and cells and rewritten in the language of physics and chemistry. What had gone before, "traditional" biology—*my* biology—was infested by stamp collectors who lacked the wit to transform their subject into a modern science.[16]

Wilson deeply resented Watson's assault on his biology. In the course of his biological "stamp collecting" Wilson had spent the summer of 1952 searching for and cataloging insects across North America: from Massachusetts to Ontario, the Great Plains states, Montana, Idaho, California, Nevada, Arizona, New Mexico, the Gulf states. In 1953 he added Cuba and Mexico, completing his original vision. The next year he toured islands in the South Pacific, advancing the study of ants. He departed Boston in November 1954 on a tour of the outer Melanesian archipelagoes, then Australia, and finally New Guinea. "At every opportunity I collected ants," he wrote.[17] If this was stamp collecting, it was certainly a very sophisticated variant of that hobby.

Wilson's work was well received, and he gradually emerged as a leading authority in entomology, especially in myrmecology (the study of ants). The data collected on his 1954 tour led to his theory of the *taxon cycle*, a cycle noted especially in the evolution of species in large systems of islands. Those early studies culminated with the publication, in collaboration with Robert H. MacArthur, of *The Theory of Island Biogeography*, a major technical work.[18]

Wilson was ambitious, competent, and careful. He knew that progress in empirical science occurs to the degree that we can find patterns in the natural world and explain them. We search for laws and regularities, develop explanatory hypotheses, and submit them to experiment. Repeatable experiments presuppose the existence of enduring spatiotemporal patterns, and success is evidence that those patterns really exist. Wilson looked hard for patterns in nature. "If well equipped," he wrote, "[the naturalist] can gather information swiftly while continuously thinking, every working hour, What patterns do the data form? What is the meaning of the patterns? What is the question they answer? What is the story I can tell?"[19]

Seeking patterns in traditional biology was far more difficult than in physics or chemistry, where things can be isolated and studied in a laboratory under controlled conditions. This was precisely what the new molecular biology of Crick and the sneering Watson was doing. Could Wilson, the old-fashioned naturalist, do something similar?

Wilson concentrated his efforts in a narrow and well-defined area, hoping for results that would compare favorably with those of molecular biology. He wanted to know how ants communicate with each other. He proceeded to find the chemical substance they use, where this substance is produced in the body of the ants, and how the ants use the substance to communicate. It was a remarkable achievement.

> A new sensory world was opening to biologists. We came fully to appreciate the simple fact that most kinds of organisms communicate by taste and smell, not by sight and sound. Animals, plants, and microorganisms employ among their millions of species an astonishing diversity of devices for transmitting the chemicals. The pheromones are usually sparse enough in the bodies of the organisms to make detection difficult for human beings. Animals are unfailingly ingenious in the methods by which they manufacture and deploy these substances. In the late 1950s I was one of no more than a dozen researchers who studied them in ants and other social insects. It was a bonanza that lay before us. We discovered new forms of chemical messages everywhere we looked, and with minimal effort.[20]

Wilson eagerly pursued ever more challenging enterprises. His goal was to conduct his projects with the rigor required in the hardest of the empirical sciences, and in many ways he succeeded. But he also launched big projects beyond the limits of established science, forever pushing the boundaries, and eventually finding himself outside of science altogether.

Big Projects

Illinois Institute of Technology sociologist Ullica Segerstråle has written:

> For a reader of Wilson's autobiography, it becomes obvious that
> naturally shy Wilson in fact was deadly ambitious—he was driven
> by the quest to be the best. What is more, it seems that Wilson in fact
> often deliberately threw himself into adrenaline-producing situa-
> tions: for instance, in his youth he competed as a long-distance run-
> ner. After giving up the running prospect early in his life, later visions
> of great intellectual feats gave him the needed stimulation. Note,
> for instance, his description of how he felt about the very idea of
> formulating a comprehensive sociobiological theory: "Once again
> I was roused by the amphetamine of ambition" (*Naturalist*, p. 323).
> It was unusual—and honest—of Wilson to reflect on the role of am-
> bition in his life.[21]

Wilson's projects, despite their grand scale, remained comfortably within
the scope of traditional biology until the 1970s. In his autobiography he devotes
a chapter to the "Florida Keys experiment." He had already done work, with
Robert MacArthur, on island biogeography. They wondered how they could
study the dynamic equilibrium of species of insects, where new "colonists" are
steadily arriving, seemingly balancing the old residents' becoming extinct. How
do you study this? Wilson wondered: "I brooded over the problem, imagined
scenarios of many kinds, and finally came up with the solution: a *laboratory* of
island biogeography. We needed an archipelago where little Krakataus could be
created at will and their recolonization watched at leisure."[22] (Krakatau is a
small island that had been wiped clean of all life in the great volcanic explosion
of August 27, 1883; scientists studied the recolonization of the island, mainly by
birds.)

How was Wilson to get his own personal archipelago for such an experiment? In the sixteenth century, the king of Denmark gave Tycho Brahe the
entire island of Hveen to establish an astronomical observatory. Wilson needed
his own island and got permission to use some islets in the Florida Keys for his
grand experiment in extinction and recolonization. His team carefully examined the insect populations before they were fumigated to extinction and
watched to see what happened afterward. It was difficult to verify that the entire
insect population was completely destroyed, with the live vegetation still intact,
as they had promised the National Park Service. But they succeeded, and in
1969, together with Daniel Simberloff, Wilson published the results. In 1971

they received the Mercer Award of the Ecological Society of America for their research, despite the fumigation. After all, due to its many natural catastrophes, gigantic "fumigations" were common to Florida. The Florida Keys experiment is a measure of Wilson's determination to turn his studies into genuine hard science, just like Watson's molecular biology.

After the Florida Keys experiment, Wilson embarked on a much larger project that would come to define his substantial stature in the scientific community. He published a trilogy—*The Insects Societies* (1971), *Sociobiology* (1975), and *On Human Nature* (1978)—successively developing a revolutionary new theme: the biological basis for behavior. Looking first at social insects, like ants, continuing with social animals in general, and culminating in a wide-ranging and speculative look at the social instincts of humans, Wilson launched a revolution. His project was deceptively simple, and firmly rooted in science. A world expert on ants, Wilson fully understood the complex social structure of the ant colony. Operating almost entirely by instinct, ant colonies have a highly specialized "society," with well-defined roles for the various members of the colony—soldiers, queens, workers, and so on. Many of the individual ants are, by evolutionary standards, quite "unfit." Some of them are actually sterile and incapable of passing on their genes. But if you put these very different and narrowly specialized ants together in a colony, the result is a highly unified "society" that is remarkably successful by just about any standard. Somehow ants have evolved in such a way that they instinctively create elaborate colonies in which most of the ants apparently sacrifice "personal" agendas for the good of the whole. Higher-level animals also organize themselves naturally and instinctively into societies: Wolves run in packs with well-defined leadership, fish swim in schools, barnyards have pecking orders, and so on. Social structures grounded in biology are ubiquitous in nature.

But what about humans? Are human social behaviors also rooted in their biology? Can insights from the ant colony and the wolf pack illuminate the more complex social world that humans have constructed? Wilson answered yes and was drawn into one of the greatest scientific controversies since Darwin published his revolutionary work.

The Sociobiology Wars

Wilson's projects were ambitious and difficult. Nobody could deny, of course, Wilson's competence to generalize about ants in particular and social insects in general. But as he worked his way into the study of vertebrates in *Sociobiology*, he was clearly extrapolating, though not unreasonably, and always with great care. *Sociobiology* became the foundational text of a new discipline with the same name. In it, Wilson synthesized the gamut of previously existing studies, launching a barrage of new perspectives. *Sociobiology* was, in the main, noncontroversial and well received by biologists, but as had previously happened with Darwin, when the explanatory agenda was extended to human beings, all hell broke loose.

Sociobiology was greeted with a broad cross section of objections. Michael Ruse synthesized the initial reactions:

> As expected, there were many objections to the new field of sociobiology. Social scientists became tense because they felt that biologists were poaching on their domain. Rather than accepting biology as a complement or an aid to social science, they saw it as a threat and feared sociology would vanish and sociobiology . . . would take its place. Feminists abhorred what they considered a direct attack on their ideology, which held sexual differences and family structures to be purely cultural rather than biological constructions. Darwin was painted as the archetypal Victorian male chauvinist, and sociobiology was seen as an excuse for the status quo that oppresses women and children. Marxists, and this included some eminent biologists, felt that a biological approach was a travesty of the truth, because it pretended that evolution and natural selection had accomplished what was truly a function and result of economic deprivation. . . . Interestingly, the one group that might have been expected to explode—those members of the Christian community interested seriously in science—was far more receptive.[23]

Ruse's comments about Christians are interesting. He notes that sociobiology does not require an atheistic interpretation. Sociobiology is entirely consistent with belief in God and, in particular, can be embraced by Christians:

> If one is a believer, one can (and must) surely interpret the situation as God's way of instilling an ethical sense in humankind. After all, the believer has to agree that God has instilled an ethical sense, and if one is an evolutionist then surely the sociobiological scenario is as plausible a scenario as any other. In fact, the Christian—certainly the Christian who takes seriously the teaching of Thomas Aquinas— knows this already. Natural law is something imposed upon us by the way that God has created humans. . . . For the theist who accepts sociobiology, ethics is part of creation, and the emotions and reasons

that constitute it are very much part of the God-made natural order. Hence, inasmuch as one's moral sense (and the awareness to which it leads) is something natural, it is something to be cherished and obeyed and respected by God's creatures.[24]

Reading Wilson through the lens of Christianity provides a certain unsettling ambivalence. On the one hand, Wilson is developing a full-fledged version of scientific materialism completely incompatible with any claim that religion might be objectively true. On the other hand, Wilson's scientific claims resemble traditional Christian theology. Wilson highlights the existence of a real *human nature* (one of his books even bore the title *On Human Nature*), a premise for a good part of traditional Christian reasoning. He also insists that the material and the cultural dimensions of human nature are closely interwoven, an idea that resonates with the Christian view of the soul as the *substantial form* of the body, which means that human beings are not composed of two distinct substances, body and soul, that are merely united or juxtaposed. The widely accepted juxtaposition idea is Platonic and was developed by Descartes in modern times, but it is not the way that the Christian tradition has understood the soul.[25]

Wilson's sociobiology would clash with Christian doctrine if interpreted as a materialist account of the whole of reality leaving no room for God or the spiritual dimensions of life. But this kind of materialism, however much it may be defended as *scientific*, ultimately is still a philosophical doctrine far outside the domain of science.

Creative and Risky Science

Some of the assaults on Wilson's sociobiology were quite aggressive and launched from entirely secular constituencies. His main opponents, in fact, were as materialist as he was and were also his departmental colleagues at Harvard University—Richard Lewontin and Stephen Jay Gould.

Lewontin and Gould charged Wilson with racism and genetic determinism. Wilson's insistence that human behavior had a biological, specifically genetic basis was interpreted as constraining both human freedom and individuality.

Both Lewontin and Gould were Jewish and therefore mindful of the atrocities perpetrated by the Nazis, in the name of science, to engineer a master race. They recalled only too well the "scientifically based" restrictions on immigration to the United States imposed in the first decades of the twentieth century. Concern also remained about measuring intelligence with IQ tests, and Lewontin was an active critic of this practice. Last but not least, this was a time of student unrest, backed by the cultural Left. Both Lewontin and Gould were leftist to the point of being Marxist, something they freely admitted. The idea of a biologically based human nature, constrained by one's genes to a limited range of cultural possibilities, was anathema to social progressives like Gould and Lewontin.

Wilson chronicled the sociobiology wars in several of his books, portraying himself as the winner.[26] The Marxism of his adversaries, he notes, has all but disappeared, while his biological approach to the study of the human nature grows steadily. Both claims are surely true. At the same time, however, two different problems were coming into focus: the scientific rigor of Wilson's theories, now floating far above the anthills of Alabama, and the ideological component of those theories, which was getting increasing scrutiny. The two problems are related in important ways.

In her extended analysis of the sociobiology debate, Ullica Segerstråle makes an interesting point:

> In my three long interviews with Lewontin, he persistently criticized Wilson for only one thing: failing to do "serious" science. Indeed, from the very beginning of the controversy, in an interview in *Harvard Gazette*, Lewontin insisted that Wilson's sociobiological theory "does not belong in the corpus of natural science, because he provides so many ways and gimmicks to make his theory work, it is by nature self-confirming and violates scientific method." Thus, whatever his nonverbal cues of dominance, Lewontin's relationship to Wilson probably had less to do with primate-type competition than with the basic fact that he disapproved of Wilson on *intellectual* grounds.[27]

The involvement in the sociobiology controversy of groups like the anti-capitalist Science for the People could easily lead to confusion about the agenda of Wilson's critics. Certainly Lewontin was involved in these leftist movements, which included people with a variety of very different concerns. But Lewontin was also recognized as a rigorous scientist in his own domain. By the lights of science, Wilson considered himself a progressive adventuring into unexplored territory, leaving the final judgment for the future, while he judged Lewontin, paradoxically, a conservative. Segerstråle notes: "Thus, the situation could be described as an opposition between a purist, critical, logical approach with slightly negative overtones (Lewontin), and a practically oriented, opportunistic, speculative, and generally 'positive' model-building approach, where judgment is postponed until later (Wilson). From the pro-tagonists' own perspectives, the first approach is 'serious science' (Lewontin) or 'too safe' (Wilson), while the latter one is either 'creative and risky' (Wilson) or 'not serious' (Lewontin)."[28]

Wilson's incursions into the cultural arena are tainted by the charges of dubious science, to say the least. His proposals contain interesting sugges-tions that may lead to further advance in the future as, indeed, they have been doing for several decades. Nevertheless, in their attempt to explain and explain away so much of human culture on as-yet-ungrounded scientific speculation, Wilson's proposals must be considered tentative and hypothetical.

Gould versus Wilson

Gould critiqued Wilson on more than sociobiology. His posthumously pub-lished 2003 book, *The Hedgehog, the Fox and the Magister's Pox: Mending the Gap between Science and the Humanities,* contained a wide-ranging assault on Wilson's program. Responding to Wilson's *Consilience,* which proposed in-troducing biology into the study of human society and culture, Gould spent an entire seventy-page chapter criticizing Wilson.[29]

Gould's criticism was not that of a scientist preoccupied with the purity of his science. Quite the contrary, for Gould was convinced that science is in-terwoven with cultural influences. He had also formulated the theory of *punc-tuated equilibrium* in evolutionary biology that has not been unanimously accepted by the scientific community, so he was familiar with controversy. Furthermore, Gould's work had contributed to widespread recognition of the philosophical consequences of Darwinism, something akin to what Wilson's was doing. The main difference between the two scientific Olympians was that Gould did not share the "reductionism" in Wilson's ideas. Wilson en-larges the explanatory domain of biology to encompass all levels of human culture. Gould thought this approach lacked rigor, and he demanded that the characteristics of the different levels of human experience be respected. Gould saw the sciences, the humanities, and religion occupying distinct plateaus of human experience. In contrast, Wilson tried to unify science with religion and ethics in a combination dominated by, and ultimately reduced to, science. Gould described himself as a "materialist in practical scientific work and as an agnostic in religious matters." He agreed with Wilson "that mental processes have physical groundings and, if knowable at all, must be consistent with the natural sciences."[30]

Gould criticizes Wilson's proposal on two grounds: He notes first "that reductionism will not suffice even within its potentially applicable domain of subjects traditionally assigned to the natural sciences," and he comments: "The 'higher' we mount, the less we can rely on reductionism for the twinned reasons of (1) ever greater influence of emergent principles, and (2) ever greater accumulation of historical accidentals requiring narrative explanations as contingencies."[31]

The second argument that Gould makes is more radical, highlighting the differing natures of science and the humanities: "By the logic of its enterprise and the nature of its fundamental questions, the concerns of traditional subjects in humanities (and also in ethics and religion) cannot be addressed and resolved by the methods of scientific inquiry, reductionistic or otherwise."[32]

Gould's appraisal is quite realistic. Certainly humans are unitary beings, in the sense that we are not combinations of matter and spirit as mutually exclusive components (as in Cartesian dualism). But clearly we have material and spiritual dimensions. We can represent the natural world as an object, building models that represent particular aspects of the world; we can theorize about our models and test them against empirical evidence; and we can evaluate the results of the tests to ascertain whether or not our models are correct. Even though we are a *part* of the natural world, we can also *transcend* the natural world in our ability to know it, to represent it, and even to dominate it. We can even theorize about ourselves, to consider the reach of our knowledge and to pose problems about the ultimate foundations of the world and the meaning of our lives.

Scientific knowledge, although partial and imperfect, provides interesting clues enabling us to grasp deeper problems as we try to understand our rich and complex human nature. The natural sciences provide no proof of a naturalist perspective. In fact, they help us understand the order existing in the natural world, our mysterious and unexplained capacities to know that order and, therefore, to know ourselves as subjects that belong to the natural world but, at the same time, transcend it.

Gould probably would not agree with this conclusion. Nevertheless, as an evolutionary biologist strongly committed to spreading the Darwinian view of life, he did not feel obliged to accept Wilson's reductionist approach. Instead, he highlighted that the sciences and the humanities are different and that the latter could not and should not be reduced to the former.

Wilson is obviously correct when he says we must take into account the material basis for all aspects of human experience when we deal with human problems. And this must also be considered when we examine cultural, ethical, and religious expressions of our common human experience. The problem with Wilson is that he wants to reduce culture, ethics, and religion to biology, rather than simply consider biology as one of many influences on the various things that comprise human culture.

Morality from Science?

Although he has not contributed any specific theory to evolutionary thinking, Wilson could be considered the most Darwinian of the Darwinians. He does not elaborate on or even discuss Darwinism: He takes it for granted and uses it to articulate a grand all-purpose explanation covering all aspects of human life.

Among the many complex and rich aspects of human life, *mind* and *culture* represent twin holy grails that seem to evade scientific explanation. Wilson is well aware of the mystery surrounding them and has tried to explain them via their evolutionary origins. He did this in two books written in collaboration with Charles J. Lumsden of the University of Toronto. The first, titled *Genes, Mind, and Culture* and published in 1981, was written for scientific specialists.[33] The book is difficult, filled with technical jargon and mathematics, and tries to explain scientifically the origin of the human mind through the interaction of genes and culture in the process of evolution. Two years later Lumsden and Wilson published *Promethean Fire*, a more popular version of the same ideas. In its preface they wrote:

> We believe that an explanation of this postulated evolutionary mechanism will be of interest to a larger audience with a nonprofessional yet keen interest in human nature. At issue is the ultimate nature of man as it might eventually come to be interpreted with the aid of scientific investigation. For the first time we also link the research on gene-culture co-evolution to other, primarily anatomic studies of human evolution, and use the combined information to reconstruct the actual steps of mental evolution. We explore the implications of these and related ideas for the development of a more potent human science, which can serve as the basis for informed social action and new techniques in moral reasoning.[34]

Many people, including hard-nosed Darwinists, object to deriving moral directives from evolution. Even Richard Dawkins, the hardest of the hardnosed, believes it is a fallacy to derive ethics from science. Evolution is a theory that explains certain facts about the world; how can an understanding of those facts lead to moral or ethical directives about right and wrong? This particular error in reasoning—getting *ought* from *is*—is so well known that it has a name—the *naturalistic fallacy*. Philosophers since David Hume have generally been quite careful to avoid this fallacy. This creates challenges, of course, for those who, like Dawkins, take ethics seriously but reject the possibility that ethics can be found within religion.

This changes dramatically if we accept the existence of a God who created the world and in whom ethics can be grounded. And if we accept that, in some form, this God has revealed the moral nature of the created order to us, it then becomes reasonable to derive moral values from the facts of this created order. The naturalistic fallacy occurs when one obtains values from *natural facts* alone. If the facts of nature are joined to sources of morality, those facts take on an entirely new character, and they may provide us with moral values.

The majority of thinkers agree that evolution by itself is not an adequate source of moral values. Evolution, however, can be interwoven with the belief that God created the world, and thus brought into conversation with religious values. Darwin himself introduced a reference to God the Creator at the end of the sixth edition of *The Origin of Species*, the last edition published while he was still alive. And today there are many religious believers among the ranks of evolutionary biologists, who consider their faith entirely compatible with a robust belief in evolution.[35]

In spite of this, Wilson speaks as a kind of secular priest, entrusted with the mission of opening our eyes and illuminating us. He offers a full-fledged version of evolution that explains all the big questions: who we are, what our destiny is, and how we should behave, following the dictates of our common human nature.

One is compelled to ask whether Wilson is fully aware of the difficulties of his enterprise. Has he examined the difficulties outlined above? How does he get around the naturalistic fallacy? What does he make of the many evolutionists who are at the same time religious believers?

The answer, surprisingly, is yes: Wilson *has* examined these difficulties at length. Ullica Segerstråle has written:

> Another belief that Wilson, but few others, entertained was that we could and should derive moral values from knowledge of evolutionary biology. Although he hesitated on this around the time of *Sociobiology* (1975), he later reasserted his belief. For instance, in 1982 he said: "To put the matter as succinctly as possible, I do not think that the is/ought distinction is necessary. I believe that we should work to eliminate it as soon as possible." He also returned to this in his papers coauthored with Michael Ruse (1985 and 1986). And in his newest book, *Consilience*, Wilson restated his view with full force.[36]

In the eleventh chapter of *Consilience* Wilson assaults the naturalistic fallacy. According to Wilson, moral reasoning does not have a special status, and its problems should be solved by the scientific approach:

> We do not have to put moral reasoning in a special category, and use transcendental premises, because the posing of the naturalistic fallacy is itself a fallacy. For if *ought* is not *is*, what is? To translate *is* into *ought* makes sense if we attend to the objective meaning of ethical precepts.... They are more likely to be physical products of the brain and culture. From the consilient perspective of the natural sciences, they are no more than principles of the social contract hardened into rules and dictates, the behavioral codes that members of a society fervently wish others to follow and are willing to accept themselves for the common good.[37]

Wilson's idea is straightforward: The ethical *ought* reduces to the factual *is*. In other words, there is no room and indeed no need for ethical rules over and above the world of facts described by science. To take one of Wilson's clearest and most thought-provoking examples, consider the apparently universal moral injunction against incest. Virtually every culture condemns the practice of having sex with one's siblings, parents, or children. Now it also happens that this practice is unwise from a biological point of view, as any offspring that result from these unions are disproportionately likely to have genetically derived weaknesses. Furthermore, it is also the case that most people have a personal revulsion against committing incest. Unlike conventional adultery, for example, which poses a genuine temptation to many married people, incest is so undesirable that few people are ever even tempted by it. Is this a coincidence? How is it that the unhealthy practice of incest happens to be considered both morally wrong and pragmatically undesirable by just about everyone? Wilson's answer, which exemplifies his overall approach to ethics, is that evolution has "programmed" us to reject incest. Since an aversion to incest is likely to result in stronger offspring than an attraction to it, the aversion contributes to evolutionary "fitness" and is thus likely to be naturally selected whenever it appears.[38]

At this point Wilson slips from the "is" of our rejection of incest to the "ought" of our moral injunction against incest. Our human natures have a "moral law" written into them by our evolution. This moral law originated in the exactly the same way as our sweet tooth—because it had survival value. If we are willing to define "moral law" in this way, and if we can find plausible evolutionary mechanisms for the origination of all such moral laws, then Wilson's program must be said to work. But both of these requirements pose enormous challenges, not the least of which is the large number of disturbing counterexamples. Racism, for example, can be explained by appealing to evolutionary mechanisms,[39] but nobody—certainly not Wilson—is prepared to argue that racism is moral.

Like so much of Wilson's work, the preceding proposal is suggestive and intriguing. But it is also hopelessly inadequate. More explanation is required to justify this radical approach that falls so far short of explaining the full range of the human experience of morality. Wilson seems to think that a complete explanation of human evolution would contain a complete explanation of the origin and development of our sense of morality. This, however, is not a problem that can be decided by science alone. A consilience of the natural sciences cannot prove that there is no room for ethics outside the scope of the natural sciences. In fact, it cannot say anything about what might lie outside the scope of the natural sciences.

Wilson's Strategy

Wilson's far-reaching optimism may at times seem unwarranted and even naive, but he is careful with his arguments. He is a thorough-going materialist presenting arguments that look as though they were backed by science, but he exercises restraint. For instance, he does not say that ethical precepts are physical products of the brain—intuitions hardwired by natural selection; rather, he says that "ethical precepts are more likely to be physical products of the brain and culture." This is a typical articulation—presented as though supported by sciences, but ultimately tied to additional concepts beyond the sciences. In fact, in the first pages of *Consilience* he writes: "The belief in the possibility of consilience beyond science and across the great branches of learning is not yet science. It is a metaphysical worldview, and a minority one at that, shared by only a few scientists and philosophers.... The strongest appeal of consilience is in the prospect of intellectual adventure and, given even modest success, the value of understanding the human condition with a higher degree of certainty."[40] Then he invites the reader to share his adventure.

Wilson cannot be critiqued for lack of clarity when he articulates his vision: "If the consilience worldview is correct," he writes, "the traverse of the gaps will be a Magellanic voyage that eventually encircles the whole of reality. But that view could be wrong: The exploration may be proceeding across an endless sea. The current pace is such that we may find out which of the two images is correct within a few decades."[41] Of course, while Wilson notes that he may be wrong, he is clearly devoted, throughout the entire book, to persuading the reader he is right. On the other hand, Wilson wrote *Consilience* as he was approaching age seventy and was thus unlikely to witness the fate of proposals to be debated over subsequent decades. His bet is typical of what sometimes has been labeled "promissory materialism"—a materialism in which partial successes are extrapolated into grand and final conclusions. Wilson's work, while intriguing and suggestive, hardly constitutes a proof of materialism, which awaits dramatic new progress across a broad front.

Wilson's proposal possesses the advantage that current and future scientific progress can always be interpreted as favoring materialism, for those are the kinds of explanations that science provides. But this argument is deceptive. Empirically based scientific investigation concentrates on those aspects of the world that can be studied by the experimental method. Typically this is done by constructing theories that make empirical predictions that can be verified through observation and experiment. These explanations are overwhelmingly materialistic, at least under current scientific paradigms. But these successes do not in any way imply that all aspects of the world can be treated that way. Materialists can always argue, however, as they learned to do so effectively during modernity, that the future is theirs, because further scientific progress will steadily conquer new territories thought to be unassailable. Counterarguments are usually dismissed with the question, Who can pose limits to scientific progress in advance?

The truth is that some limits can be safely posed in advance, and we now have reservations about where science might take us. For instance, if God exists (and science certainly cannot prove that God does not exist), a domain of religious reality exists that can be studied by science only in a partial and limited way.

This is why materialists, even those as polite and restrained as Wilson, must employ their best weapons to counteract arguments that come from religion.

The Tribalistic Roots of Religion

Wilson employs the usual arguments against traditional religion of the sort that he embraced as a young man: It has fostered wars, confrontation, and cruelty; it is intolerant; and all this is what we should have expected because, after all, religion originated in tribalism.

The "overwhelming attraction of religion" for the human mind (the expression is Wilson's) as largely beneficent and a source of love, devotion, and, above all, hope are counterbalanced, says Wilson, by religion's dark side: We all know the stories of the great cruelties perpetrated across the centuries by religion. Wilson explains the attraction of religion as deriving from our well-developed instinct for survival: "*Anything* will serve, as long as it gives the individual meaning and somehow stretches into eternity that swift passage of the mind and spirit lamented by St. Augustine as the short day of time." Also, "the understanding and control of life is another source of religious power. Doctrine draws on the same creative springs as science and the arts, its aim being the extraction of order from the mysteries of the material world. To explain the meaning of life it spins mythic narratives of the tribal history, populating the cosmos with protective spirits and gods. The existence of the supernatural, if accepted, testifies to the existence of that other world so desperately desired." Then, "Religion is also empowered mightily by its principal ally, tribalism." Wilson concludes, "If the religious mythos did not exist in a culture, it would be quickly invented, and in fact it has been everywhere, thousands of times through history."[42]

Understanding religion, for Wilson, means providing an evolutionary explanation for its origins. He quotes approvingly the Roman poet Lucretius, who wrote, "Fear was the first thing on earth to make gods,"[43] implying that primitive human beings were afraid in the midst of so many natural phenomena they could not control, and they invented supernatural deities and religion as a source of consolation. We may wonder, however, if this conclusion was obtained scientifically. The argument takes for granted that God does not exist, which implies that things must be explained by their evolutionary origins, as determined by science. But no convincing arguments against the existence of God are advanced, and the evolutionary explanations of the origin of religion are speculative, inadequate, and supported by the scantiest of evidence.

In dealing with this complex and controversial issue, Wilson makes several substantial assertions one after the other, with little analysis. He says that the tribalistic roots of religion and those of moral reasoning are similar and may be identical; that religion arose on an ethical foundation; that religion has probably always been used in one manner or another to justify moral codes; that gods are primarily the product of fear; that religion draws on the same creative springs as science and the arts; that the principal ally of religion is tribalism.[44] We are compelled to ask Wilson to back up and explain these sweeping generalizations one by one, citing the empirical evidence for each: How do we know they are true? Are we asked to believe that "fear made the gods" because Lucretius said so? Wilson provides only speculative generalizations, not convincing arguments. He does little more than offer superficial criticisms of religion and point out that the empiricist perspective on religion has roots that go back to Aristotle's *Nichomachean Ethics*, to David Hume in the modern era, and to Charles Darwin for their first clear evolutionary elaboration.

Religion is not so much explained as "explained away" without serious argument. To be fair, we should add that Wilson treated religion in "primitive" peoples in his book *On Human Nature*. But one comes away from that discussion with the uneasy feeling that only evolutionary arguments and primitive peoples count for Wilson. He knows that thinkers like Kant, G. E. Moore, and John Rawls have proposed ethical arguments different from his own, but he easily finds why they are mistaken: They didn't know much biology. The same limitation holds not only for contemporary "religious believers" but also for "countless scholars in the social sciences and humanities who, like Moore and Rawls before them, have chosen to insulate their thinking from the natural sciences."[45] Once again, the natural sciences are presumed to have the last word, and other perspectives are dismissed simply on the basis that they are not rooted in science.

Wilson thinks religion is successful because it fulfils passions and emotions deeply rooted in human nature. In contrast, science is more of a "by-product" of evolution, rooted not in passions or desires but in objective truth. Wilson writes:

> If history and science have taught us anything, it is that passion and desire are not the same as truth. The human mind evolved to believe in the gods. It did not evolve to believe in biology. Acceptance of the supernatural conveyed a great advantage throughout prehistory, when the brain was evolving. Thus it is in sharp contrast to biology, which was developed as a product of the modern age and is not underwritten by genetic algorithms. The uncomfortable truth is that the two beliefs are not factually compatible. As a result those who hunger for both intellectual and religious truth will never acquire both in full measure.[46]

This passage is notable. Each of Wilson's assertions could be discussed and debated, for none of them have rigorous scientific foundations. For instance, many nonbelievers, comfortable in their nonbelief, might dispute the statement "The human mind evolved to believe in the gods," something that could be pleasant, if true, for believers.

The most important of Wilson's several claims here is, in any case, the final assertion that religion and science are incompatible. Perhaps it is here that we locate the core of Wilson's materialist program.

A False Dichotomy

Wilson's scientific authority in his field cannot be disputed: He is a distinguished entomologist and a world-class myrmecologist. His competence as a philosopher of science, however, falls woefully short of the minimum standards. Wilson's "conversion" from fundamentalist Southern Baptist to evolutionary evangelist provides a clue for understanding his philosophical adventure.

Michael Ruse, who has collaborated with Wilson, has written a revealing passage on this issue: "The post-Christian Wilson has always thought of his science in some way as a religion substitute and has used Darwinism not to banish faith but to find a more satisfying creed for the modern age." Ruse notes the following quote from Wilson's *On Human Nature*:

> The core of scientific materialism is the evolutionary epic. Let me repeat its minimum claims: that the laws of the physical sciences are consistent with those of the biological and social sciences and can be linked in chains of causal explanation; that life and mind have a physical basis; that the world as we know it has evolved from earlier worlds obedient to the same laws; and that the visible universe today is everywhere subject to these materialist explanations. The epic can be indefinitely strengthened up and down the line, but its most sweeping assertions cannot be proved with finality.[47]

Ruse goes on: "We are dealing with a 'myth'; but, when all is said and done, 'the evolutionary epic is probably the best myth we will ever have.' "[48]

The bad news for Wilson is that science and religion are compatible, at least in the view of those who have studied it most carefully.[49] What he presents in the quote above as "materialism" is not real materialism; it is simply an acknowledgment that the material dimension of the natural world studied by science is relevant. There is nothing there that deserves to be called "evolutionary epic" and worshiped. Wilson does speak here of the "minimum claims" of materialism and his grand evolutionary epic, but determining why he considers them incompatible with religion is difficult.

In one of his declarations about his own religious beliefs, Wilson offers a provocative and puzzling comment:

> On religion I lean toward deism but consider its proof largely a problem in astrophysics. The existence of a cosmological God who created the universe (as envisioned by deism) is possible, and may

eventually be settled, perhaps by forms of material evidence not yet imagined. Or the matter may be forever beyond human reach. In contrast, and of far greater importance to humanity, the existence of a biological God, one who directs organic evolution and intervenes in human affairs (as envisioned by theism) is increasingly contravened by biology and the brain sciences.... And yes—lest I forget—I may be wrong.[50]

This is a remarkable claim, both in its clarity and scope. But there are some obvious difficulties with this position, as Wilson outlines it: (1) How is the problem of the existence of God to be settled by astrophysics? Wilson refers to what has been called the "fine-tuning" of the laws of physics, but there is no sense in which an appeal to fine-tuning can "settle" the question of the existence of God. (2) What is the basis for the view of God as simply a deistic creator? Why does Wilson presume that a Creator God would not possess the full range of characteristics usually attributed to God? There is no reason, of course, why Wilson is obligated to use the Christian concept of God exclusively, but there should be at least some rationale presented for the restrictive concept he is using. Is he perhaps defining "God" in such a way as to rule out any possibility of religion? (3) Why do we have a distinction between a "cosmological God" who created the universe and a different "biological God," who Wilson says does not exist? The concepts of "cosmological God" and "biological God" may be catchy, but they can hardly be used if we desire to discuss religion seriously.

When Wilson speaks of "God," it is hard to see that he is referring to the God of the Abrahamic faiths. In these religious traditions you cannot distinguish a cosmological and a biological God, as if God is like a professor in a university department with a well-defined focus of attention. All developed concepts of God make it clear that God transcends both cosmology and biology. Wilson approaches the concept of God with the same mechanistic, reductionistic paradigm that he employs when working in entomology and that he praises for its capacity to advance science.

Wilson's reductionist approach, which has been wildly successful in science, entails dissecting objects into their most basic and elementary components and carefully studying each of the parts. The knowledge of the parts is then synthesized into knowledge of the whole. In contrast to this strategy, the God of the Abrahamic faiths is generally understood as an infinite Being that exists on its own and is the source of all that exists. Our pattern of distinguishing astrophysics from biology does not imply a corresponding distinction that can be applied to God; God does not relate to "parts" differently than "wholes." Wilson's search for consilience among the disciplines fails most precisely where this consilience could really be complete. If God is the prime cause of everything that exists, then the distinction of different scientific disciplines is theologically irrelevant. Consilience should not be interpreted as a metaphysical problem that characterizes reality as a whole; rather, the need for consilience grows out of the way that human knowledge is organized. Every scientific discipline adopts partial perspectives, and these do not always fit together into a coherent whole. Reality is very complex, our knowledge is very limited, and we must adopt restricted perspectives if we want to progress in the scientific study of the world. We must be satisfied with limited knowledge of parts of the world. This is very different than the way that God relates to that world, understood traditionally as the prime cause of all that exists.

The Consilient Perspective

Wilson's *consilience* is more than a unification of human knowledge. It also represents an alternative to religious thinking, free of the difficulties of religion, and, above all, supported by the natural sciences. The thrust of Wilson's approach is that valid explanations, in whatever ambit we explore, should be informed by the natural sciences. This also applies to religion, which Wilson represents in a very peculiar way: "The same reasoning that aligns ethical philosophy with science can also inform the study of religion. Religions are analogous to superorganisms. They have a life cycle. They are born, they grow, they compete, they reproduce, and, in the fullness of time, most die. They express a primary rule of human existence, that whatever is necessary to sustain life is also ultimately biological."[51] We wonder what scientific evidence supports this, for Wilson certainly presents his ideas as a consequence of science. "From the consilient perspective of the natural sciences, they [ethical precepts] are no more than principles of the social contract hardened into rules and dictates,"[52] says Wilson. Thus, we must ask whether "the consilient perspective of the natural sciences" is correct.

Wilson's inspiration for consilience—indeed, the word itself—derives from the nineteenth-century philosopher of science William Whewell (1794–1866). In his classical work *The Philosophy of the Inductive Sciences*, Whewell wrote:

> The evidence in favour of our induction is of a much higher and more forcible character when it enables us to express and determine cases of a *kind different* from those which were contemplated in the

formation of our hypothesis. The instances in which this occurred, indeed, impress us with a conviction that the truth of our hypothesis is certain. No accident could give rise to such an extraordinary co-incidence. No false supposition could, after being adjusted to one class of phenomena, so exactly represent a different class, when the agreement was unforeseen and uncontemplated. That rules springing from remote and unconnected quarters should thus leap to the same point, can only arise from *that* being the point where truth resides.[53]

Whewell's *consilience of inductions* can be interpreted as the convergence of varied and independent lines of evidence supporting one and the same hypothesis. It is similar to the testimony of varied and independent witnesses in a trial, all pointing in the same direction. In science we usually address the problem at hand with the hypothetico-deductive method. We formulate a hypothesis to explain something of interest, deduce consequences in the form of predictions that can be empirically tested, and evaluate the hypothesis by considering the result of the experiments. This method does not lead by itself to definitive conclusions, because the same data explained by our hypothesis could perhaps be explained also by a different hypothesis. This was the case in the sixteenth century for the retrograde motion of the planets, for example, which could be explained equally well by Ptolemy's geocentric epicycles or by Copernicus's heliocentric parallax. If we know only one consequence that has been well tested, we cannot be certain of any particular explanation. However, when several consequences coming from disparate domains support the same hypothesis, we can be much more certain of its truth. Again, by way of example, by the time Newton was finished, Copernican heliocentricity had so many different evidences that virtually everyone was certain of its truth. This is why Whewell considered the *consilience of inductions* as the strongest support that a scientific hypothesis can receive.

Wilson's thesis is that a *consilience* progressing from the basic levels of the natural world to the upper levels could reach the humanities, including ethics and religion. Or, seen the other way round, that all kinds of human experience could be explained on the basis of the natural sciences. But this is not Whewell's notion of consilience, nor is it compatible with Whewell's religious ideas. Whewell's consilience applies when independent lines of evidence support the same hypothesis, increasing the likelihood that the hypothesis is true. Atomic theory is an especially good example, applied successfully in entirely different branches of science: in statistical mechanics, in chemistry, in biochemistry, and so on. Many well-known phenomena in those areas can be explained and even predicted by atomic theory. In contrast, Wilson is talking about very different things, like culture, ethics, and religion, and he supposes that they have the same underlying natural causes. Thus, roughly speaking, ethics and religion would be explained through sociobiology, which in turn would be explained by biology, which in turn would be explained by chemistry, which in turn would be explained by physics.

Wilson, as we have seen, admits that his idea of consilience is a metaphysical program. In the related passage, quoted above, he adds: "Its best support [of consilience] is no more than an extrapolation of the consistent past success of the natural sciences. Its surest test will be its effectiveness in the social sciences and humanities."[54] Presently, however, there is little evidence that the social sciences and the humanities can be reduced to the natural sciences; the most one can claim is that some tiny insights into the higher level have floated up from below, such as the example we gave above about incest taboos. There are, to be sure, an increasing number of illuminating publications in evolutionary psychology, the current label for sociobiology; we are discovering the biological basis of mental activity; we anticipate that the deciphering of the human genome will make possible unforeseen advances in understanding a host of interesting phenomena. All this is true, and we affirm it, but it has little to do with Wilson's materialist ideology. We simply point out that, in spite of the great advances of science, we remain as ignorant as ever about the simplest and most basic question in all of science: How is it that physical events in the brain correspond to subjective states of the mind? Until materialism begins to illuminate this question, it can make no claim to being an appropriate metaphysical foundation for all of human experience.

Not surprisingly, Wilson has a strongly scientistic overtone when he speaks of the superiority of science over religion:

> I consider the scientific ethos superior to religion: its repeated triumphs in explaining and controlling the physical world; its self-correcting nature open to all competent to devise and conduct the tests; its readiness to examine all subjects sacred and profane; and now the possibility of explaining traditional religion by the mechanistic models of evolutionary biology. The last achievement will be crucial. If religion, including the dogmatic secular ideologies, can be systematically analyzed and explained as a product of the brain's evolution, its power as an external source of morality will be gone forever.[55]

Wilson makes no acknowledgment that the sciences deal with much simpler phenomena than does religion. It is no coincidence that physics, the most successful science and the one most often taken as a paradigm for all the sciences, is the science that addresses the simplest problems. The physicists study electrons; the psychologists study people; the reader is invited to guess which one is most likely to "solve" the problems they are addressing. Wilson also takes for granted that science and religion occupy the same territory, provide the same kind of explanations, and compete for the same goals and with the same methods. This is simply not the case. Wilson's hope that religion will be explained as a product of the evolution of the brain is a pipe dream.

Overexplanation

Steve Jones, professor of genetics at the Galton Laboratory of University College London, is coeditor of *The Cambridge Encyclopedia of Human Evolution* and author of *The Language of the Genes: Biology, History, and the Evolutionary Future*, winner of the 1994 Science Book Prize. Reviewing *Consilience*,[56] he notes: "The main problem is in over-explanation; in the relentless application of biology to social issues even when it has nothing much to say (or when what it says is stupefyingly banal).... Most human sociobiology is a restatement of the obvious in biological language."

Perhaps Jones, a geneticist himself, wanted to avoid the devastating assault on genetic determinism stirred up by Wilson's sociobiology. But Jones does clearly believe that Wilson overestimates the relevance of biology for sociology:

> Although Wilson makes a good case that man is a social animal
> because he evolved that way, he fails to point out that it is impossible
> to interpret any particular society in evolutionary terms. Evolution
> has been an alibi for socialism, for capitalism, and for racism.... We
> have evolved, of course; that is why we breathe air and need vitamin C:
> but everyone is the same in that regard. The interesting question is
> what makes us different. When it comes to society, biology has pre-
> cisely nothing to say about that.

"There is a danger in Wilson's book of accepting all possible patterns of human behavior as evidence for its thesis," warns Jones.

> Nowhere is this more clear than in its discussion of religion. When
> it comes to ants, Wilson is as rigorous as any of his colleagues.
> Ideas are tested with experiments. Some of them classics. As soon as
> God walks in, though, he becomes strangely flaccid. Rigor disap-
> pears in the face of assertion. Culture and religion are, he says,

superorganisms—but what does this mean? How do you recognize one when you see it? How many are there? What is the "basic unit of culture" measured in? Is there really a selective advantage for faith, as Wilson writes—even in Northern Ireland? And if all creeds are dominance hierarchies, why does the Bible say "Blessed are the meek"?

Freeman Dyson, one of the most distinguished contemporary physicists and a gifted science writer, also has reservations regarding *Consilience*. Reviewing a book written by Henri Broch and Nobel Prize–winner Georges Charpak, Dyson mentions Wilson's *Consilience*:

> There are two extreme points of view concerning the role of science in human understanding. At one extreme is the reductionist view, holding that all kinds of knowledge, from physics and chemistry to psychology and philosophy and sociology and history and ethics and religion, can be reduced to science. Whatever cannot be reduced to science is not knowledge. The reductionist view was forcibly expressed by Edward Wilson in his recent book *Consilience*. At the other extreme is the traditional view, that knowledge comes from many independent sources, and science is only one of them.... Most people hold views intermediate between the two extremes.... I am close to the traditional extreme.[57]

The Future of Life

John Horgan interviewed Wilson at Harvard for his book *The End of Science*. He writes,

> Everything would have been easy for Edward O. Wilson if he had just stuck to ants. Ants lured him into biology when he was a boy growing up in Alabama, and they remain his greatest source of inspiration. He has written stacks of papers and several books on the tiny creatures. Ant colonies line Wilson's office at Harvard University's Museum of Comparative Zoology. Showing them off to me, he was as proud and excited as a 10-year-old child. When I asked Wilson if he had exhausted the topic of ants yet, he exulted, "We're only just beginning!" He had recently embarked on a survey of *Pheidole*, one of the most abundant genera in the animal kingdom. *Pheidole* is thought to include more than 2,000 species of ants, most of which have never been described or even named. "I guess with that same

urge that makes men in their middle age decide that at last they are going to row across the Atlantic in a rowboat or join a group to climb K2, I decided that I would take on *Pheidole*," Wilson said.[58]

Wilson's ambitions, as we have seen, were much higher. He expanded the study of ants into the study of social insects into the study of social animals into the study of human beings, always seeking a unified perspective guided by the natural sciences. It was a risky plan labeled by Wilson himself as a metaphysical adventure—he dreamed an impossible dream—and it was that of the materialist. In his dream the elementary particles of the physicist combined to create atoms, molecules, proteins, and then life. Life evolved into ever more complex forms capable of various behaviors, and ultimately thinking and consciousness appeared, but guided by ancient instincts relevant to survival. Each successive layer of complexity built on the one before it, extending and refining basic patterns and algorithms that emerged at the lowest level of complexity. Human beings are ultimately made of elementary particles, and what a glorious explanation it would be to explain them as such. This was Wilson's dream.

To be sure, various aspects of the human condition are indeed rooted in a material reality, which is why Wilson's program can foster productive scientific studies. But although the mechanistic worldview produced abundant insights in the seventeenth and eighteen centuries, considered as a complete worldview, it turned out to be false. Today, even within science, few would claim the mechanical view was right. It reduced the whole fabric of the world to matter in motion, conceiving of natural processes as the collision of bits of matter. This idea, however, while marvelous at explaining things like the formation of stars, or the diffusion of gases, could not account for many aspects of the natural world. Materialism provides the same opportunity. But we must not consider it as an *ontological* doctrine that nothing is real except material things. Rather, we must treat materialism as a more limited tool, a *methodological* mode of inquiry that looks for whatever can be explained by it, without assuming that it can explain everything.

Consilience was, in both the final analysis and its original conception, more a manifesto than a guide for future studies. After *Consilience* Wilson embarked on another big project, revisiting his earlier passion about the almost spiritual connection that humans have with the rest of the living world, published as *Biophilia*[59] and *The Diversity of Life*.[60] In the 1970s he had joined a small group of scientists active in the global conservation movement. But at that time "the role played by the nongovernmental groups we advised was basically that of evangelists and beggars."[61] The moment arrived finally for

Wilson to actively join the conservation movement on a much greater scale, contributing with his wide knowledge of the biological world. In 2002, Wilson published *The Future of Life*, where he describes the problem as he sees it and refers to big projects on a grand scale. In the preface we read: "The situation is desperate—but there are encouraging signs that the race can be won.... A global land ethic is urgently needed. Not just any land ethic that might happen to enjoy agreeable sentiment, but one based on the best understanding of ourselves and the world around us that science and technology can provide.... Science and technology led us into this bottleneck. Now science and technology must help us find our way through and out."[62]

Wilson never abandoned the ants that captured his adolescent heart, even as his vision expanded to embrace and even protect the entire biosphere. In 2003, at the age of seventy-four, he published *Pheidole in the New World: A Dominant, Hyperdiverse Ant Genus*. The book is a magisterial 800-page opus on ants, filled with drawings he had done personally. Included is an associated CD-ROM with color images and tables.[63] In early 2006 he released *Nature Revealed*, a compilation of sixty-one pieces starting with his first scientific paper in 1949; he wrote an essay placing each piece in its historical and scientific context. The wide-ranging volume spans six decades of original and highly influential work; the author's constantly expanding scientific and cultural vision is clearly on display.[64]

Wilson's growing stature as a public intellectual gave him a grand public platform for his ideas, an opportunity he used wherever possible to mobilize concern for earth's increasingly threatened biodiversity. His public appearances and writings acquired an increasingly prophetic tone as he warned that humankind's reckless disregard for other species threatened the planet's rich biosphere and our own future. In late 2006 he released *The Creation: A Meeting of Science and Religion*, which offered an interesting and curious return to his roots. Written as a letter to a Southern Baptist pastor, of the sort that would have presided over Wilson's childhood spiritual development, the book calls Christians everywhere to cherish the many lifeforms they believe were created by God.[65]

Into his late seventies, Wilson's passion for science and reverence for the rich canvas of life painted by biological evolution continues undiminished. He remains active as both a theorist and a participant in big international projects, doing what he can to save species from extinction. But in so many ways he remains the curious little boy from Alabama, blinded in one eye by a pinfish, but forever able to see so much with the other.

Conclusion

Science and Beyond

We have examined the scientific and cultural impact of our six Oracles independently, so that each chapter can be read on its own, in any order. We can find no relevant criteria by which to order them; they also do not depend or build on each other in any meaningful sense. The Oracles are more or less contemporary, each with his own personal and public career that has unfolded apart from any significant interaction with the others. Nevertheless, as a careful reading of the previous chapters will have made clear, they have much in common, as well as great diversity.

We conclude our study by examining some of these similarities and differences, focusing on the connections that the Oracles make between science and culture, particularly their ideas about religion. This brief conclusion does not, of course, provide a systematic scholarly study that might uncover, for example, the sources of some of their common notions. That would take another book. Nor do the following reflections synthesize or summarize the present book. We simply offer some comparative highlights that round out our picture of the Oracles and their cultural impact.

Ambitious Oracles

Carl Sagan, Stephen Weinberg, Richard Dawkins, Stephen Hawking, Edward O. Wilson, and Stephen Jay Gould are the architects of wildly successful and wide-ranging projects. Like all scientists, they have done important work in specific areas, but unlike many scientists, they have a grand view of reality and have elected to engage the deeper scientific and cultural issues of our time. Their ability to do this so effectively accounts for their success and for the impact of their opinions. A list of the top one hundred living world intellectuals published in October 2005 includes Dawkins, Weinberg, and Wilson. Hawking's notable absence was highlighted by many of the voters as a sort of "write-in."[1]

Consider Wilson, who describes himself in his autobiography as an ambitious man. His *first* project as a university student was to classify *all* the ants of Alabama. Years later he did something even greater in *The Ants*, an impressive analysis of all kinds of ants from around the globe. He went from being an expert in the ants of Alabama to being the world's foremost authority on ants in general. Wilson's vision always had a grandeur, not only in science but also in his humanistic attempt to unify the sciences and the human condition. He is driven by a strong and consuming personal ambition to accomplish great things. And he has succeeded; he has been strongly influential in the new sciences of sociobiology and evolutionary psychology; he has published best-selling books, two of which have won Pulitzers; and his cultural impact can hardly be measured with the same yardsticks that calibrate ordinary human achievement.

Sagan's "big project" was finding extraterrestrial intelligence, and his enthusiasm for it was similar. His belief that contact with aliens could change the course of human history inspired him to give the complex and controversial search for alien life a fighting chance. His *Cosmos* television series was another huge achievement, making him a popular and influential celebrity all over the world.

The most extraordinary case is Hawking. His determination to overcome a crippling illness and do world-class physics is nothing short of heroic. How can we not be impressed by the human drama of a brilliant mind, hiding in a withered body, and yet still able to plumb the deepest depths of science?

Gould's prowess as an essayist is such that, even if he were not also a scientist, he would be an important cultural figure. His monthly articles in *Natural History* were published continuously for thirty years, and consistently compiled into best-selling books. He overcame a serious cancer when he was forty years old, combining his considerable intelligence and determination to escape the gloomy prognosis. His still-controversial theory of punctuated equilibrium was an ambitious contribution to evolutionary theory, made when he was young. And his great 1,433-page opus on evolution is nothing if not ambitious.

Weinberg's contribution to contemporary physics is considerable and was recognized with a Nobel Prize. And his popular book on the big bang has occupied a definitive niche for three decades now. Weinberg has also, out of sheer personal interest, turned himself into an authority on military history, a topic he has chosen to engage as a leading public intellectual, speaking out on American policy. [2]

Finally, Dawkins is a most enthusiastic and energetic advocate of his scientific, cultural, and religious ideas. Ambition is the signature of everything he does, from trying to introduce new ways of thinking into evolutionary theory to assaulting religion. He calls himself the "devil's chaplain," giving himself a cosmic role in his crusade against religion. If indeed the devil exists, he must surely be pleased with his good and faithful servant Richard Dawkins.

The Oracles of Science combine great ambition with great talent to address great problems. In doing so they have become major public intellectuals, household names to the well educated. They have real enthusiasm for science and for the rest of their ideas, and the talent to communicate this enthusiasm. Their oracular status is not accidental, nor simply the product of media hype (although the media certainly played an important role in Hawking's ascendancy to stardom). The Oracles are interesting and important simply because they are masters of science and want to bring that science to bear on the great questions of our time.

Points of Departure

The Oracles of Science, for the most part, create the impression that science is hostile to religion. But we have seen that this must be qualified. Gould, for example, claims otherwise. He devoted an entire book to showing the compatibility between science and religion. His "non-overlapping magisteria" (NOMA) proposal recommends that science and religion be kept completely separate from each other, thus avoiding conflict. Some think this is naive. But it echoes a bit of seventeenth-century wisdom immortalized by perhaps the greatest scientific Oracle of all time, Galileo, when he quoted Cardinal Cesare Baronio: "The intention of the Holy Spirit is to teach us how to go to heaven, not how the heavens go."[3] Galileo argued eloquently that the Bible was written to provide not scientific knowledge but religious teaching, a position routinely embraced by many scholars of religion today, but not at the time of Galileo. Gould notes, as a simple matter of fact, that many scientists, including evolutionary biologists, are religious, and he sensibly infers that this implies that evolution and religion must be compatible. So while Gould promotes positions that undermine some traditional religious ideas, it would be unfair to consider him an enemy of religion.

Dawkins and Weinberg, in contrast to Gould, are openly hostile to religion and make no apology for their hope that it will pass away. Dawkins's *The Blind Watchmaker* is a book-length argument that evolution explains the marvels of the living world much better than religion. Darwin, says Dawkins, showed that God is an unnecessary hypothesis for explaining the natural world. But as we pointed out earlier, this is not something that needs to be ascribed to God anyway, so it hardly implies that evolution and religion are incompatible, any more than showing that God is not needed to explain plumbing makes plumbing incompatible with religion. Dawkins makes a more general argument when he opposes the reliability of science, based on empirically testable, intersubjective hypotheses, to opinions based on authority, tradition, and revelation. And he strongly criticizes religion as a source of fanaticism and evil. After the events of September 11, 2001, Dawkins brought out all his rhetorical weapons to fight religion, which he presented as the source of the major evils in the world. His considerable rhetorical skills were also on display in his article "Opiate of the Masses," where he lists the negative effects of an addictive drug named "Gerin oil" (or "Geriniol"). The reader quickly realizes that the effects described actually derive from religious fanaticism at its worst and that Dawkins is playing an ancient game: "Gerin oil" or "Geriniol" are anagrams formed by rearranging the letters of "religion."[4]

Weinberg's views are similar to Dawkins's, but because Weinberg is a Jew who had many relatives killed in the Holocaust, his aversion to religion is profoundly shaped by the problem of how a good God could permit the evil in the world.

Wilson is different and somewhat more interesting. Growing up as a Southern Baptist, he had a "born-again" conversion experience and worshiped a traditional, biblical God. After becoming one of the world's most articulate evolutionists, he now calls for us to worship "the evolutionary epic." In his abandonment of his childhood religion, he did not simply shrug his shoulders and bid his faith farewell, as he did some years earlier with his belief in Santa Claus. Instead, he reconstituted his faith. He replaced the Genesis creation story with the modern scientific creation story; he replaced Christian ethical directives with ones derived from evolution and ecology; and he replaced the worship of God with the worship—*celebration* might be a better word—of the grand story of evolution. Perhaps because of his background Wilson understands the importance of religion. But, more important, the science that he did so much to create—evolutionary psychology, which looks at the way human evolution has shaped not just our bodies, but also the way we think—suggests that we have developed the natural predisposition that we have toward religion. Evolutionary psychologists are quite convinced that humans have a genetically based intuition to seek out or create religions. Wilson knows that religion is not simply going to "go away" just because, in his mind, science has triumphed over it. But Wilson does not exactly want religion to go away. He just wants to swap out its traditional obsolete contents and replace them with new scientific ones.

Hawking's attitude toward religion is a bit of a puzzle, and he enjoys being cryptic on this topic. Sometimes he seems to rule out any legitimate reflection on God and religion. But at other times he seems to knowingly locate himself on the side of a bounded science, leaving open the door for religion on the other side of that boundary. The brevity of his writings on this subject makes it difficult to determine exactly where he stands.

We have quoted Sagan earlier, from *The Demon-Haunted World*, as saying "many religions, devoted to reverence, awe, ethics, ritual, community, family, charity, and political and economic justice, are in no way challenged, but rather uplifted, by the findings of science. There is no necessary conflict between science and religion." He also believes that the reductionist program of science and its findings "are perfectly consonant with many religions." Sagan also made efforts to distinguish serious religion from superstition, and he sought to collaborate with religious groups as a part of his campaign to raise concern about environmental issues.

Our six Oracles are thus not a uniform body of thinkers, all rejecting religion in the name of science. None of them, however, are religious in the usual sense of the word, or in any sense, for that matter. Their writings produce the impression that science supersedes religion and even explains it away. But this requires further explanation.

Theology Out of Science?

The Oracles of Science should not be criticized for promoting their opinions on cultural and religious matters. That is their right, their choice, and something that a great many public figures do. A different issue, however, is whether they are justified in presenting their views as if they are derived from science. The immediate response has to be no: The Oracles are not justified in extrapolating from science to religion. But this response may be too simple.

The most surprising case is Gould. His NOMA proposal argues that the empirical study of the material world, which is the subject of the sciences, has no relation to the world of spirituality and meaning, which is the domain of religion. So far so good. However, since he first put pen to paper and began writing, he has set out an agenda quite incompatible with his own NOMA scheme and has developed this agenda consistently for many years. As we have seen, his agenda entails drawing "the radical philosophical content of Darwin's message—in its challenge to a set of entrenched Western attitudes that we are not yet ready to abandon." This message includes three claims: *Evolution has no purpose, evolution has no direction,* and the inferred *philosophy of materialism* implies that "mind, spirit, and God as well, are just words that express the wondrous results of neuronal complexity." How is this to be squared with the religious acceptance of a God who created the world? Gould is breaking his own commandments, invading theology in the name of science.

Wilson derives ethics and humanism from science in a most interesting way. He presents the "evolutionary epic" as a new source for ethics and religion, meeting our need for a big framework that provides meaning for our lives. But he acknowledges that something of traditional religion will have to stay in order to meet the very real human need for religion. It is quite hard to see, however, exactly how one is going to grow a new religion out of the worship of evolution.

Sagan and Dawkins exalt the wonders of the natural world as a source of excitement they hope surpasses the religious perspective. But this "sounds like a thief who chides his victims for lacking the items he has just taken from them."[5] The great monotheistic traditions praise God for the wonderful works of nature and consider this sense of wonder to be a road to God. Scientific progress provides us with new sources of excitement and awe, to be sure, but why would we suppose that this excitement competes with religion? Is it not simply an extension of the celebration of nature that has long been a part of religion?

Dawkins rejects the derivation of ethics from his "genes' eye" view of human nature. But he provides no alternative, or even an argument for why we should admit any ethics at all. He defends animal rights, though, which is an ethical stance; and he calls for respect for human life, assaulting as ethically inconsistent those who oppose abortion but support the death penalty. But on what does this ethical stance reside? Applying Dawkins's own criterion, it cannot be based on science. Dawkins is a brilliant and clever critic of ideas he rejects, but he proves quite inept at proposing alternatives to the rejected positions.

The Oracles of Science have not articulated a new vision that would provide meaning to the human experience. The closest they come is the suggestion that there is something to be reverenced in the evolutionary worldview. The biologists (Dawkins, Gould, and Wilson) are enthusiastic evolutionists, and the physicists (Hawking, Sagan, and Weinberg) are deeply involved with the origin and evolution of the universe. How evolution provides meaning to human experience remains unclear. Gould simply denies it, arguing that the process that "created us" is just a series of accidents, no more a source of meaning than a gambling casino, where some people strike it rich. Dawkins, the devil's chaplain, thinks that the evolutionary epic is a grand and meaningful tale compared to its pitiful analogue in religion, but he certainly offers no suggestions for how ordinary people, uninterested in the creation story of science, should make their way in the world. Sagan's view is more positive but sometimes seems to rest on the speculation that we will one day establish a cosmic connection with extraterrestrial intelligent beings. This would certainly be exciting but may very well never happen. Weinberg is pessimistic about the quest for meaning, seeing human experience as a farce. Wilson is the more optimistic of the Oracles, but his optimism relies on developing an understanding of the biological basis of human behavior that will prove adequate to provide meaning. This understanding, like Sagan's extraterrestrials, may never be discovered.

The Oracles do not offer a consistent new humanism as a replacement of religion. All of them defend humanist values but, with the exception of Wilson, they do not claim that we can extract from science a humanistic worldview and ethics.

Nevertheless, the Oracles have all challenged traditional religion in various ways, despite their failure to produce viable replacements. These assaults on religion have created an image of them as crusaders for an agnostic materialism in the name of science. Their cryptic and oracular utterances have taken on a life of their own, being quoted broadly with both approval and disapproval, appearing as epigrams at the beginning of chapters, and on Web sites devoted to "quotable quotes." We noted that Weinberg, at the end of a best-seller on the origin of the universe, says, "The more the universe seems comprehensible, the more it also seems pointless." If you type this famous phrase into Google, more than 30,000 references appear. And Hawking writes, at the end of a book even more famous than Weinberg's, that we are searching for a complete physical theory, "for then we would know the mind of God." We have met other similar examples. These oracular utterances, prominently located in books written by eminent science writers, are more effective than a hundred pages of dense argumentation, and their mysterious tone and great ubiquity provides them with the air of importance.

There must be more than this to the explanation, though. The books of the Oracles contain good popular science mixed with the philosophy of "scientific naturalism." But it is curious that they do not share a common view of scientific truth, a necessary step for establishing naturalism as a consequence of science.

Scientific Truth

There are important differences among the Oracles regarding the nature of scientific truth. Gould defends a *realist* position: "I espouse a rigorously conventional and rather old fashioned 'realist' view that an objective factual world exists 'out there' and that science can access its ways and modes."[6] But Gould also tends to contextualize science in a wider context. He is the only one of the Oracles proud to have collaborated with philosophers to clarify scientific problems: "Professional training in philosophy," he comments, "does provide a set of tools, modes and approaches, not to mention a feeling for common dangers and fallacies, that few scientists (or few 'smart folks' of any untrained persuasion) are likely to possess by the simple good fortune of superior raw brainpower."[7] Of course, Gould's early affinity for Marxism may explain his positive evaluation of approaches usually bypassed by other Oracles.

Wilson, for instance, says that the account of knowledge provided by the neopositivists (also called "logical positivists") in the 1930s, definitively abandoned long ago by philosophers as untenable, failed simply because they lacked sufficient knowledge of the brain, implying that positivism will succeed when new empirical knowledge about the brain becomes available: "Logical positivism was the most valiant concerted effort ever mounted by modern philosophers. Its failure, or put more generously, its shortcoming, was caused by ignorance of how the brain works. That in my opinion is the whole story."[8] This is a good example of oracular style, a big dramatic statement unsupported by science, and far outside the arena of anything remotely empirical. Wilson defends neopositivist ideas but simultaneously and inconsistently presents himself as a realist, noting that his belief in an objective and attainable truth risks heresy.[9] In contrast, Hawking embraces a thoroughly positivist account of science that would provide only models useful for predictions. However, this somewhat narrow view of science did not preclude him from presenting solutions for the most intricate problems relating to the origin of the universe.

Dawkins examines a roster of truth claims and concludes with his unique oracular style: "Scientific truth is the only member of the list which regularly persuades converts of its superiority. People are loyal to other belief systems for one reason only: they were brought up that way, and they have never known anything better."[10] He sharply criticizes nonrealist accounts of scientific truth, dismissing them as "unworthy of adult attention."[11] Weinberg also adopts a realist stance, defending the position that Sokal so cleverly articulated in his celebrated hoax.

These disagreements about the nature of scientific truth are important. Any evaluation of the cultural or religious impact of science must rely on ideas about the nature of the truth claims made by science. The Oracles are good scientists and excellent communicators, but these disagreements indicate that they do not possess a unique solution for the important question of the reach of science, and how far its conclusions can be extrapolated. We thus should not expect to find a well-articulated and consistent defense of scientific naturalism in their writings.

In the Name of Science

In his *Oxford Dictionary of Philosophy*, Simon Blackburn defines *naturalism* as "the view that ultimately nothing resists explanation by the methods characteristic of the natural sciences."[12] The undeniably spectacular progress of the sciences has led to their current stature as the paradigm for reliable knowledge.

There is a general agreement that science concentrates on aspects of the world that can be studied through theories that can be tested by doing experiments. Those aspects relate to spatiotemporal patterns in nature, for this is what makes experiments possible. If other dimensions of reality exist, they simply cannot be studied using the methods of the empirical sciences. The Royal Astronomer Sir Arthur Eddington (1882–1944) used an image that can help us here:

> Let us suppose that an ichthyologist is exploring the life of the ocean. He casts a net into the water and brings up a fishy assortment. Surveying his catch, he proceeds in the usual manner of a scientist to systematize what it reveals. He arrives at two generalizations:
>
>   (1) No sea-creature is less than two inches long.
>   (2) All sea-creatures have gills.
>
> These are both true of his catch, and he assumes tentatively that they will remain true however often he repeats it.
>
> In applying this analogy, the catch stands for the body of knowledge which constitutes physical science, and the net for the sensory and intellectual equipment which we use in obtaining it. The casting of the net corresponds to observation; for knowledge which has not been or could not be obtained by observation is not admitted into physical science.

An onlooker may object that the first generalisation is wrong. "There are plenty of sea-creatures under two inches long, only your net is not adapted to catch them." The ichthyologist dismisses this objection contemptuously. "Anything uncatchable by my net is *ipso facto* outside the scope of ichthyological knowledge, and is not part of the kingdom of fishes which has been defined as the theme of ichthyological knowledge. In short, what my net can't catch isn't fish." Or—to translate the analogy—"If you are not simply guessing, you are claiming a knowledge of the physical universe discovered in some other way than by the methods of physical science, and admittedly unverifiable by such methods. You are a metaphysician. Bah!"[13]

The same mistake is made when naturalism is presented as a consequence of the progress of science. There is a world of difference between the "methodological naturalism" used in the sciences (seeking natural explanations) and an "ontological naturalism" that denies the reality of anything outside the reach of science. While methodological naturalism has no problems, except for creationists and the advocates of Intelligent Design, scientific naturalism is self-defeating. The claim that nothing exists aside from what can be studied by the scientific method is a *philosophical* position. If you want to determine what science is and how far its reach extends, you must place yourself outside science, taking a philosophical perspective. But if there is no territory outside science, how are we going to stand there?

Our Oracles are aware of this problem, but they appear impatient and dissatisfied with the implications. They want a way out. The result is that sometimes their opinions—"the universe is pointless"—appear as though they were science, or a consequence of science.

We have been describing the Oracles of Science as ambassadors, messengers from the scientific community to the public at large. They play an important role in our scientific culture. We are in sympathy with their scientific findings and their cultural role. We applaud their capacity to communicate challenging ideas and their ability to provoke enthusiasm for the scientific enterprise. We would desire, however, that they would treat the humanistic issues that lie beyond the boundaries of science with the same careful rigor they employ when dealing with scientific problems. This would be a great service to society, effectively undermining the arguments of those who, like the proponents of Intelligent Design, see science as dangerously allied with materialism.

Modern science is an enormously wonderful and powerful achievement of our species, a culturally transcendent, universal method for studying the natural world. It should never be used as an ideological weapon. Scientific progress demands a respect for truth, rigor, and objectivity, three ethical values implied in the ethos of science. We can nevertheless draw different conclusions from our analyses of science, but we should always present them carefully, distinguishing what can be said in the name of science from personal interpretations that must be supported by independent reasons, or acknowledged simply as personal opinions. Our analysis shows that the Oracles differ in important points and are not consistently fighting for a common cause. When they go beyond their science, they use different arguments and arrive at different conclusions.

We conclude with one final insight. Science is compatible with a broad cross section of very different views on the deepest human problems. Weinberg, an agnostic Jew from New York, shared his Nobel Prize with Abdus Salam, a devout Muslim from Pakistan. They spoke different languages and had very different views on many important topics. But these differences were of no consequence when they came together to do science. Modern science can be embraced by any religion, any culture, any tribe, and brought to bear on whatever problems are considered most urgent, whether it be tracing their origins, curing their diseases, or cleaning up their water. Science should never be fashioned into a weapon for the promotion of an ideological agenda. Nevertheless, as history has shown, science is all too frequently enlisted in the service of propaganda; and, as we have argued in this book, we must be on guard against intellectual nonsense masquerading as science.

Notes

INTRODUCTION

1. See Keay Davidson, *Carl Sagan: A Life* (New York: J. Wiley, 1999), or William Poundstone, *Carl Sagan: A Life in the Cosmos* (New York: Henry Holt, 1999).

2. Richard Dawkins, *The Blind Watchmaker: Why the Evidence of Evolution Reveals a Universe without Design* (New York: Norton, 1987), 6.

3. Richard Dawkins, "Time to Stand Up," in *A Devil's Chaplain. Selected Essays by Richard Dawkins* (London: Weidenfeld and Nicolson, 2003), 156–61.

4. Steven Weinberg, *The First Three Minutes: A Modern View of the Origin of the Universe,* updated ed. (New York: Basic, 1993), 155.

5. Stephen Jay Gould, *Wonderful Life: Burgess Shale and the Nature of History* (New York: Norton, 1990), 323.

6. Edward O. Wilson (with Bert Hölldobler), *The Ants* (Berlin: Springer, 1990); *On Human Nature* (Cambridge, Mass.: Harvard University Press, 1978).

7. Edward O. Wilson, *Consilience: Unity of Knowledge* (New York: Knopf, 1998), 266.

8. C. P. Snow, *The Two Cultures and the Scientific Revolution* (Cambridge: Cambridge University Press, 1959).

9. C. P. Snow, *The Two Cultures,* 2d ed. (Cambridge: Cambridge University Press, 1993).

10. John Brockman, *The Third Culture* (New York: Touchstone, 1995).

11. Carl Sagan, *Cosmos* (New York: Ballantine, 1985), 4.

12. Stephen Weinberg, *Dreams of a Final Theory: The Scientist's Search for the Ultimate Laws of Nature,* with a new afterword (New York: Vintage, 1994), 245.

13. Poundstone, *Carl Sagan*, 355.

14. Available online at www.americanhumanist.org/humanism/.

15. Stephen Jay Gould, *Rocks of Ages*, 4.

16. Sagan, *Cosmos*, chap. 10: "The Edge of Forever," 212.

17. Stephen Hawking, *Black Holes and Baby Universes and Other Essays* (New York: Bantam, 1994), 172–73.

18. Wilson, *On Human Nature*, 192.

19. Stephen Weinberg, *Facing Up: Science and Its Cultural Adversaries* (Cambridge, Mass.: Harvard University Press, 2003), 242.

20. Dawkins, *A Devil's Chaplain*, 160–61.

21. Alister McGrath, *Dawkins' God: Genes, Memes, and the Meaning of Life* (Oxford: Blackwell, 2005).

22. Edward J. Larson and Larry Witham, "Scientists Are Still Keeping the Faith," *Nature* 386 (1997): 435–36. See also Larson and Witham, "Scientists and Religion in America," *Scientific American* (September 1999), 88–93 and Witham, *Where Darwin Meets the Bible* (New York: Oxford University Press, 2002).

23. Leuba found in 1916 that 40 percent of 1,000 surveyed scientists believed in God. See James H. Leuba, *The Belief in God and Immortality: A Psychological, Anthropological, and Statistical Study* (Boston: Sherman, French and Co., 1916).

24. Lea Plante, "Spirituality Soars Among Scientists," *Science and Theology News* 6.2 (October 2005): 7–8.

25. W. Mark Richardson, Robert John Russell, Philip Clayton, and Kirk Wegter-McNelly, eds., *Science and the Spiritual Quest: New Essays by Leading Scientists* (London: Routledge, 2002), 52–63.

26. Weinberg, *The First Three Minutes*, 154.

27. Matt Donnelly, "From the Other Side: Richard Dawkins Responds," *Science and Theology News* 6.2 (October 2005): 38.

28. Weinberg, *Dreams of a Final Theory*, 166–90.

29. Weinberg, *The First Three Minutes*, 154.

30. Gould, *Wonderful Life*, 323.

31. Richard Dawkins, *The Ancestor's Tale: A Pilgrimage to the Dawn of Evolution* (Boston: Houghton Mifflin, 2004), 614.

32. Issac Asimov, "Is Big Brother Watching?" *The Humanist* 44.4 (1984): 6–10.

33. Dawkins, *The Blind Watchmaker*.

34. Richard Dawkins, "Book Review," of Donald Johanson and Maitland Edey's *Blueprint, New York Times*, section 7, 9 April 1989.

35. Henry Morris, *The Long War against God: History and Impact of the Creation/Evolution Conflict* (Grand Rapids, Mich.: Baker, 1989).

36. William A. Dembski and Jay Wesley Richards, eds., *Unapologetic Apologetics: Meeting the Challenges of Theological Studies* (Downers Grove, Ill.: InterVarsity, 2001).

37. William Dembski, *Intelligent Design: The Bridge between Science and Theology* (Downers Grove, Ill.: InterVarsity Press, 1999), 13.

38. Ibid.

39. Phillip Johnson, *Reason in the Balance: The Case against Naturalism in Science, Law and Education* (Downers Grove, Ill.: InterVarsity, 1995).

40. Ibid., 16.

41. William R. Shea and Mariano Artigas, *Galileo in Rome: The Rise and Fall of a Troublesome Genius* (New York: Oxford University Press, 2003).

42. Karl Giberson, *Worlds Apart: The Unholy War between Religion and Science* (Kansas City, Mo.: Beacon Hill, 1993), and Karl Giberson and Donald A. Yerxa, *Species of Origins: America's Search for a Creation Story* (New York: Rowman and Littlefield, 2002).

CHAPTER I

1. Phillip E. Johnson, *Darwin on Trial* (Washington: Regnery Gateway, 1991).

2. Major figures of the modern synthesis, established in the 1930s and 1940s, include, among others, Sir Ronald Aylmer Fisher (1890–1962), John Burdon Sanderson Haldane (1892–1964), Theodosius Dobzhansky (1900–1975), and Sewall Wright (1889–1988). The titles of their works clearly show the central place that genetics occupies in neo-Darwinism. Fisher published the book *The Genetical Theory of Natural Selection* in 1930. Wright published his article *Evolution in Mendelian Populations* in 1931. The book *Genetics and the Origin of Species* was published by Dobzhansky in 1937.

3. Richard Dawkins, *The Selfish Gene*, 30th anniversary edition with a new Introduction by the author (New York: Oxford University Press, 2006), 11.

4. Ibid., 90.

5. H. Allen Orr, "A Passion for Evolution" (review of Dawkins' book *A Devil's Chaplain*), *New York Review of Books* 51.3 (February 26, 2004): 27.

6. Dawkins, *The Selfish Gene*, xv.

7. Ibid., xvi.

8. Ibid., xxii.

9. Stephen Jay Gould, *The Panda's Thumb: More Reflections in Natural History* (New York: Norton, 1992), 85–86.

10. Ibid., 90.

11. Ibid., 91.

12. Ibid., 91–92.

13. Robert Wright, "The Accidental Creationist: Why Stephen Jay Gould Is Bad for Evolution," *New Yorker* 75 (December 1999), 56–65.

14. Kim Sterelny, *Dawkins vs. Gould: Survival of the Fittest* (Cambridge: Icon, 2001).

15. Orr, "A Passion for Evolution," 27.

16. "Junk" DNA is present in the chromosomes but is not used to make proteins.

17. John S. Mattick, "The Hidden Genetic Program of Complex Organisms," *Scientific American* 291.4 (October 2004), 30–37; W. Wayt Gibbs, "The Unseen Genome: Gems among the Junk," *Scientific American* 289.5 (November 2003), 26–33.

18. Dawkins, *The Selfish Gene*, 12.

19. Richard Dawkins, *The Extended Phenotype: The Long Reach of the Gene* (New York: Oxford University Press, 1989), viii.

20. Ibid., v.

21. Dawkins, *The Selfish Gene*, 235.

22. Dawkins, *The Extended Phenotype*, 4.

23. Ibid., 1.

24. Ibid., 83.

25. Dawkins, *The Selfish Gene*, 191.

26. Susan Blackmore, *The Meme Machine* (New York: Oxford University Press, 2000), 192.

27. Dawkins, *The Selfish Gene*, 322–23.

28. Daniel Dennett, *Darwin's Dangerous Idea: Evolution and the Meanings of Life* (London: Penguin, 1995).

29. Blackmore, *The Meme Machine*.

30. Richard Dawkins, *Unweaving the Rainbow: Science, Delusion, and the Appetite for Wonder* (Boston: Houghton Mifflin, 1998), 302.

31. Jacques Monod, *Chance and Necessity: On the Natural Philosophy of Modern Biology* (London: Penguin, 1997), 180.

32. Richard Dawkins, *The Blind Watchmaker: Why the Evidence of Evolution Reveals a Universe without Design* (New York: Norton, 1987), ix.

33. Ibid., 21–41.

34. Ibid., 46.

35. Ibid., 47.

36. John A. Zahm, *Evolution and Dogma* (Chicago: D. H. McBride, 1896).

37. Christian de Duve, *A Guided Tour of the Living Cell* (New York: Scientific American, 1984), 357.

38. Dawkins, *The Blind Watchmaker*, 178.

39. Ibid.

40. Ibid., 193.

41. Ibid., x.

42. Richard Dawkins, *River Out of Eden: A Darwinian View of Life* (London: Phoenix, 1996), xiv.

43. Ibid.

44. Ibid., 154.

45. Ibid., 155.

46. Thomas Aquinas, *Summa Theologica*, pars 1, question 2, article 3 (Westminster, Md.: Christian Classics, 1981), 13–14.

47. Richard Dawkins, "God's Utility Function," *Scientific American* 273.5 (November 1995): 62–67.

48. Richard Dawkins, *A Devil's Chaplain. Selected Essays by Richard Dawkins* (London: Weidenfeld and Nicolson, 2003), 8.

49. Ibid., 118.

50. Ibid., 117.

51. Ibid., 145.

52. Mariano Artigas, *The Mind of the Universe* (Philadelphia: Templeton Foundation Press, 2000), chap. 7: "Scientific Values," 251–98.

53. Dawkins, *A Devil's Chaplain*, 149–50.

54. Ibid., 150.

55. Ibid.

56. Ibid., 154.

57. Ibid., 156.

58. Brian Goodwin, in *The Third Culture*, ed. John Brockman (New York: Touchstone, 1996), 88–89.

59. Dawkins, *A Devil's Chaplain*, 160–61.

60. Ibid., 158.

61. Blackmore, *The Meme Machine*, 191–92.

62. Dawkins, *A Devil's Chaplain*, 242–48.

63. Ibid., 117.

64. Richard Dawkins, *Climbing Mount Improbable* (London: Viking, 1996), 68.

65. Orr, "A Passion for Evolution," 28.

66. Ibid., 29.

67. Ibid.

68. See David C. Lindberg and Ronald N. Numbers, eds., *God and Nature: Historical Essays on the Encounter between Christianity and Science* (Berkeley: University of California Press, 1986); John Hedley Brooke, *Science and Religion: Some Historical Perspectives* (Cambridge: Cambridge University Press, 1991); Gary B. Ferngren, ed., *Science and Religion: A Historical Introduction* (Baltimore: Johns Hopkins University Press, 2002).

69. Orr, "A Passion for Evolution," 29.

70. Richard Dawkins, *The Ancestor's Tale: A Pilgrimage to the Dawn of Evolution* (Boston: Houghton Mifflin, 2004), 613–14.

71. Michael Ruse, "The Confessions of a Skeptic," *Research News and Opportunities in Science and Theology* 1.6 (February 2001): 20.

72. Michael Ruse, *Mystery of Mysteries: Is Evolution a Social Construction?* (Cambridge, Mass.: Harvard University Press, 1999), 132.

73. Richard Dawkins, "A Survival Machine," in *The Third Culture*, ed. John Brockman (New York: Simon and Schuster, 1996), 85–86.

74. Kenneth R. Miller, *Finding Darwin's God: A Scientist's Search for Common Ground between God and Evolution* (New York: Cliff Street, 2000), 213.

75. Karl W. Giberson and Donald A. Yerxa, *Species of Origins: America's Search for a Creation Story* (Lanham, Md.: Rowman and Littlefield, 2002), 119–50.

76. Alister McGrath, *Dawkins' God: Genes, Memes, and the Meaning of Life* (Oxford: Blackwell, 2005), 83–84.

77. Dawkins, *The Selfish Gene*, 198.

78. McGrath, *Dawkins' God*, 83–84.

79. Ibid., 95.

80. Alan Grafen and Mark Ridley, eds. *Richard Dawkins: How a Scientist Changed the Way We Think* (Oxford: Oxford University Press, 2006), xiii.

81. Richard Dawkins, "Opiate of the Masses," *Prospect* (October, 2005): 16–17.

82. Richard Dawkins, *The God Delusion* (Boston: Houghton Mifflin, 2006).

CHAPTER 2

1. Stephen Jay Gould, *I Have Landed: End of a Beginning in Natural History* (New York: Three Rivers, 2003), 15.

2. Stephen Jay Gould, *Rocks of Ages: Science and Religion in the Fullness of Life* (New York: Ballantine, 1999), 7–9.

3. Gould, *I Have Landed*, 3.

4. "Baseball," dir. Ken Burns, written by Ken Burns and Geoffrey C. Ward. Documentary miniseries, PBS, September 18, 1994.

5. Stephen Jay Gould, *Triumph and Tragedy in Mudville: A Lifelong Passion for Baseball* (New York: Norton, 2003).

6. Ibid., 17.

7. Stephen Jay Gould, *The Lying Stones of Marrakech: Penultimate Reflections in Natural History* (New York: Three Rivers, 2000), 228.

8. Stephen Jay Gould, *The Mismeasure of Man*, rev./exp. ed. (New York: Norton, 1996).

9. Robert Wright, "The Accidental Creationist: Why Stephen Jay Gould Is Bad for Evolution," *New Yorker* 75 (December 1999), 56–65.

10. Stephen Jay Gould, *The Structure of Evolutionary Theory* (Cambridge, Mass.: Harvard University Press, 2002), 759.

11. Ibid., 759–61.

12. Niles Eldredge and Stephen Jay Gould, "Punctuated Equilibria: An Alternative to Phyletic Gradualism," in *Models in Paleobiology*, ed. T. Schopf (San Francisco: Freeman, 1972), 82–115.

13. Ernst Mayr, *What Evolution Is* (New York: Basic, 2001), 175.

14. Mendel's work, which could have helped Darwin a bit, was not generally known at this time: Peter Bowler, *Evolution: History of an Idea* (Berkeley: University of California Press, 1989), 270–75.

15. Mayr, *What Evolution Is*, 176–83.

16. Eldredge and Gould, "Punctuated Equilibria: An Alternative to Phyletic Gradualism," 84.

17. Mayr, *What Evolution Is*, 193, 270.

18. Stephen Jay Gould and Niles Eldredge, "Punctuated Equilibrium Comes of Age," *Nature* 366 (November 18, 1993): 227.

19. John S. Mattick, "The Hidden Genetic Program of Complex Organisms," *Scientific American* 291.4 (October 2004): 30–37. See also W. Wayt Gibbs, "The Unseen Genome: Gems among the Junk," *Scientific American* 289.5 (November 2003): 26–33; and "The Unseen Genome: Beyond DNA," *Scientific American* 289.6 (December 2003): 106–13.

20. Stephen Jay Gould, *Ontogeny and Phylogeny* (Cambridge, Mass.: Harvard University Press, 1977).

21. Stephen Jay Gould, *Ever Since Darwin: Reflections in Natural History* (New York: Norton, 1977).

22. Ibid., 12–13 (italics are ours).

23. Gould, *I Have Landed*, 15.

24. For a colorful account of one theologian's experience in the Arkansas trial, see the late Langdon Gilkey's *Creationism on Trial: Evolution and God at Little Rock* (Minneapolis: Winston Press, 1985).

25. William R. Overton, "Creationism in Schools: Decision in McLean versus the Arkansas Board of Education," *Science* 215 (1982): 934–43.

26. *McLean v: Arkansas Documentation Project*, "Deposition of Dr. Stephen Jay Gould": www.antievolution.org/projects/mclean/new_site/depos/pf_gould_dep.htm, 15 (accessed December 17, 2004).

27. Ibid., 67.

28. Stephen Jay Gould, *Bully for Brontosaurus: Reflections in Natural History* (New York: Norton, 1991), 452–57.

29. Gould, *The Structure of Evolutionary Theory*, 1338.

30. Stephen Jay Gould, *Wonderful Life: Burgess Shale and the Nature of History* (New York: Norton, 1990), 14.

31. Ibid., 13.

32. Ibid., 23–24.

33. Ibid., 25.

34. Ibid., 35.

35. Michael Ruse, *Mystery of Mysteries: Is Evolution a Social Construction?* (Cambridge, Mass.: Harvard University Press, 1999), 135–52.

36. Gould, *Wonderful Life*, 43.

37. Ibid., 44.

38. Gould, *Ever Since Darwin*, 16–17.

39. Gould, *Wonderful Life*, 44–45.

40. Stephen Jay Gould, "The Evolution of Life on the Earth," *Scientific American* 271.4 (October 1994): 86.

41. Ibid., 87.

42. Ibid., 91.

43. Stephen Jay Gould, *The Panda's Thumb: More Reflections in Natural History* (New York: Norton, 1992), 136.

44. Ibid., 137.

45. Ibid., 138.

46. Ibid., 138–39.

47. Sigmund Freud, *A General Introduction to Psycho-Analysis*, in *Great Books of the Western World*, ed. Mortimer J. Adler, vol. 54: *Freud* (Chicago: Encyclopedia Britannica, Inc., 1993), 449–638.

48. Ibid., 449.

49. Ibid., 562.

50. Ibid.

51. Stephen Jay Gould, *Time's Arrow, Time's Cycle: Myth and Metaphor in the Discovery of Geological Time* (Cambridge, Mass.: Harvard University Press, 1987), 1–3.

52. Gould, *Ever Since Darwin*, 50.

53. Ibid.

54. Ibid., 21–23.

55. Ibid., 24.

56. Ibid., 24–25.

57. Ibid., 26–27.

58. Stephen Jay Gould, *Dinosaur in a Haystack: Reflections in Natural History* (New York: Three Rivers, 1997), xi–xii.

59. Gould, *Bully for Brontosaurus*, 475.

60. Gould, *I Have Landed*, 217.

61. Stephen Jay Gould, *Hen's Teeth and Horse's Toes: Further Reflections in Natural History* (New York: Norton, 1994), 285.

62. Piltdown Man was a fossil that combined a human skull and a simian jaw in a very convenient way so as to be construed as a crucial missing link in evolution. The alleged discoveries took place between 1908 and 1912, and the fraud was not discovered until 1953.

63. Gould, *Hen's Teeth and Horse's Toes*, 201–50.

64. Ibid., 250.

65. Stephen Jay Gould, *An Urchin in the Storm: Essays about Books and Ideas* (New York: Norton, 1988), 206.

66. John A. Zahm, *Evolution and Dogma* (Chicago: D. H. McBride, 1896), 312–13.

67. Thomas Aquinas, *Summa Theologica*, pars 1, question 19, article 8 (Westminster, Md.: Christian Classics, 1981), 109–10.

68. Ibid., pars 1, question 22, 120–25.

69. Thomas Aquinas, *Summa contra Gentiles*, book 1, chap. 85 (Notre Dame, Ind.: University of Notre Dame Press, 2003), 266–67.

70. Ibid., book 3, chaps. 70–77, 235–60.

71. Gould, *An Urchin in the Storm*, 12.

72. Gould, *Mismeasure of Man*.

73. Gould, *Rocks of Ages*, 4.

74. Ibid., 5.

75. Denyse O'Leary, *By Design or by Chance?* (Minneapolis: Augsburg, 2004), 112. See Karl W. Giberson and Donald A. Yerxa, *Species of Origins: America's Search for a Creation Story* (New York: Rowman and Littlefield, 2002), 136–37.

76. Stephen Jay Gould, *The Hedgehog, the Fox, and the Magister's Pox: Mending the Gap between Science and the Humanities* (New York: Harmony, 2003), 87.

77. H. Allen Orr, "Gould on God: Can Religion and Science Be Happily Reconciled?" *Boston Review*, October/November 1999, 33–38. All the quotations by Orr in this section are taken from this review.

78. Gould, *Rocks of Ages*, 213–20.

79. Gould, *The Hedgehog, the Fox, and the Magister's Pox*, 29.

80. Ibid., 234.

81. Ibid., 89.

82. Ibid., 141–42.

83. Ibid., 142–43.

84. Ibid., 143.

85. Ibid., 6.

CHAPTER 3

1. Michael White and John Gribbin, *Stephen Hawking: A Life in Science*, new ed. (Washington: Joseph Henry Press, 2002), 3.

2. Stephen W. Hawking, *A Brief History of Time*, updated and exp. 10th anniversary ed. (New York: Bantam, 1998), 191.

3. Martin Rees, *Before the Beginning: Our Universe and Others* (London: Simon and Schuster, 1997), 97–98.

4. Ibid., 6.

5. Ibid., 99.

6. Much biographical data can be found in his book: Stephen Hawking, *Black Holes and Baby Universes and Other Essays* (New York: Bantam, 1994), especially 1–26, 33–39, 157–75. Also in White and Gribbin, *Stephen Hawking*, and Kitty Ferguson, *Stephen Hawking: Quest for a Theory of Everything* (New York: Bantam, 1992).

7. Hawking, *Black Holes and Baby Universes*, 168.

8. White and Gribbin, *Stephen Hawking*, 67–68.

9. Ibid., 72.

10. S. W. Hawking and R. Penrose, "The Singularities of Gravitational Collapse and Cosmology," *Proceedings of the Royal Society of London*, Series A, vol. 314.1519 (January 27, 1970): 529–48.

11. Stephen W. Hawking, "Quantum Cosmology," in *Three Hundred Years of Gravitation*, ed. S. W. Hawking and W. Israel (Cambridge: Cambridge University Press, 1989), 632.

12. Hawking, *A Brief History of Time*, 53–54.

13. Ibid., 63.

14. Ibid., 81.

15. Stephen W. Hawking, "The Quantum Mechanics of Black Holes," *Scientific American* 236.1 (January 1977): 34.

16. Stephen W. Hawking, "Black Hole Explosions," *Nature* 248 (1974): 30.

17. Ferguson, *Stephen Hawking*, 91–92.

18. Hawking, *A Brief History of Time*, 116–17.

19. "Allocution of His Holiness John Paul II," in *Astrophysical Cosmology, Proceedings of the Study Week on Cosmology and Fundamental Physics*, eds. H. A. Bruück, G. V. Coyne, and M. S. Longair. Vatican City: Pontifica Academia Scientiarum, 1982, xxvii–xxxii.

20. John Paul II, Address to the Plenary Session and to the Study Week on the Subject," Cosmology and Fundamental Physics (3 October 1981), in *Papal Addresses to*

the Pontifical Academy of Sciences 1917–2002 (Vatican City: Pontifical Academy of Sciences, 2003), 250.

21. Ibid.

22. Ibid., 250–51.

23. White and Gribbin, *Stephen Hawking*, 202–3.

24. Hawking, *A Brief History of Time*, 119–20.

25. J. McEvoy and Oscar Zarate, *Introducing Stephen Hawking* (Cambridge: Icon, 1997), 146–52, 156.

26. Hawking, *A Brief History of Time*, 49.

27. Pius XII, "The Proofs of the Existence of God in the Light of Modern Natural Science" (November 22, 1951), in *Papal Addresses to the Pontifical Academy of Sciences 1917–2002*, 130.

28. Ibid., 131.

29. Ibid., 139.

30. Ibid., 139–40.

31. Ibid., 141.

32. Quoted by Dominique Lambert, *Un atome d'univers: La vie et l'oeuvre de Georges Lemaître* (Brussels: Lessius, 2000), 278.

33. Lambert, *Un atome d'univers*, 275–92; Valérie de Rath, *Georges Lemaître, le Père du big bang* (Brussels: Labor, 1994): 101–5; Pius XII, Speech to the International Astronomical Union (September 7, 1952): *Acta Apostolicae Sedis* 44 (1952): 732–39.

34. Quoted in Ferguson, *Stephen Hawking*, 85, and White and Gribbin, *Stephen Hawking*, 19.

35. Renée Weber, *Dialogues with Scientists and Sages* (1986; reprint, London: Arkana, 1990), interview with Stephen Hawking: "If there's an edge to the universe, there must be a God," 214.

36. Ibid., 209.

37. Hawking, *A Brief History of Time*, 146.

38. *Aquinas on Creation*, Writings on the Sentences of Peter Lombard, Book 2, Distinction 1, Question 1, translated with an introduction and notes by Steven E. Baldner and William E. Carroll (Toronto: Pontifical Institute of Medieval Studies, 1997), 119. In Appendix B (pp. 114–22), a translation of Aquinas's *On the Eternity of the World* is included.

39. Ibid., 114.

40. Ibid.

41. Ibid., 116.

42. Hawking, *A Brief History of Time*, 190.

43. Ibid., 53.

44. Hawking, "The Boundary Conditions of the Universe," in *Astrophysical Cosmology*, 563.

45. See Yakov B. Zeldovich, "Spontaneous Birth of the Closed Universe and the Anthropic Principle," in *Astrophysical Cosmology*, 578.

46. Hawking, *A Brief History of Time*, 141.

47. Stephen W. Hawking and J. B. Hartle, "Wave Function of the Universe," *Physical Review* D 28 (December 15, 1983): 2961.

48. Ibid., 2974.

49. Ibid., 2975.

50. Hawking, *A Brief History of Time*, 202.

51. Ibid., 143–44.

52. Roger Penrose, *The Road to Reality: A Complete Guide to the Laws of the Universe* (New York: Knopf, 2005), 769–72.

53. Hawking, *A Brief History of Time*, 141–42.

54. Ibid., viii–ix.

55. Lee Smolin, "The Future of the Nature of the Universe," in *The Next Fifty Years*, ed. John Brockman (New York: Vintage, 2002), 12.

56. Hawking, *Black Holes and Baby Universes*, 33–39.

57. Ferguson, *Stephen Hawking*, 88, 91, 127.

58. White and Gribbin, *Stephen Hawking*, 220–21.

59. Ibid., 221–29.

60. Hawking, *A Brief History of Time*, 191.

61. Ibid., 190.

62. Ferguson, *Stephen Hawking*, 121.

63. Ibid., 121–22; the quotation is from Hawking, *A Brief History of Time*, 190.

64. Kitty Ferguson, *The Fire in the Equations: Science, Religion and the Search for God* (Grand Rapids, Mich.: Eerdmans, 1994).

65. Stephen Hawking, *Black Holes and Baby Universes*, 172–73.

66. White and Gribbin, *Stephen Hawking*, 154.

67. Ibid., 157–58.

68. Ibid., 168.

69. Don Page, "Hawking's Timely Story," *Nature* 332 (April 21, 1988): 742.

70. Ibid.

71. Ibid., 742–43.

72. Ibid., 743.

73. Stephen Hawking, *The Universe in a Nutshell* (New York: Bantam, 2001), vii.

74. Ibid., 31.

75. Ibid., 54.

76. Ibid., 59.

77. Ibid., 118, 127, 180, 198.

78. Stephen Hawking, *The Illustrated A Brief History of Time*, updated and exp. ed. (New York: Bantam, 1996), 15–17.

79. Michael Atiyah, "Foreword," in Stephen Hawking and Roger Penrose, *The Nature of Space and Time* (Princeton, N.J.: Princeton University Press, 2000), vii.

80. Ibid., 120.

81. Stephen Hawking, "Chronology Protection: Making the World Safe for Historians," in *The Future of Spacetime*, ed. Stephen Hawking et al. (New York: Norton, 2002), 87–108.

82. Hawking, *The Illustrated A Brief History of Time*, 243.

83. Ibid., 204.

84. Ibid., 210.

85. Ibid., 210–11.

86. Hawking, *The Universe in a Nutshell*, 153.

87. Peter Coles, *Hawking and the Mind of God* (Cambridge: Icon, 2000), 61.

88. Ibid., 64.

89. Ibid., 66.

90. Ibid., 67.

91. John Horgan, *The End of Science: Facing the Limits of Knowledge in the Twilight of the Scientific Age* (New York: Broadway, 1997), 93.

92. Ibid., 95.

CHAPTER 4

1. Keay Davidson, *Carl Sagan: A Life* (New York: J. Wiley, 1999), 9.

2. Davidson, *Carl Sagan*, 390–91. See also William Poundstone, *Carl Sagan: A Life in the Cosmos* (New York: Henry Holt, 1999), 355–58.

3. Ann Druyan, "Carl Sagan: A New Sense of the Sacred," in Jerome Agel, *Carl Sagan's Cosmic Connection: An Extraterrestrial Perspective*, ed. Carl Sagan (Cambridge: Cambridge University Press, 2000), xx.

4. Carl Sagan, *The Demon-Haunted World: Science as a Candle in the Dark* (London: Headline, 1997), 3.

5. Poundstone, *Carl Sagan*, xvi.

6. Ibid., xvii.

7. Carl Sagan, *Cosmos* (New York: Ballantine, 1985), 134. We quote the text of the *Cosmos* TV series with the indication: *Cosmos* TV series.

8. Davidson, *Carl Sagan*, 168.

9. Ibid., 168–69.

10. Ibid., 267.

11. Ibid., 210–11.

12. Carl Sagan, ed. Jerome Agel, *Carl Sagan's Cosmic Connection: An Extraterrestrial Perspective* (Cambridge: Cambridge University Press, 2000), xxix.

13. Davidson, *Carl Sagan*, 258.

14. Carl Sagan, *Carl Sagan's Cosmic Connection: An Extraterrestrial Perspective*.

15. Freeman J. Dyson, foreword to ibid., xii–xiii.

16. Ibid., xiv–xv.

17. Davidson, *Carl Sagan*, 263.

18. Ibid., 15. See more details on the time capsule in Poundstone, *Carl Sagan*, xiii–xv.

19. Carl Sagan, *The Dragons of Eden: Speculations of the Evolution of Human Intelligence* (New York: Ballantine, 1978), 4–5.

20. Ibid., 239–45.

21. Sagan, *Cosmos*, 285.

22. Sagan, *Cosmos* TV series, episode 7, scene 11, "Evidence of Other Planets." See a similar text in the book *Cosmos*, 159–60.

23. Sagan, *Cosmos*, chap. 5: "Blues for a Red Planet," 105.

24. Davidson, *Carl Sagan*, 274.

25. Sagan, *Cosmos*, chap. 10: "The Edge of Forever," 212.

26. Sagan, *Cosmos* TV series, episode 1, scene 3, "The Cosmos."

27. See, for example, John Hedley Brooke, *Science and Religion: Some Historical Perspectives* (Cambridge: Cambridge University Press, 1991).

28. Sagan, *Cosmos* TV series, episode 7, scene 5, "Ancient Greek Scientists."

29. Sagan, *Cosmos*, 141 (almost textual in *Cosmos* TV series, episode 7, scene 5).

30. Sagan, *Cosmos* TV series, episode 7, scene 5.

31. Sagan, *Cosmos*, 154.

32. Werner Jaeger, *The Theology of the Early Greek Philosophers* (Oxford: Clarendon Press, 1964), 21.

33. Sagan, *Cosmos*, 147–48 (*Cosmos* TV series, episode 7, scene 7, "Democritus," almost identical with the book).

34. Ibid., 150–51.

35. Sagan, *Cosmos* TV series, episode 7, scene 9, "Plato and Others."

36. Ibid.

37. Steven Weinberg, *Dreams of a Final Theory: Scientist's Search for the Ultimate Laws of Nature* (New York: Vintage, 1994), 7.

38. Sagan, *Cosmos*, 142.

39. David Lindberg, *The Beginnings of Western Science* (Chicago: University of Chicago Press, 1992).

40. Thomas Kuhn, *The Copernican Revolution: Planetary Astronomy in the Development of Western Thought* (Cambridge, Mass.: Harvard University Press, 1957), 122.

41. Davidson, *Carl Sagan*, 322.

42. Sagan, *Cosmos*, 278–79.

43. See Maria Dzielska, *Hypatia of Alexandria* (Cambridge, Mass.: Harvard University Press, 1998), 105–6.

44. Ibid., 1.

45. Davidson, *Carl Sagan*, 342.

46. Carl Sagan, *Contact* (New York: Pocket, 1997).

47. Davidson, *Carl Sagan*, 409–10.

48. Ibid., 409.

49. Ibid.

50. Ibid., 377–78.

51. Carl Sagan, *Billions and Billions: Thoughts on Life and Death at the Brink of the Millennium* (New York: Ballantine, 1997), 167.

52. Ibid., 166–67.

53. Michael Shermer, "An Awful Hole: A Wonderful Life," *Skeptic* 4.4 (1996): 13.

54. Ann Druyan, "Carl Sagan: A New Sense of the Sacred," xviii–xix.

55. Davidson, *Carl Sagan*, 136–37.

56. Ibid., 55–58.

57. Poundstone, *Carl Sagan*, 20.

58. Ibid., 21.

59. Davidson, *Carl Sagan*, 112.

60. Ibid., 58.

61. Sagan, *The Demon-Haunted World*, 19.

62. Ibid., 264.

63. Ibid., 264–65.

64. Ibid., 262.

65. Ibid., 263.

66. Ibid., 254–55.

67. Davidson, *Carl Sagan*, 420.

68. Ibid., 1.

69. Ibid., 30–31.

70. Ibid., 237.

71. Carl Sagan, *Broca's Brain: Reflections on the Romance of Science* (New York: Ballantine, 1980), 324.

72. Davidson, *Carl Sagan*, 240.

73. Sagan, *The Demon-Haunted World*, 28–31.

74. Ibid., 32.

75. Sagan, *Broca's Brain*, 332–33.

76. See, for example, Colin A. Russell, "The Conflict of Science and Religion," in *Science and Religion: A Historical Introduction*, ed. Gary B. Ferngren (Baltimore: Johns Hopkins University Press, 2002), 3–12; David B. Wilson, "The Historiography of Science and Religion," in ibid., 13–29.

77. Sagan, *Broca's Brain*, 333.

78. Ibid.

79. Andrew Dickson White, *A History of the Warfare of Science with Theology in Christendom* (Buffalo, NY: Prometheus, 1993), 142.

80. William R. Shea and Mariano Artigas, *Galileo in Rome: The Rise and Fall of an Uneasy Genius* (New York: Oxford University Press, 2003), 179–97.

81. Sagan, *The Demon-Haunted World*, 33–38.

82. Ibid., 261.

83. See Stanley L. Jaki, *Science and Creation: From Eternal Cycles to an Oscillating Universe* (Edinburgh: Scottish Academic Press, 1986), and *The Road of Science and the Ways to God* (Chicago: Chicago University Press, 1978). For critique, see Rolf Gruner, "Science, Nature, and Christianity," *Journal of Theological Studies* 26 (1975): 55–81.

84. Tom Head, ed. *Conversations with Carl Sagan* (Jackson: University Press of Mississippi, 2006), 68–75.

CHAPTER 5

1. Weinberg's autobiography in *Nobel Lectures: Physics, 1971–1980*, ed. Stig Lundqvist (Singapore: World Scientific Publishing, 1994), 541.

2. Ibid.

3. Steven Weinberg, "What Price Glory?" *New York Review of Books* 50.17 (November 6, 2003): 55.

4. Bengt Nagel, "The Nobel Prize for Physics," in *Nobel Lectures, Physics, 1971–1980*, 487.

5. Ibid.

6. George Gamow, *Thirty Years That Shook Physics: Story of Quantum Theory* (New York: Dover, 1985).

7. Steven Weinberg, *Facing Up: Science and Its Cultural Adversaries* (Cambridge, Mass.: Harvard University Press, 2003), 185.

8. Ibid., 185–86.

9. Steven Weinberg, *Dreams of a Final Theory* (New York: Vintage, 1994), 120–21.

10. Bengt Nagel, "The Nobel Prize for Physics," 488.

11. Steven Weinberg, "Unified Theories of Elementary-Particle Interaction," *Scientific American* 231.1 (July 1974): 57.

12. David B. Cline, Alfred K. Mann, and Carlo Rubbia, "The Detection of Neutral Weak Currents," *Scientific American* 231.6 (December 1974): 108.

13. For a detailed report of the experiments leading to the detection of weak neutral currents, see Peter Galison, *How Experiments End* (Chicago: University of Chicago Press, 1987), a study performed with the help of Weinberg: "Conversations with Steven Weinberg led me first to the history of the neutral-current experiments and then to problems in the phenomenology of electroweak interactions" (ibid., xi).

14. David B. Cline, Carlo Rubbia, and Simon van der Meer, "The Search for Intermediate Vector Bosons," *Scientific American* 246.3 (March 1982): 38.

15. Steven Weinberg, *The First Three Minutes: A Modern View of the Origin of the Universe*, updated ed. (New York: Basic, 1993), vii.

16. Ibid., ix.

17. Ibid., 154.

18. Ibid., 154–55.

19. Alan Lightman and Roberta Brawer, *Origins: Lives and Worlds of Modern Cosmologists* (Cambridge, Mass.: Harvard University Press, 1990), 466.

20. Ibid., 66, 83–84, 100–101, 119, 135, 152–53, 168–69, 248–49.

21. Ibid., 358.

22. Ibid., 398.

23. Ibid., 409.

24. Weinberg, *Facing Up*, 46.

25. Ibid., 47.

26. Ibid., 42–43.

27. J. David Jackson, Maury Tigner, and Stanley Wojcicki, "The Superconducting Supercollider," *Scientific American* 254.3 (March 1986): 56.

28. John Horgan, "Particle Metaphysics," *Scientific American* 270.2 (February 1994): 96–106.

29. Weinberg, *Dreams of a Final Theory*, 5.

30. Weinberg, *Facing Up*, x.

31. Ibid., 182.

32. Weinberg, *Dreams of a Final Theory*, 241.

33. Mariano Artigas, *The Mind of the Universe: Understanding Science and Religion* (Philadelphia: Templeton Foundation Press, 2000), 300–301.

34. Weinberg, *Dreams of a Final Theory*, 242.

35. Ibid., 245.

36. Ibid., 245–46.

37. Ibid., 250.

38. Ibid., 244.

39. Ibid., 253–54.

40. Ibid., 254.

41. Ibid., 250–51.

42. Ibid., 256.

43. Ibid., 260.

44. Ibid., 261.

45. John Horgan, *The End of Science: Facing the Limits of Knowledge in the Twilight of the Scientific Age* (New York: Broadway, 1997), 76.

46. Ibid., 77.

47. Weinberg, *Facing Up*, ix–x.

48. Ibid., 182.

49. Weinberg, *Dreams of a Final Theory*, 249–50.

50. John Hedley Brooke, *Science and Religion: Some Historical Perspectives* (Cambridge: Cambridge University Press, 1991).

51. Weinberg, *Dreams of a Final Theory*, 248.

52. Francisco J. Ayala, "Intelligent Design: Original Version," *Theology and Science* 1 (2003): 30–31.

53. Abdus Salam, *Ideals and Realities: Selected Essays of Abdus Salam*, 2d ed., ed. C. H. Lai (Singapore: World Scientific, 1987), 160–61.

54. Weinberg, *Facing Up*, 230.

55. Ibid., 231.

56. Ibid., 242.

57. Ibid., 241.

58. Ibid., 242.

59. Ibid., 231.

60. Ibid., 255.

61. Weinberg, "What Price Glory?" 55.

62. Weinberg, *Facing Up*, 232.

63. Ibid., 237.

64. Ibid., 239–40.

65. Ibid., 240.

66. Ibid., 242.

67. Alister McGrath, *The Twilight of Atheism: Rise and Fall of Disbelief in the Modern World* (New York: Doubleday, 2004).

68. Weinberg, *Facing Up*, 269.

69. Thomas S. Kuhn, *The Essential Tension: Selected Studies in Scientific Tradition and Change* (Chicago: University of Chicago Press, 1977), xi–xiii.

70. Weinberg, *Facing Up*, 203–4.

71. Horgan, *The End of Science*, 47.

72. Weinberg, *Facing Up*, 190–91.

73. Ibid., 197

74. Ibid., 200–201.

75. Ibid., 205–6.

76. See, for example, Nick Herbert, *Quantum Reality. Beyond the New Physics* (New York: Anchor, 1987).

77. Rom Harré, *Varieties of Realism: A Rationale for the Natural Sciences* (Oxford: Blackwell, 1986).

78. Steven Weinberg, "A Unified Physics by 2050?" *Scientific American* 281.6 (December 1999): 70.

79. Ibid., 74–75.

80. Alain Sokal, "Transgressing the Boundaries: Toward a Transformative Hermeneutics of Quantum Gravity," *Social Text* (Spring-Summer 1996): reproduced in *The Sokal Hoax: The Sham That Shook the Academy*, ed. editors of *Lingua Franca* (Lincoln: University of Nebraska Press, 2000), 11–45. This book contains the contributions of many authors to the discussion. The already classic book on the affair is Alan Sokal and Jean Bricmont, *Intellectual Impostures: Postmodern Philosophers' Abuse of Science*, 2d ed. (London: Profile, 2003).

81. Alain Sokal, "Revelation: A Physicist Experiments with Cultural Studies," *Lingua Franca* (May–June 1996), reproduced in *The Sokal Hoax*, 49–53.

82. Steven Weinberg, "Sokal's Hoax, and Selected Responses," in *The Sokal Hoax*, 152 (also in *Facing Up*, 145–46).

83. Karl R. Popper, *The Logic of Scientific Discovery* (New York: Routledge, 1980), 36.

84. Freeman Dyson, "The Scientist as Rebel," in *Nature's Imagination: Frontiers of Scientific Vision*, ed. John Cornwell (New York: Oxford University Press, 1995), 5, 11.

85. Weinberg, *Facing Up*, 109.

86. Ibid., 111.

87. Ibid., 112.

88. Ibid., 57.

89. Philip W. Anderson, "More Is Different," *Science* 177.4047 (August 4, 1972): 393.

90. Ibid.

91. Ibid., 396.

92. Weinberg, *Facing Up*, 119.

93. Weinberg, *Dreams of a Final Theory*, 18.

94. Ibid., 17.

CHAPTER 6

1. Bert Hölldobler and Edward O. Wilson, *The Ants* (Berlin: Springer, 1990). See also Hölldobler and Wilson, *Journey to the Ants: A Story of Scientific Exploration* (Cambridge, Mass.: Belknap Press of Harvard University Press, 1994).

2. Edward O. Wilson, *The Insect Societies* (Cambridge, Mass.: Belknap Press of Harvard University Press, 1971).

3. Edward O. Wilson, *Sociobiology: New Synthesis*, 25th anniversary ed. (1975; Cambridge, Mass.: Belknap Press of Harvard University Press, 2000).

4. Edward O. Wilson, *On Human Nature* (Cambridge, Mass.: Harvard University Press, 1978).

5. Edward O. Wilson, *Consilience: Unity of Knowledge* (New York: Knopf, 1998).

6. Edward O. Wilson, *Biophilia* (Cambridge, Mass.: Harvard University Press, 1984).

7. Edward O. Wilson, *Naturalist* (New York: Warner, 1994), 5.

8. Ibid., 15.

9. For a pictorial essay on why Wilson thinks we prefer hilltop mansions, see E. O. Wilson, "Never Out of Africa," *Science and Spirit* (September–October 2003): 50–56.

10. Wilson, *Consilience*, 3–7. All the quotations by Wilson in this section are taken from this chapter.

11. Gerald Holton, Wilson's Harvard colleague and a leading historian of science, is well known for his penetrating analyses of the deep intuitions that have shaped various scientific advances. See, for example, his *Thematic Origins of Scientific Thought* (Cambridge, Mass.: Harvard University Press, 1988), or his *Scientific Imagination* (Cambridge: Cambridge University Press, 1978).

12. Just how nostalgic can be seen from an episode related by Robert Wright in *Three Scientists and Their Gods* (New York: HarperCollins, 1989). While attending an old-fashioned "southern-Baptist-style" chapel service in honor of Martin Luther King Sr., Wilson was observed crying during the singing of one of hymns. When queried, he explained, "It was tribal. It was the feeling that I had been a long way away from the tribe" (192).

13. Wilson, *Consilience*, 247–48.

14. Ibid., 248.

15. Ibid., 55.

16. Wilson, *Naturalist*, 218–19.

17. Ibid., 187.

18. Robert H. MacArthur and Edward O. Wilson, *The Theory of Island Biogeography* (Princeton, N.J.: Princeton University Press, 1967).

19. Wilson, *Naturalist*, 167.

20. Ibid., 296–97.

21. Ullica Segerstråle, *Defenders of the Truth: The Sociobiology Debate* (New York: Oxford University Press, 2001), 49.

22. Wilson, *Naturalist*, 261.

23. Michael Ruse, "Sociobiology," in *Encyclopedia of Science and Religion*, ed. J. Wentzel Vrede van Huyssteen (New York: Macmillan, 2003), 810.

24. Ibid., 811–12.

25. The Fifteenth Ecumenical Council, held in the French city of Vienne in 1311–13, decreed: "We reject as erroneous and contrary to the truth of the Catholic faith every doctrine or proposition rashly asserting that the substance of the rational or intellectual soul is not of itself and essentially the form of the human body, or casting doubt on this matter. In order that all may know the truth of the faith in its purity and all error may be excluded, we define that anyone who presumes henceforth to assert, defend or hold stubbornly that the rational or intellectual soul is not the form of the human body of itself and essentially, is to be considered a heretic." See *Decrees of the Ecumenical Councils*, ed. Norman Tanner (London: Sheed and Ward, 1990), 361. Certainly, according to Catholic doctrine, when a person dies, the spiritual dimensions continue to exist for the afterlife, but this should not be interpreted as though the soul were something like a preexisting substance superimposed upon the body from outside. Obviously we do not intend to develop here a whole exposition of this doctrine. We intend to show only that the intertwining of the spiritual and material dimensions in the human being is far from being anything new for Christian thinking.

26. Wilson, *Naturalist*, 330–53; Charles J. Lumsden and Edward O. Wilson, *Promethean Fire: Reflections on the Origin of Mind* (Cambridge, Mass.: Harvard University Press, 1983), 23–50.

27. Segerstråle, *Defenders of the Truth*, 49.

28. Ibid., 50.

29. Stephen Jay Gould, *The Hedgehog, the Fox, and the Magister's Pox: Mending the Gap between Science and the Humanities* (New York: Harmony, 2003), 189–260.

30. Ibid., 232–33.

31. Ibid., 227–28, 233.

32. Ibid., 233.

33. Charles J. Lumsden and Edward O. Wilson, *Genes, Mind, and Culture: Coevolutionary Process* (Cambridge, Mass.: Harvard University Press, 1981).

34. Lumsden and Wilson, *Promethean Fire*, v.

35. Perhaps the best example in the United States is Brown University biologist and practicing Roman Catholic Kenneth Miller, who is both a staunch defender of evolution and an outspoken critic of scientific creationism and Intelligent Design. Miller provides an articulate overview of his beliefs and how he reconciles biology and faith in *Finding Darwin's God* (New York: HarperCollins, 1999).

36. Segerstråle, *Defenders of the Truth*, 291.

37. Wilson, *Consilience*, 249–50.

38. Wilson, *On Human Nature*, 36–39.

39. The argument is based on the concept of the "out-group." One's "in-group," or tribe, originally was probably essentially an extended family, which meant that the members of one's in-group were very likely to share some of one's genes, making it advantageous, at least genetically, to care for and protect the members of the in-group.

In contrast, the out-group—another race—was the enemy because they posed various challenges, such as competing for resources, and the survival of their genes was of no value.

40. Wilson, *Consilience*, 9.

41. Ibid., 268.

42. Ibid., 257.

43. Ibid.

44. Ibid., 256–57.

45. Ibid., 249.

46. Ibid., 262.

47. Wilson, *On Human Nature*, 201.

48. Michael Ruse, *Mystery of Mysteries: Is Evolution a Social Construction?* (Cambridge, Mass.: Harvard University Press, 1999), 188.

49. The past few years have witnessed the growth of what amounts to a discipline looking at the interaction of science and religion and, while there are a wide variety of perspectives advanced within this new field, there is an emerging consensus that the incompatibility of science and religion is an outmoded nineteenth-century notion that originated with some overeager secularists. For a sustained and authoritative critique of the view that the relationship between science and religion is simple incompatibility, see John Hedley Brooke, *Science and Religion: Some Historical Perspectives* (Cambridge: Cambridge University Press, 1991).

50. Wilson, *Consilience*, 241.

51. Ibid., 256.

52. Ibid., 250.

53. William Whewell, *The Philosophy of the Inductive Sciences* (1840; reprint, London: Routledge/Thoemmes, 1996) 2:230.

54. Wilson, *Consilience*, 9.

55. Wilson, *On Human Nature*, 201.

56. Steve Jones, "In the Genetic Toyshop," *New York Review of Books* 45.7 (April 23, 1998): 14–16.

57. Freeman J. Dyson, "One in a Million" (review of *Debunked! ESP, Telekinesis, Other Pseudoscience*, by Georges Charpak and Henri Broch), *New York Review of Books* 51.5 (March 25, 2004): 5.

58. John Horgan, *The End of Science: Facing the Limits of Knowledge in the Twilight of the Scientific Age* (London: Little, Brown, 1997), 143.

59. Wilson, *Biophilia*.

60. Edward O. Wilson, *The Diversity of Life* (Cambridge, Mass.: Belknap Press of Harvard University Press, 1992).

61. Edward O. Wilson, *The Future of Life* (New York: Vintage, 2003), 170.

62. Ibid., xxiii–xxiv.

63. Edward O. Wilson, *Pheidole in the New World: A Dominant, Hyperdiverse Ant Genus* (Cambridge, Mass.: Harvard University Press, 2003).

64. Edward O. Wilson. *Nature Revealed: Selected Writings, 1949–2006* (Baltimore: Johns Hopkins Press, 2006).

65. Edward O. Wilson. *The Creation: A Meeting of Science and Religion* (New York: Norton, 2006).

CONCLUSION

1. See *Prospect*, October 2005, 25.

2. Steven Weinberg, *Glory and Terror: Growing Nuclear Danger* (New York: New York Review of Books, 2004).

3. Galileo Galilei, *Letter to the Grand Duchess Christina*, in *Le Opere di Galileo* (Florence: Barbèra, 1968), vol. 5, 319; English translation, *Letter to the Grand Duchess Christina*, in *Discoveries and Opinions of Galileo*, ed. Stillman Drake (New York: Doubleday, 1957), 186.

4. Richard Dawkins, "Opiate of the Masses," *Prospect* (October 2005): 16–17.

5. A comparison is taken from Paul K. Feyerabend, *Problems of Empiricism: Philosophical Papers*, vol. 2 (Cambridge: Cambridge University Press, 1981), 233.

6. Stephen Jay Gould, *The Structure of Evolutionary Theory* (Cambridge, Mass.: Harvard University Press, 2002), 31.

7. Ibid., 28.

8. Edward O. Wilson, *Consilience: The Unity of Knowledge* (New York: Knopf, 1998), 63–64.

9. Ibid., 60.

10. Richard Dawkins, *A Devil's Chaplain. Selected Essays by Richard Dawkins* (London: Weidenfeld and Nicolson, 2003), 15.

11. Ibid., 19.

12. Simon Blackburn, *Oxford Dictionary of Philosophy* (New York: Oxford University Press, 1996), 255.

13. Arthur S. Eddington, *The Philosophy of Physical Science* (1939; reprint, Ann Arbor: University of Michigan Press, 1974), 16.

Bibliography

WORKS BY THE ORACLES

Dawkins, Richard. *The Ancestor's Tale: A Pilgrimage to the Dawn of Evolution.* Boston: Houghton Mifflin, 2004.

———. *The Blind Watchmaker: Why the Evidence of Evolution Reveals a Universe without Design.* New York: Norton, 1987.

———. *Climbing Mount Improbable.* London: Viking, 1996.

———. *A Devil's Chaplain. Selected Essays by Richard Dawkins.* London: Weidenfeld and Nicolson, 2003.

———. *The Extended Phenotype: The Long Reach of the Gene.* New York: Oxford University Press, 1983.

———. *The God Delusion.* Boston: Houghton Mifflin, 2006.

———. "God's Utility Function." *Scientific American* 273.5 (November 1995): 62–67.

———. "Opiate of the Masses," *Prospect,* October 2005, 16–17.

———. Review of Donald Johanson and Maitland Edey's *Blueprint, New York Times,* section 7, April 9, 1989.

———. *River Out of Eden: A Darwinian View of Life.* London: Weidenfeld and Nicolson, 1995; reprint, London: Phoenix, 1996.

———. *The Selfish Gene.* 1976; 30th Anniversary edition with a new Introduction by the author. New York: Oxford University Press, 2006.

———. "A Survival Machine." In *The Third Culture,* ed. John Brockman, 74–95. New York: Simon and Schuster, 1996.

———. *Unweaving the Rainbow: Science, Delusion, and the Appetite for Wonder.* Boston: Houghton Mifflin, 1998.

Gould, Stephen Jay. *Bully for Brontosaurus: Reflections in Natural History.* New York: Norton, 1991.

———. *Dinosaur in a Haystack: Reflections in Natural History*. New York: Three Rivers Press, 1997.

———. *Ever Since Darwin: Reflections in Natural History*. New York: Norton, 1977.

———. "The Evolution of Life on the Earth." *Scientific American* 271.4 (October 1994): 84–91.

———. *The Hedgehog, the Fox, and the Magister's Pox: Mending the Gap between Science and the Humanities*. New York: Harmony Books, 2003.

———. *Hen's Teeth and Horse's Toes: Further Reflections in Natural History*. 1983; reprint, New York: Norton, 1994.

———. *I Have Landed: The End of a Beginning in Natural History*. New York: Three Rivers Press, 2003.

———. *The Lying Stones of Marrakech: Penultimate Reflections in Natural History*. New York: Three Rivers Press, 2000.

———. *The Mismeasure of Man*. 1981; rev./exp. ed., New York: Norton, 1996.

———. *Ontogeny and Phylogeny*. Cambridge, Mass.: Harvard University Press, 1977.

———. *The Panda's Thumb: More Reflections in Natural History*. 1980; reprint, New York: Norton, 1992.

———. *Rocks of Ages: Science and Religion in the Fullness of Life*. New York: Ballantine, 1999.

———. *The Structure of Evolutionary Theory*. Cambridge, Mass.: Harvard University Press, 2002.

———. *Time's Arrow, Time's Cycle: Myth and Metaphor in the Discovery of Geological Time*. Cambridge, Mass.: Harvard University Press, 1987.

———. *Triumph and Tragedy in Mudville: A Lifelong Passion for Baseball*. New York: Norton, 2003.

———. *An Urchin in the Storm: Essays about Books and Ideas*. New York: Norton, 1988.

———. *Wonderful Life: The Burgess Shale and the Nature of History*. New York: Norton, 1990.

Gould, Stephen Jay, with Niles Eldredge. "Punctuated Equilibria: An Alternative to Phyletic Gradualism." In *Models in Paleobiology*, ed. T. Schopf, 82–115. San Francisco: Freeman, 1972.

———. "Punctuated Equilibrium Comes of Age." *Nature*, November 18, 1993, 223–27.

Hawking, Stephen. *Black Holes and Baby Universes and Other Essays*. New York: Bantam, 1994.

———. "Black Hole Explosions." *Nature* 248 (1974): 30–31.

———. "The Boundary Conditions of the Universe." In *Astrophysical Cosmology: Proceedings of the Study Week on Cosmology and Fundamental Physics*, ed. H. A. Brück, G. V. Coyne, and M. S. Longair, 563–72. Vatican City: Pontificia Academia Scientiarum, 1982.

———. *A Brief History of Time*. 1988; updated/exp. 10th anniv. ed., New York: Bantam, 1998.

———. "Chronology Protection: Making the World Safe for Historians." In Stephen Hawking et al., *The Future of Spacetime*, 87–108. New York: Norton, 2002.

———. *The Illustrated A Brief History of Time,* updated/exp. ed. New York: Bantam Books, 1996.

———. "Quantum Cosmology." In *Three Hundred Years of Gravitation,* ed. S. W. Hawking and W. Israel, 631–51. Cambridge: Cambridge University Press, 1989.

———. "The Quantum Mechanics of Black Holes." *Scientific American* 236.1 (January 1977): 34–40.

———. *The Universe in a Nutshell.* New York: Bantam, 2001.

Hawking, Stephen, with J. B. Hartle. "Wave Function of the Universe." *Physical Review* D, 28.12 (December 1983): 2960–75.

Hawking, Stephen, with Roger Penrose. *The Nature of Space and Time.* 1996; reprint, Princeton, N.J.: Princeton University Press, 2000.

———. "The Singularities of Gravitational Collapse and Cosmology." *Proceedings of the Royal Society of London,* series A, 314.1519 (January 1970): 529–48.

Sagan, Carl. *Billions and Billions: Thoughts on Life and Death at the Brink of the Millenium.* New York: Ballantine, 1997.

———. *Broca's Brain: Reflections on the Romance of Science.* 1974; reprint, New York: Ballantine, 1980.

———. *Carl Sagan's Cosmic Connection: An Extraterrestrial Perspective.* Ed. Jerome Agel. Cambridge: Cambridge University Press, 2000.

———. *Cosmos.* 1980; reprint, New York: Ballantine, 1985.

———. *Cosmos TV series* DVD (7-disc collector's ed.). Studio City, Calif.: Cosmos Studios, 2000.

———. *The Demon-Haunted World: Science as a Candle in the Dark.* London: Headline, 1997.

———. *The Dragons of Eden: Speculations of the Evolution of Human Intelligence.* New York: Ballantine, 1978.

Weinberg, Steven. *Autobiography.* In *Nobel Lectures, Physics 1971–1980,* ed. Stig Lundqvist. Singapore: World Scientific Publishing, 1992.

———. *Dreams of a Final Theory: The Scientist's Search for the Ultimate Laws of Nature,* with a new afterword. New York: Vintage Books, 1994.

———. *Facing Up: Science and Its Cultural Adversaries.* Cambridge, Mass.: Harvard University Press, 2003.

———. *The First Three Minutes: A Modern View of the Origin of the Universe.* 1977; updated ed., New York: Basic Books, 1993.

———. "Sokal's Hoax, and Selected Responses." In *The Sokal Hoax: The Sham that Shook the Academy,* ed. the editors of *Lingua Franca,* 148–71. Lincoln: University of Nebraska Press, 2000.

———. "A Unified Physics by 2050?" *Scientific American* 281.6 (December 1999): 68–75.

———. "Unified Theories of Elementary-Particle Interaction." *Scientific American* 231.1 (July 1974): 50–59.

———. "What Price Glory?" *New York Review of Books,* November 6, 2003, 55–60.

Wilson, Edward O. *Biophilia.* Cambridge, Mass.: Harvard University Press, 1984.

———. *Consilience: The Unity of Knowledge.* New York: Knopf, 1998.

————. *The Creation: A Meeting of Science and Religion*. New York: Norton, 2006.

————. *The Diversity of Life*. Cambridge, Mass.: The Belknap Press of Harvard University Press, 1992.

————. *The Future of Life*. New York: Vintage Books, 2003.

————. *The Insect Societies*. Cambridge, Mass.: The Belknap Press of Harvard University Press, 1971.

————. *Naturalist*. New York: Warner Books, 1994.

————. *Nature Revealed: Selected Writings, 1949–2006*. Baltimore: The Johns Hopkins Press, 2006.

————. "Never Out of Africa." *Science and Spirit*, September/October 2003, 50–56.

————. *On Human Nature*. Cambridge, Mass.: Harvard University Press, 1978.

————. *Pheidole in the New World: A Dominant, Hyperdiverse Ant Genus*. Cambridge, Mass.: Harvard University Press, 2003.

————. *Sociobiology: The New Synthesis*. 1975; 25th anniv. ed., Cambridge, Mass.: The Belknap Press of Harvard University Press, 2000.

Wilson, E. O., with Bert Hölldobler. *The Ants*. Berlin: Springer, 1990.

————. *Journey to the Ants: A Story of Scientific Exploration*. Cambridge, Mass.: The Belknap Press of Harvard University Press, 1994.

Wilson, Edward O., with Charles J. Lumsden. *Genes, Mind, and Culture: The Coevolutionary Process*. Cambridge, Mass.: Harvard University Press, 1981.

————. *Promethean Fire: Reflections on the Origin of Mind*. Cambridge, Mass.: Harvard University Press, 1983.

Wilson, Edward O., with Robert H. MacArthur. *The Theory of Island Biogeography*. Princeton, N.J.: Princeton University Press, 1967.

WORKS BY OTHERS

Anderson, Philip W. "More Is Different." *Science*, August 4, 1972, 393–96.

Aquinas, Thomas. *Summa contra Gentiles*. Notre Dame, Ind.: University of Notre Dame Press, 2003.

————. *Summa Theologica*. Westminster, Md.: Christian Classics, 1981.

Artigas, Mariano. *The Mind of the Universe: Understanding Science and Religion*. Philadelphia: Templeton Foundation Press, 2000.

Asimov, Isaac. "Is Big Brother Watching?" *The Humanist* 44.4 (1984): 6–10.

Atiyah, Michael. "Foreword." In Stephen Hawking and Roger Penrose, *The Nature of Space and Time*, vii–viii. Princeton, N.J.: Princeton University Press, 2000.

Ayala, Francisco J. "Intelligent Design: The Original Version." *Theology and Science* 1 (2003): 9–32.

"Baseball." Dir. Ken Burns. Written by Ken Burns and Geoffrey C. Ward. Documentary miniseries. PBS. September 18, 1994.

Blackmore, Susan. *The Meme Machine*. New York: Oxford University Press, 2000.

Bowler, Peter. *Evolution: The History of an Idea*. Berkeley: University of California Press, 1989.

Brockman, John. *The Third Culture*. New York: Touchstone, 1996.

Brooke, John Hedley. *Science and Religion: Some Historical Perspectives*. Cambridge: Cambridge University Press, 1991.

Brück, H. A., G. V. Coyne, and M. S. Longair, eds. *Astrophysical Cosmology: Proceedings of the Study Week on Cosmology and Fundamental Physics*. Vatican City: Pontificia Academia Scientiarum, 1982.

Cline, David B., Alfred K. Mann, and Carlo Rubbia. "The Detection of Neutral Weak Currents." *Scientific American* 231.6 (December 1974): 108–19.

Cline, David B., Carlo Rubbia, and Simon van der Meer. "The Search for Intermediate Vector Bosons." *Scientific American* 246.3 (March 1982): 38.

Coles, Peter. *Hawking and the Mind of God*. Cambridge: Icon, 2000.

Davidson, Keay. *Carl Sagan: A Life*. New York: J. Wiley, 1999.

Dembski, William. *Intelligent Design: The Bridge Between Science and Theology*. Downers Grove, Ill.: InterVarsity Press, 1999.

Dembski, William A., and Jay Wesley Richards, eds. *Unapologetic Apologetics: Meeting the Challenges of Theological Studies*. Downers Grove, Ill.: InterVarsity, 2001.

Dennett, Daniel. *Darwin's Dangerous Idea: Evolution and the Meanings of Life*. London: Penguin, 1995.

Donnelly, Matt. "From the Other Side: Richard Dawkins Responds." *Science and Theology News* 6.2 (October 2005): 38.

Druyan, Ann. "Carl Sagan: A New Sense of the Sacred." In *Carl Sagan's Cosmic Connection: An Extraterrestrial Perspective*, ed. Jerome Agel, xvii–xxvii. Cambridge: Cambridge University Press, 2000.

Duve, Christian de. *A Guided Tour of the Living Cell*. New York: Scientific American, 1984.

Dyson, Freeman J. "Foreword." In *Carl Sagan's Cosmic Connection: An Extraterrestrial Perspective*, ed. Jerome Agel, xi–xv. Cambridge: Cambridge University Press, 2000.

———. "One in a Million" (review of *Debunked! ESP, Telekinesis, Other Pseudoscience*, by Georges Charpak and Henri Broch). *New York Review of Books*, March 25, 2004, 4–6.

———. "The Scientist as Rebel." In *Nature's Imagination: The Frontiers of Scientific Vision*, ed. John Cornwell, 1–11. New York: Oxford University Press, 1995.

Dzielska, Maria. *Hypatia of Alexandria*. Cambridge, Mass.: Harvard University Press, 1998.

Ferguson, Kitty. *The Fire in the Equations: Science, Religion, and the Search for God*. Grand Rapids, Mich.: Eerdmans, 1994.

———. *Stephen Hawking: Quest for a Theory of Everything*. New York: Bantam, 1992.

Ferngren, Gary B., ed. *Science and Religion: A Historical Introduction*. Baltimore: Johns Hopkins University Press, 2002.

Freud, Sigmund. *A General Introduction to Psycho-Analysis*, in *Great Books of the Western World*, ed. Mortimer J. Adler, vol. 54: *Freud*, 449–638. Chicago: Encyclopaedia Britannica, 1993.

Galison, Peter. *How Experiments End*. Chicago: University of Chicago Press, 1987.

Gamow, George. *Thirty Years That Shook Physics: The Story of Quantum Theory*. New York: Dover, 1985.

Gibbs, W. Wayt. "The Unseen Genome: Beyond DNA." *Scientific American* 289.6 (December 2003): 106–113.

———. "The Unseen Genome: Gems among the Junk." *Scientific American* 289.5 (November 2003): 26–33.

Giberson, Karl. *Worlds Apart: The Unholy War between Religion and Science*. Kansas City, Mo.: Beacon Hill, 1993.

Giberson, Karl W., and Donald A. Yerxa. *Species of Origins: America's Search for a Creation Story*. Lanham, Md.: Rowman and Littlefield, 2002.

Gilkey, Langdon. *Creationism on Trial: Evolution and God at Little Rock*. Charlottesville: University Press of Virginia, 1998.

Grafen, Alan, and Mark Ridley, eds. *Richard Dawkins: How a Scientist Changed the Way We Think*. Oxford University Press, 2006.

Gruner, Rolf. "Science, Nature, and Christianity." *Journal of Theological Studies* 26 (1975): 55–81.

Harré, Rom. *Varieties of Realism: A Rationale for the Natural Sciences*. Oxford: Blackwell, 1986.

Head, Tom, ed. *Conversations with Carl Sagan*. Jackson: University Press of Mississippi, 2006.

Herbert, Nick. *Quantum Reality: Beyond the New Physics*. New York: Anchor, 1987.

Holton, Gerald. *Scientific Imagination*. Cambridge: Cambridge University Press, 1978.

———. *Thematic Origins of Scientific Thought*. Cambridge, Mass.: Harvard University Press, 1988.

Horgan, John. *The End of Science: Facing the Limits of Knowledge in the Twilight of the Scientific Age*. New York: Broadway, 1997.

———. "Particle Metaphysics." *Scientific American* 270.2 (February 1994): 96–106.

Jackson, J. David, Maury Tigner, and Stanley Wojcicki. "The Superconducting Supercollider." *Scientific American* 254.3 (March 1986): 56–67.

Jaeger, Werner. *The Theology of the Early Greek Philosophers*. Oxford: Clarendon Press, 1964.

Jaki, Stanley L. *The Road of Science and the Ways to God*. Chicago: Chicago University Press, 1978.

———. *Science and Creation: From Eternal Cycles to an Oscillating Universe*. Edinburgh: Scottish Academic Press, 1986.

John Paul II. "Address to the Plenary Session and to the Study Week on the Subject 'Cosmology and Fundamental Physics'" (October 3, 1981), in *Papal Addresses to the Pontifical Academy of Sciences 1917–2002*, 249–52. Vatican City: Pontifical Academy of Sciences, 2003.

———. "Allocution of His Holiness John Paul II." In *Astrophysical Cosmology: Proceedings of the Study Week on Cosmology and Fundamental Physics*, xxvii–xxxii. Vatican City: Pontificia Academia Scientiarum, 1982.

Johnson, Phillip E. *Darwin on Trial*. Washington: Regnery Gateway, 1991.

———. *Reason in the Balance: The Case against Naturalism in Science, Law and Education*. Downers Grove, Ill.: InterVarsity, 1995.

Jones, Steve. "In the Genetic Toyshop" (review of Wilson's book *Consilience*). *New York Review of Books*, April 23, 1998, 14–16.

Kuhn, Thomas. *The Copernican Revolution: Planetary Astronomy in the Development of Western Thought*. Cambridge, Mass.: Harvard University Press, 1957.

———. *The Essential Tension: Selected Studies in Scientific Tradition and Change*. Chicago: University of Chicago Press, 1977.

Lambert, Dominique. *Un atome d'univers: La vie et l'oeuvre de Georges Lemaître*. Brussels: Lessius, 2000.

Larson, Edward J., and Larry Witham. "Scientists and Religion in America." *Scientific American*, September 1999, 88–93.

———. "Scientists Are Still Keeping the Faith." *Nature* 386 (1997): 435–36.

Leuba, James H. *The Belief in God and Immortality: A Psychological, Anthropological and Statistical Study*. Boston: Sherman, French and Co., 1916.

Lightman, Alan, and Roberta Brawer. *Origins: The Lives and Worlds of Modern Cosmologists*. Cambridge, Mass.: Harvard University Press, 1990.

Lindberg, David. *The Beginnings of Western Science*. Chicago: University of Chicago Press, 1992.

Lindberg, David C., and Ronald N. Numbers, eds. *God and Nature: Historical Essays on the Encounter between Christianity and Science*. Berkeley: University of California Press, 1986.

Lundqvist, Stig, ed. *Nobel Lectures, Physics 1971–1980*. Singapore: World Scientific Publishing, 1992.

Mattick, John S. "The Hidden Genetic Program of Complex Organisms." *Scientific American* 291.4 (October 2004): 30–37.

Mayr, Ernst. *What Evolution Is*. New York: Basic, 2001.

McEvoy, J. P., and Oscar Zarate. *Introducing Stephen Hawking*. Cambridge: Icon, 1997.

McGrath, Alister. *Dawkins' God: Genes, Memes, and the Meaning of Life*. Oxford: Blackwell, 2005.

———. *The Twilight of Atheism: The Rise and Fall of Disbelief in the Modern World*. New York: Doubleday, 2004.

McLean v. Arkansas Documentation Project. "Deposition of Dr. Stephen Jay Gould." Available at www.antievolution.org/projects/mclean/new_site/depos/pf_gould_dep.htm, p. 15 (accessed December 17, 2004).

Miller, Kenneth R. *Finding Darwin's God: A Scientist's Search for Common Ground between God and Evolution*. New York: Cliff Street, 2000.

Mivart, St. George. *On the Genesis of Species*. New York: Appleton, 1871.

Monod, Jacques. *Chance and Necessity: On the Natural Philosophy of Modern Biology*. 1971; reprint, London: Penguin, 1997.

Morris, Henry. *The Long War against God: The History and Impact of the Creation/Evolution Conflict*. Grand Rapids, Mich.: Baker, 1989.

Nagel, Bengt. "The Nobel Prize for Physics" (speech). In *Nobel Lectures, Physics 1971–1980*, ed. Stig Lundqvist, 487–88. Singapore: World Scientific Publishing, 1992.

O'Leary, Denyse. *By Design or by Chance?* Minneapolis: Augsburg, 2004.

Orr, H. Allen. "Gould on God: Can Religion and Science Be Happily Reconciled?" *Boston Review*, October/November 1999, 33–38.

———. "A Passion for Evolution" (review of Dawkins' book *A Devil's Chaplain*). *New York Review of Books*, February 26, 2004, 27–29.

Overton, William R. "Creationism in Schools: The Decision in McLean versus the Arkansas Board of Education." *Science* 215 (1982): 934–43.

Page, Don. "Hawking's Timely Story." *Nature* 332 (April 21, 1988): 742–43.

Penrose, Roger. *The Road to Reality: A Complete Guide to the Laws of the Universe.* New York: Knopf, 2005.

———. *Shadows of the Mind.* New York: Oxford University Press, 1996.

Pius XII. "The Proofs of the Existence of God in the Light of Modern Natural Science" (November 22, 1951), in *Papal Addresses to the Pontifical Academy of Sciences 1917–2002*, 130–42. Vatican City: Pontifical Academy of Sciences, 2003.

———. "Speech to the International Astronomical Union" (September 7, 1952). *Acta Apostolicae Sedis* 44 (1952): 732–39.

Plante, Lea. "Spirituality Soars among Scientists." *Science and Theology News* 6.2 (October 2005): 7–8.

Popper, Karl R. *The Logic of Scientific Discovery.* 1934; reprint, New York: Routledge, 1980.

Poundstone, William, *Carl Sagan: A Life in the Cosmos.* New York: Henry Holt, 1999.

Rath, Valérie de. *Georges Lemaître, le Père du big bang.* Brussels: Labor, 1994.

Rees, Martin. *Before the Beginning: Our Universe and Others.* London: Simon and Schuster, 1997.

Richardson, Mark W., Robert John Russell, Philip Clayton, and Kirk Wegter-McNelly, eds. *Science and the Spiritual Quest: New Essays by Leading Scientists*, 52–63. London: Routledge, 2002.

Ruse, Michael. "The Confessions of a Skeptic." *Research News and Opportunities in Science and Theology* 1.6 (February 2001): 20.

———. *Mystery of Mysteries: Is Evolution a Social Construction?* Cambridge, Mass.: Harvard University Press, 1999.

———. "Sociobiology." In *Encyclopedia of Science and Religion*, ed. J. Wentzel Vrede van Huyssteen, 807–14. New York: Macmillan, 2003.

Salam, Abdus. *Ideals and Realities: Selected Essays of Abdus Salam.* 2d ed., ed. C. H. Lai. Singapore: World Scientific, 1987.

Segerstråle, Ullica. *Defenders of the Truth: The Sociobiology Debate.* New York: Oxford University Press, 2001.

Shea, William R., and Mariano Artigas. *Galileo in Rome: The Rise and Fall of a Troublesome Genius.* New York: Oxford University Press, 2003.

Shermer, Michael. "An Awful Hole. A Wonderful Life." *Skeptic* 4.4 (1996): 13.

Smolin, Lee. "The Future of the Nature of the Universe." In *The Next Fifty Years*, ed. John Brockman, 3–17. New York: Vintage, 2002.

Snow, C. P. *The Two Cultures.* 1959; 2d. ed. Cambridge: Cambridge University Press, 1993.

Sokal, Alan. "Revelation: A Physicist Experiments with Cultural Studies." *Lingua Franca*, May–June 1996. In *The Sokal Hoax: The Sham That Shook the Academy*, ed. Editors of *Lingua Franca*, 49–53. Lincoln: University of Nebraska Press, 2000.

———. "Transgressing the Boundaries. Toward a Transformative Hermeneutics of Quantum Gravity." In *The Sokal Hoax: The Sham That Shook the Academy*, ed. Editors of *Lingua Franca*, 11–45. Lincoln: University of Nebraska Press, 2000.

Sokal, Alan, and Jean Bricmont. *Intellectual Impostures: Postmodern Philosophers' Abuse of Science*. 2d ed. London: Profile, 2003.

Sterelny, Kin. *Dawkins vs Gould: Survival of the Fittest*. Cambridge: Icon, 2001.

Tanner, Norman P., ed. *Decrees of the Ecumenical Councils*. London: Sheed and Ward, 1990.

Weber, Renée. "If There's an Edge to the Universe, There Must Be a God" (interview with Stephen Hawking). In *Dialogues with Scientists and Sages*, ed. Weber, 201–14. London: Arkana, 1990.

Whewell, William. *The Philosophy of the Inductive Sciences*. 1840; reprint, London: Routledge/Thoemmes, 1996.

White, Andrew Dickson. *A History of the Warfare of Science with Theology in Christendom*. Buffalo, N.Y.: Prometheus, 1993.

White, Michael, and John Gribbin. *Stephen Hawking: A Life in Science*. New ed. Washington, D.C.: Joseph Henry Press, 2002.

Witham, Larry. *Where Darwin Meets the Bible*. New York: Oxford University Press, 2002.

Wright, Robert. "The Accidental Creationist: Why Stephen Jay Gould Is Bad for Evolution." *New Yorker* 75 (December 1999): 56–65.

———. *Three Scientists and Their Gods*. New York: HarperCollins, 1989.

Zahm, John A. *Evolution and Dogma*. Chicago: D. H. McBride, 1896.

Zeldovich, Yakov B. "Spontaneous Birth of the Closed Universe and the Anthropic Principle." In *Astrophysical Cosmology: Proceedings of the Study Week on Cosmology and Fundamental Physics*, ed. H. A. Bruck, G. V. Coyne, and M. S. Longair, 575–78. Tuscon: University of Arizona Press, 1989. Reprint ed.

Index